Social Entrepreneurship in the Water Sector

Getting Things Done Sustainably

Rafael Ziegler

Coordinator of the Social Entrepreneurship Research Group GETIDOS, Universität Greifswald, Germany

Lena Partzsch

University of Freiburg, Germany

Jana Gebauer

IÖW, Germany

Marianne Henkel

Universität Greifswald, Germany

Justus Lodemann

Universität Greifswald, Germany

Franziska Mohaupt

IÖW, Germany

Edward Elgar

Cheltenham, UK • Northampton, MA, USA

Published by
Edward Elgar Publishing Limited
The Lypiatts
15 Lansdown Road
Cheltenham
Glos GL50 2JA
UK

Edward Elgar Publishing, Inc.
William Pratt House
9 Dewey Court
Northampton
Massachusetts 01060
USA

A catalogue record for this book
is available from the British Library

Library of Congress Control Number: 2014932599

This book is available electronically in the ElgarOnline.com
Business Subject Collection, E-ISBN 978 1 78347 131 7

ISBN 978 1 78347 130 0 (cased)

Typeset by Servis Filmsetting Ltd, Stockport, Cheshire
Printed and bound in Great Britain by T.J. International Ltd, Padstow

Contents

Figures

Tables

Maps

Boxes

Preface

This book suggests that social entrepreneurship centrally involves collaboration. The book itself is the result of a collaborative process. Six main authors – the core GETIDOS team – worked together to address people working in and on social entrepreneurship related to water and sustainability issues. This is a diverse group and we hope the book contributes to further reflection and collaboration. Chapter 1 introduces the issues and our approach, Chapters 2 through 6 present our case studies and Chapter 7 offers our conclusions on them. Finally, Chapter 8 presents our experiment in collaborative campaigning.

This book would not have been possible without the support and encouragement from a great number of people, organizations and institutions; we would like to acknowledge them here even if we cannot acknowledge everyone specifically.

GETIDOS has been supported by the social-ecological research programme of the German Ministry of Education and Research (BMBF), which has generously financed this research from 2009–2013 at the University of Greifswald and at the Institute for Ecological Economy Research, Berlin. First Hermann Flau and then Claudia Müller ensured that there was always sufficient flexibility to conduct a dynamic research project.

Professor Johanna Mair and Professor Konrad Ott both agreed to serve as mentors of the research group and from the start they supported this project in many ways. In particular we discussed an early version of the introductory chapter in Konrad Ott's environmental ethics research colloquium, and different aspects of case study methodology with Johanna Mair. We are also very thankful for the support of Ashoka: Dr. Nir Tsuk helped get the project started and David Strelneck and Michal Vollmann accompanied further development of the research project and helped us bridge the gap between theory and practice. We also acknowledge the support of our advisory board members Dorothea Härlin, Dr. Esther Hoffmann, Dr. Johannes Merck and especially Nicole Maisch, who as a member of parliament helped us with the Big Jump Challenge and hosted the final event in the German Parliament.

At the heart of this book are the case studies. We would specifically like to thank the social entrepreneurship initiatives presented here, both social entrepreneurs and staff within the organizations as well as network participants, for being very cooperative by patiently answering numerous questions, offering data and contacting partners. The case studies would clearly not have been possible without this openness. We are very grateful to Benjamin Adrion and Viva con Agua, Marta Echavarria and Ecodecision, Roberto Epple and the European Rivers Network, David Kuria and Ecotact, Michal Kravčík and People and Water, and Marcella D'Souza and WOTR.

These case studies were conducted in and across a wide variety of watersheds, not only geographically but also culturally. We are therefore very thankful to have conducted this research in cooperation with young researchers from the respective areas who helped us turn linguistic and cultural 'problem-sheds' into 'opportunity-sheds' for working together. Pavol Varga, the first visitor to our new offices in Greifswald, not only filled the empty space immediately with pictures and music from his native Slovakia, he also ensured that we could conduct our Slovakian case study in a way that was informed and respectful, in particular with a view to the rural people for whom he cares. Dr. Michal Gazovic, following the completion of his PhD in Greifswald, joined the Slovak team and provided invaluable and patient help with the survey and interviews. Benson Karanja endured a snowy and cold winter in Greifswald to prepare our Ecotact case study; always in a good spirit, he was of invaluable help for conducting interviews and the survey in Nairobi. Dr. Christian Dietsche accompanied Rafael during the first trip to Nairobi and generously offered his methodological insight. He also stoically endured joint sessions counting toilet users in a dusty marketplace, where he stood out as a very tall foreigner, with whom local market visitors liked to take pictures (while we studied toilets as 'toilet monuments', people studied him as a 'basketball star'). Balachandra Hegde participated in a seminar in Greifswald, where we saw his keen interest in nature conservation and social entrepreneurship. He helped conduct the WOTR case study and through numerous conversations about the capabilities approach, sustainability and poverty, he greatly improved our background understanding of the rich complexity of Indian traditions, which not only informed WOTR but also provided much inspiration for the Ashoka approach to social entrepreneurship. Grace Viera Andrade first came to Greifswald to join the team and then made us feel at home at her family's place in Quito, Ecuador, helping us to conduct the Marta Echavarria case study and to get a glimpse of Ecuadorian life. Léa Bigot arrived on a sunny afternoon in Greifswald to support the Roberto Epple case study. While the evening brought rain and prevented us from having dinner at the Museum's harbour, the rest of the case study went smoothly because of Léa's consistent and highly competent backing, not only in organizational matters but also with regards to content. Christoph Buschmann, who unfortunately did not get to travel, enormously supported the Viva con Agua case study as a desk scout who thoroughly mapped the Viva con Agua cosmos, patiently collecting ever more information and continuously keeping track of all the developments of the case.

The case studies in this book have benefitted from much prior discussion. Change reports, including our non-public recommendations, were sent to the initiatives named above and then jointly discussed at a conference in Frankfurt in September 2012. In preparation for this conference, as well as the research on sanitation more generally, Danica Straith was of great assistance as an intern in Berlin, who cheerfully endured never-ending scaling-taxonomy discussions and helped bring them together for the Frankfurt conference.

Our experiment with a collaborative competition – the Big Jump Challenge discussed in Chapter 8 – is the joint product of working together with the betterplace lab, the Deutsche Umwelthilfe, Grüne Liga Berlin, the European Rivers Network and Viva con Agua. We gratefully acknowledge their inputs. Central for this experiment were the challenge coordinators Nele Kapretz and Sabrina Schultz, who coordinated the various partners, especially the contact with youth groups; we thank them for their tireless work. In organizing and evaluating collaborative campaigns and Ryck jumps, Lukas Richter, Jassa Best, Nando Hamker, Juliane Fritzsch, Kathrin Mangelsen, Julia Pohlers, Martin Schreck and Wencke Wendlandt greatly helped with the survey, media analysis and organizational matters. We gratefully acknowledge the work of Martin Grov in preparing the index and Doro Will in preparing the water maps.

Six authors could not write a book together without important people in the background. Our first project manager Eva Wascher managed our group of six people from six different disciplines in a spirit of getting things done together and sustainably. Our current project manager Claudia Rettich patiently helped prepare the final manuscript as well as 'keeping things together' with a view to the many loose ends at the end of a project.

Six German-speaking authors should probably not write a book together in English unless they have a good editor. We are very thankful to Amelia Pope, who not only thoroughly edited the language of the entire book but also offered very helpful comments on the entire draft, and the editors at Edward Elgar for their professional and encouraging support.

Last but certainly not least, it is almost impossible for six authors to duly thank all families and friends. Thank you to each of you for your support in this journey.

1. Introduction

Rafael Ziegler, Lena Partzsch, Jana Gebauer, Marianne Henkel, Franziska Mohaupt and Justus Lodemann

1.1 GETTING THINGS DONE SUSTAINABLY

A lake in Southern Sweden, the Darß Peninsula on the south shore of the Baltic Coast, the Island of Utila off the Honduran Coast, the Thames River in London, the River Spree in Berlin and the Ruhr River in Bochum – what do all of these places have in common? The descriptions evidently suggest some reference to water. These are the various places where the authors of this book spent ringing in the New Millennium. While few of us have memories of our specific New Year's resolutions for 2000, the majority remembers a general interest in sustainability issues and each of us can recall the specific body of water where we were.

At the turn of the millennium some people warned of radical change; social, environmental and religious groups anticipated major transformations (and also the Y2K bug). Some had high hopes; others had no specific outlook. Where were you at the turn of the millennium? Do you remember personal New Year's resolutions? What happened to them? And why should it take a new year or even a new millennium to make resolutions?

In 2000 governments worldwide agreed on Millennium Development Goals (MDG) to eradicate extreme poverty by 2015. In view of the deprivation experienced by billions of people, the goals appear to be a paradigmatic commitment to change. It is noteworthy that the MDG are based on a 25-year period with 1990 as their base year. The 1990s were years of substantive global summits, notably the Rio Earth Summit of 1992; there was also a systematic change that preceded these conferences, the end of the Cold War as symbolized by the fall of the Berlin Wall. From this base, the Millennium Declaration placed a commitment to change by 2015.

A 25-year period is roughly one generation; this particular one was the period during which we, the members of this research group, went through school and university and have become adult citizens in a world publicly committed to change. While there is a widely shared, vague agreement that change is necessary, there is a wide space as to the precise goals of such change, as well as the possible means. Recall the MDG commitment to a world without poverty – without *extreme* poverty to be precise. What does this mean? The specification of the goal is to halve the proportion of people whose income is less than 1 US$ a day by 2015. In short, the goal is a world with less relative poverty. Is this still a commitment to change? As far as means are concerned, who is responsible for such a commitment?

Change raises a question of responsibility. For personal resolutions the responsibility is at least obvious, it is yours. But who is responsible for holding government accountable to commit to international resolutions such as the MDG? Other governments? The rich and powerful? All the citizens of the world? Who takes the responsibility for societal change? *Changemaking* requires makers, or so it is often claimed. *Changemakers* may be governments, businesses or NGOs, but in everyday life they are most easily understood as persons. Biographies tell the stories of outstanding changemakers – motivated and creative, experimental and persistent, visionary and charismatic – and examples include civil society leaders such as Wangaari Mathai, who planted millions of trees, entrepreneurs like Steve Jobs, who changed information technology, and statesmen like Barack Obama, perhaps the major player today in the rhetoric of change.

Entrepreneurship receives double attention in capitalism. It is used to describe individual business entrepreneurs and increasingly as a way of talking about politicians and civil society leaders. Hence the spectre of an economic imperialism that phrases everything in economic terms, indicating entrepreneurship and innovation as somehow inevitable. On the one hand, entrepreneurs and their innovations are a driver of economic growth, and by implication also of the sustainability problems caused by economic growth. On the other hand, entrepreneurs may come up with social or ecological innovations that help overcome problems of unsustainability. One way this problem solving seems to happen is via a relatively recent type of changemaker: *social entrepreneurs* are now popular and self-identify as actors for societal change (rather than primarily for private profit). There is both attraction and doubt regarding social entrepreneurs and 'the power of their ideas to change the world' (Bornstein 2004).

It is easy to be attracted by the local, bottom-up nature of social entrepreneurs, by the many agile and non-Photoshopped faces from around the globe who stand for concrete ideas and actions for change. They express local origin yet are coupled with a larger outlook; there is a societal commitment rather than solitary project making. It is difficult not to be drawn in by the priority of the social, the relevant goal rather than the goal of profit – not more of the same stuff, but different doings and beings. The possibility to work together with such changemakers is attractive, to help make brilliant ideas visible; the brilliant ideas of regular people rather than those of the usual suspects from business, politics or culture.

Thus in 2009 a journey started that would take us from the River Ryck in Greifswald to a football player in Hamburg (Germany) and a river jump inventor at the Loire in France, to quite a different river jump in Nairobi (Kenya), to the stakeholders upstream and downstream of a fund in Quito (Ecuador), to water catchments in Maharashtra (India) and a blue forest in the High Tatra in Slovakia, almost to 'greening the desert' in Saudi Arabia and back to Greifswald and into the Ryck (more about all this later).

From the start, however, there were second thoughts. What, if anything, can local actors achieve for societal change? Do such actors have significant access to resources and know-how of scale to make a difference or do they simply legitimize the status quo? In particular, what do tales of heroes tell us about change? 'Caesar defeated the Gauls. Did he not even have a cook with him?' asks Bertolt Brecht. Who is with these actors; who gives them authority to act on behalf of others? Where does social change originate? Is the framing of changemakers as 'entrepreneurs' and 'innovators' part of a neo-liberal agenda that makes the market and its terminology the imperial language for politics and civil society? What then about environmental sustainability and social goals? Finally, what about us? Would we be able to make a contribution to our partners or to the general public, not least given the large diversity of ideas and approaches seemingly held together by the new label of *social entrepreneurship*?

According to Joseph Schumpeter the maxim of the entrepreneur is *getting things done*. The term 'social entrepreneur' indicates there is a pressure in view of large societal and environmental problems to move beyond business pragmatism. Hence we see the rise of the adjective: not the entrepreneur, but the *social* entrepreneur (and not development, but *sustainable* development and so on). Accordingly we called our project GEtting ThIngs DOne *Sustainably* (GETIDOS); pragmatism on the one hand, meeting social and environmental goals on the other. A paradox or the way forward?

Our research project set out to clarify the role and potential of social entrepreneurship for sustainable development with a specific focus on the water sector. Following a general mapping of social entrepreneurship in relation to major water challenges, we selected case studies for in-depth investigations and cooperations. The following sections provide the relevant background information, set out our approach and introduce the case studies that will be presented in depth in the following chapters.

1.2 GLOBAL CHANGE – SUSTAINABILITY AND ENTREPRENEURSHIP

Economic growth and its consequences have been at the centre of contestations over global change worldwide. On one hand it is argued that economic growth is required to promote development on a global level; on the other hand, there are large economic inequalities and, at least partly owing to economic growth, the world faces ecological challenges including climate change, biodiversity loss and freshwater shortage. Thus emerged *sustainable development*, which focuses not only on economic development but also on the non-economic dimensions, especially the environmental sustainability of the earth for present and future generations. As the World Commission on Environment and Development (WCED) put it in what is the most widely referred to political definition, 'sustainable development is development that meets the needs of the present without compromising the ability of future generations to meet their own needs' (WCED 1989).

The WCED puts particular emphasis on the concept of needs, 'in particular the essential needs of the world's poor, to which overriding priority should be given' (WCED 1989). About a decade later this call for priority was taken up by 191 countries in the 2000 Millennium Declaration and the subsequent MDG with their primary focus on poverty eradication and its links to education, gender, health and environmental sustainability (see Box 1.1).

As far as actors are concerned, the MDG focus first on governments and intergovernmental agencies. Within each state, governments are to set appropriate targets and take responsibility for their achievement based on implementation strategies developed in dialogue with partners at home and from abroad. The MDG specify ends; the necessary means or strategies are left in principle to the respective governments and their partners. In practice, however, in spite of the wide focus on human development

---

BOX 1.1   THE MILLENNIUM DEVELOPMENT GOALS

Goal 1: Eradicate extreme poverty and hunger
Goal 2: Achieve universal primary education
Goal 3: Promote gender equality and empower women
Goal 4: Reduce child mortality rates
Goal 5: Improve maternal health
Goal 6: Combat HIV/AIDS, malaria and other diseases
Goal 7: Ensure environmental sustainability
Goal 8: Develop a global partnership for development

in the MDG, economic growth has frequently re-emerged as *the* means for development (Vandemoortele 2009, p. 364) along with a donor-centric view on aid (ibid. 365) as *the* means of development cooperation when economic growth has not yet been achieved. In spite of committing to endogenous development in principle, one global way of pursuing these goals tends to dominate.

In this light it comes as no surprise that entrepreneurship is frequently invoked in the context of achieving global change goals (Easterly 2006). Entrepreneurship has long been considered the driver of economic development. Business innovation rejuvenates economies – the train replaces the post carriage, the mobile phone, the landline and so on – triggering 'gales of creative destruction' (Schumpeter 1942). With the rise of sustainable development, entrepreneurship has been specifically placed in a context of *green growth* and more recently for the goal of *green economies* (UNEP 2011).

There is a need to look more closely into the concepts of entrepreneurship and innovation and their possible contributions to global change goals. The WCED has highlighted 'the idea of limitations imposed by the state of technology and social organization on the environment's ability to meet present and future needs' (WCED 1989). Yet the state of technology and social organization co-depends on available ideas and the ability to carry out these ideas. In view of the priority given to needs, it is noteworthy that the discussion of limits is a challenge for ecological innovation in the sense of new technologies – for example, for water saving in personal consumption, agriculture and industry – and for social innovation owing to the fact that the main limitation may be just as much social rather than technological. Cultural or political contexts may prevent the use of available instruments – for example insufficient hand-washing and personal hygiene may cause disease even in the presence of technology, and unsustainable consumption continues in the presence of greener alternatives.

We can further spell out the attraction to social entrepreneurship within the context of global commitments to change, particularly sustainable development, in terms of the following prima facie reasons for relevance. First, social entrepreneurship proposes to address societal concerns, particularly of those least-advantaged and excluded; it thereby seems highly relevant for achieving the hoped-for change.

Second, closer examination of the MDG, in particular the environmental sustainability goal (MDG 7), reveals a surprisingly strong plea for the contextual, local and endogenous. As a 2006 UNDP progress report notes, not only is there no definition of 'environmental sustainability' associated with the Millennium Development Declaration (ibid. 13), there is also a task for countries to adopt global targets and adapt them to their context, including the specification of new goals and targets where relevant (ibid. 54). In short, progress and especially realistic visions of progress are closely tied to endogenous processes. Social entrepreneurship is associated with such contextual, endogenous processes.

Third, the difficulties with donor-centric views of development suggest the need to study alternative ways of dealing with problems; ideas changing minds instead of money changing hands, as Jan Vandemoortele puts it. Social entrepreneurship is associated precisely with such a focus on ideas and their power to change the world. As social entrepreneur Roberto Epple puts it, 'Il faut changer les cerveaux' (see Chapter 3). A move beyond traditional donor-centric approaches is called for to examine the role of social entrepreneurs as putative actors in sustainable development.

Fourth, sustainable development and the MDG stand for a global mega-programme. There does not seem to be any evident way in which the contribution of social entrepreneurship could be studied in the face of such global challenges, let alone counted with a focus on specific targets. Nonetheless, a closer look is warranted. As noted above, the MDG methodology itself does not include a definition of environmental sustainability; rather there is a call to adopt and adapt more general principles (UNDP 2006). By implication, more contextual approaches are fully legitimate as long as the link to environmental sustainability is made explicit. The focus on home-grown processes particularly in relation to ideas implies a focus on very different ideas – case studies below include river jumps, toilet monuments and cup throwing – that each respond directly to specific problems and challenges, yet at best only indirectly to global aggregate targets. The fact that each idea is different also implies that appropriate contributions may fall out of the global aggregate focus. Hence a focus on the ideas of social entrepreneurs helps to make issues that may have remained excluded or were at the fringe more visible. The focus is on ideas that emerge in response to specific contextual problems; while these ideas may be highly relevant for those local problems, it is an open question whether such ideas can travel or be replicated and imitated. We will pay special attention to this issue of *scaling*. In short, even if there is no self-evident way of summing up and counting different ideas, this does not imply their irrelevance. Now that this has been said, we will say more about social entrepreneurship and our understanding of the concept.

1.3   SOCIAL ENTREPRENEURSHIP

'Social entrepreneurship' and 'social entrepreneurs' have only become more widely known expressions since the early 1980s. As we will see in the next chapters, in practice these terms refer to a diversity of individuals, organizations and networks. To do justice to this diversity, we here use the term *social entrepreneurship initiatives* (SEI) to cover both the social entrepreneur and the organization or network.

The rise of SEI coincided with a more general rise in entrepreneurship in terms of a revival of small businesses (seen for more than a decade in Europe and the United States), a shift in the ideology of political economics from Keynesianism to the more individualist, market-first ideologies of the Thatcher and Reagan administrations, and a persistently high unemployment rate, which led to the hope that entrepreneurship would create new businesses and jobs (Swedberg 2000, p. 8). The rise of civil society post-World War II added to this constellation of factors in the 1980s and 1990s with an increasing number of non-governmental organizations (NGOs) and an increasing competition amongst them for funding.

Ashoka, founded in 1980 by William Drayton, is a US-based foundation for the support of social entrepreneurs worldwide and is probably the most important organization in making the term 'social entrepreneur' more widely known. Before we turn to Ashoka in more detail, a conceptual point is in order. We approach social entrepreneurship as a contested concept (Gallie 1956). Contested concepts serve as common currency for different actors from government, civil society, business and academia. The concept of sustainable development is a prominent example. On one level contested concepts have core ideas and expectations that need to be addressed; in the example of sustainable development there is a concern with (economic) development as well as with (environmental and social) sustainability. These expectations can seem paradoxical and controversial; that is one reason why they attract attention. For example, Wolfgang Sachs has called sustainable development a paradox. For him it means economic growth *and* nature conservation; yet an ever-increasing material standard for all is not compatible with the finite resources of planet Earth and even less so with nature conservation (Sachs 1999). Likewise, social entrepreneurship opens a space for concern with social goals *and* an entrepreneurial approach. Again the first impression seems paradoxical; social entrepreneurship as promoting societal goals *and* making profit?

On another level contested concepts attract specific conceptions. Actors from government, business, civil society and academia propose specific ways of using and refining the concept. What is the social or the social mission? Can entrepreneurship be equated with business and making a profit? What difference does the qualifier 'social' make to entrepreneurship? Accordingly it is important to clarify one's conception of a contested concept and at the same time keep in mind that it is part of a larger contestation. Disagreements over the meaning of contested concepts reveal the central arguments that the concept calls forth and unite people in discussion and contestation (Jacobs 1999).

Before we turn to our working conception, we offer a few comments on the general and vague level of the contested concept. The social of social entrepreneurship requires at minimum a focus on societal issues. Paradigmatic is a focus on needs in relation to poverty reduction. The world's most famous social entrepreneur, Muhamad Yunus, illustrates the goal of his microcredit approach with the image of *museums of poverty*; poverty, not just a proportion of the poor, is to be made a matter of the past. Entrepreneurship seems to require at minimum the production of some good or service, such as the microcredits offered by Yunus's Grameen bank. These considerations show that already at the vague level a few differentiations are possible to help shape the contours of the contested concept. The production of goods and services suggests a difference to social activism, which may advocate for or against a cause but need not produce a good or service. The explicit social mission suggests a difference to primarily profit-oriented or self-interested business; a pioneer of social entrepreneurship research, Gregory W. Dees argues that this is the core that distinguishes social entrepreneurs from business entrepreneurs (Dees 2001). Finally, the production of goods and services suggests a difference to government, which sometimes provides (public) goods, yet is ultimately responsible for the *regulation* of goods (the production being a secondary question of appropriate means). These are only initial differentiations with blurry borders. We hence turn to the level of conception and more specific approaches. Actors from government, business, civil society and academia have approached social entrepreneurship from their specific yet frequently overlapping contexts. In his first speech as UK Prime Minister in 1997, Tony Blair referred to social entrepreneurs as 'those people who bring to social problems the same enterprise and imagination that business entrepreneurs bring to wealth creation' (quoted in Grenier 2009, p. 175). Business entrepreneurs have also responded to the theme of social entrepreneurship; for example, Jeffrey Skoll of eBay founded the Skoll Foundation in 1999. The foundation speaks of social entrepreneurs as 'extraordinary leaders . . .; their organizations are creating the innovative models that can spark large-scale change for seemingly intractable social problems'.[1] Furthermore, civil society organizations have been selecting, supporting and celebrating social entrepreneurship for some time now. Ashoka speaks of social entrepreneurs as 'individuals with innovative solutions to society's most pressing social problems'.[2] While there is widespread interest in social entrepreneurship, properly speaking it is only academia that has a constitutive interest in formulating conceptions of social entrepreneurship.

Specifically, Jacques Defourny and Marthe Nyssens have identified the emergence of two schools within social entrepreneurship research – the *earned income school* and the *social innovation school* (Defourny and Nyssens 2010). The earned income school defines social enterprise as 'any earned-income business or strategy undertaken by a non-profit to generate revenue in support of its charitable mission' (Defourny and Nyssens 2010, p. 41). In terms of defining elements, the focus is on the earned income of organizations while the social tends to be associated with the production of goods and services for a market. Innovation is not central for this approach. According to Defourny and Nyssens, the earned income view strongly dominates outside academia, and it usually requires a social enterprise to have at least 50 per cent market-based income. Within academia, the social enterprise incubator at Harvard Business School has been associated with this view as well as the work of Jed Emerson and Jerr Boschee.

In contrast, the social innovation school analyses social entrepreneurship centrally in terms of innovation. Unlike an invention, an innovation has to be put into practice; it has to be carried out. Like an invention, an innovation has to be novel at least relative to its place and time. For example, the microcredits of Grameen are relatively novel in the context of post-independent Bangladesh even if historians can point to earlier instances of microcredit use in the Middle Ages and in early industrialization. For the social innovation school there is a primary focus on outcomes and impact rather than on incomes. Frequently there is a focus on individuals presumably owing to the strong linkage between new ideas and persons. In terms of defining elements, we find a focus on innovation, frequently (though not necessarily) a focus on individuals and finally a focus on the social in a wide sense that is not tied to market production as an outcome or a necessary prerequisite. Earned income in this view is a question of means and not central to the phenomenon. If the earned income view has been popular outside academia, then almost the opposite seems to hold inside academia with many scholars focusing on social innovation (Nicholls 2010).

The language of schools no doubt calls for some caution so as not to downplay the diversity of positions and perspectives. More general juxtapositions have a helpful role as a heuristic for mapping and hence for situating more fine-grained positions. In particular, the above distinction is resonant with the language of practice. Consider as an example two prominent civil society organizations, Ashoka and the Social Enterprise Alliance. According to Ashoka:

Social entrepreneurs are individuals with innovative solutions to society's most pressing social problems. They are ambitious and persistent, tackling major social issues and offering new ideas for wide-scale change. Rather than leaving societal needs to the government or business sectors, social entrepreneurs find what is not working and solve the problem by changing the system, spreading the solution, and persuading entire societies to take new leaps.[3]

Here the focus is on innovation; innovations that can change systems. Ashoka selects and supports fellows according to a selection procedure that focuses on 'the new idea, creativity, entrepreneurial quality, social impact of the idea and ethical fiber'.[4] Ashoka has selected more than 3000 fellows from 80 countries and typically supports these fellows with a three-year stipend as well as network support.

According to the Social Enterprise Alliance:

> A social enterprise is an organization or venture that achieves its primary social or environmental mission using business methods. The social needs addressed by social enterprises and the business models they use are as diverse as human ingenuity. Social enterprises build a more just, sustainable world by applying market-based strategies to today's social problems.[5]

Here the focus is on the use of business approaches for social or environmental missions.

The respective approaches of these two organizations fit well with the distinction between the two schools. Moreover they suggest a rough terminological clarification: social entrepreneurship as a reference to social innovation and social enterprise as a reference to earned income. The distinction need not be viewed as a dichotomous either/or debate.[6] There is room for both earned income and social innovation approaches. In fact, both co-exist in practice. In the following chapters the focus will be on social entrepreneurship broadly within the school of innovation; we will, however, keep earned income in perspective and will return to it in our synthesis chapter (8).

Innovation is the carrying out of new ideas relative to their temporal and/or spatial context. The main focus is not the invention but the putting into practice of the invention. As is well known, not least from political visionary programmes, it is one thing to have an idea, quite something else to carry it out. We limit this practical focus to a modest requirement of novelty relative to temporal and spatial context. What is proposed as novel by an entrepreneur may be nothing new from the perspective of the historian – a point that has even been made in regards to the concept of social entrepreneurship!

A focus on the practical implications of ideas that target social problems leads to the concern of whether the product or service is available to all who need it or who could benefit from it. In social entrepreneurship research the term 'scaling' has come to be associated with this issue. In the following chapters we address this concern via an investigation of the goals of the respective SEI and their ability to achieve these goals. More specifically, we ask whether they aim at the national level and to what extent they have been able to achieve impact on the national level; this is a central reference point as the nation-state remains a central locus of the democratic discussion and implementation of the public good.

Scaling is possible through many different means – organizational growth, collaboration with others, imitation by others, and so on. In view of this diversity it is helpful to first draw a basic distinction. In the following chapters, *scaling out* refers to the growth and replication of a product and service by the SEI itself, as a franchise or by imitation. *Conditions of scaling out* refer to the use and creation of cultural, economic, political, scientific and environmental spaces that co-shape the journey of an innovation. For example, legal advocacy work may remove a barrier in regulation that the innovation faced in political space. We will first analyse ways of scaling for different SEI. In the synthesis chapter (8) we will review the results obtained via the case studies.

On this basis we will discuss the *new paradigm of scaling* that is proclaimed to have emerged from social entrepreneurship practice (McPhedran Waitzer and Paul 2011). The *old paradigm* in this debate draws on an idea of scaling from the business sector: grow your organization and with it you will grow your impact. It is said to draw on 'conventional wisdom of the business sector, where efforts at scaling-up typically focus on increasing the size of organizations' (McPhedran Waitzer and Paul 2011, p. 143). Additionally there is the idea of global reach: 'Great business ideas go global to serve customers; at their full potential they become ubiquitous. For example, people everywhere happily use soft contact lenses without having any idea where they first came from' (ibid.). In contrast, the new paradigm – pioneered in social entrepreneurship research by Jeffrey Bradach (2003) – holds a different view on organizational size and scaling. Societal impact is the goal, whereas organizational growth and size is deemphasized; 'finding ways to scale impact without scaling the size of an organization' is for Bradach the 'new frontier for our work in the field' (Bradach 2003, p. 143). 'How can we get 100x the impact with only a 2x change in the size of the organization?' (Bradach 2010). According to McPhedran Waitzer and Paul, this emerging paradigm is better adapted to the social sector: 'This emerging paradigm holds the promise of shaping strategies that succeed, thanks to the defining characteristics of the *social* sector, leveraging the collaborative potential of mission-driven innovators while keeping organizational footprints – and attendant resource needs – to a minimum'.

We will return to this paradigm debate in the final part of this book

---

BOX 1.2   THESES ON INNOVATION AND SCALING

Innovation: Social entrepreneurship initiatives carry out new ideas relative to their temporal and/or spatial contexts of action.

Scaling: Social entrepreneurship initiatives a) aim at the broad societal level and b) are able to implement their ideas at the broad societal level.

Further theses in relation to the two schools:

School of innovation: The social entrepreneur as individual is central as a driver for innovation; they are the founders and top-down leaders of their organizations.

Earned income: Earned income is central for social entrepreneurship initiatives.

(Chapter 8). For now we can note that the focus on innovation suggests the following *theses* to be examined in the following case studies (see Box 1.2).

So far our approach fails to specify the social in social entrepreneurship. Both in the earned income and the social innovation schools, the social is frequently taken for granted as a matter of obviously good goals.[7] Yet upon consideration, little is self-evident or obvious. Albert Cho points out two key problems (Cho 2006). First, if the social is taken for granted, then the social of social entrepreneurship is effectively deferred to social mission, social innovation, and so on. For example, while innovation may help clarify entrepreneurship, it is much less clear how social innovation helps clarify what is social about social entrepreneurship. The question has simply been deferred and we now need to ask what is social about social innovation? Goals and procedures are frequently controversial and thus more needs to be said about goals and procedures. Second, the problem re-emerges as one of monological definition: social is what the social entrepreneur or social enterprise claims to be social. This move seems tied to the assumption that the actor is good. Yet consider the controversies over the pros and cons of abortion, the right or not to privately own weapons, the right way of living with animals, and so on. This list could easily be extended. Real-world controversies involve a diversity of interests, value pluralism and non-inclusive public spheres. A monological definition is therefore not likely to sufficiently illuminate the social of any specific case of social entrepreneurship, let alone all of them.

It is a matter of theoretical adequacy to increase the clarity of terms used. And it is a matter of academic honesty (Max Weber) to clarify one's positions and their implicit or explicit normative stakes. This last point is especially important for social entrepreneurship research to the extent that it exhibits a strong tendency not just to study social entrepreneurship but also to promote it. Here we approach this normative explication in two steps. We first examine the place of social entrepreneurship with respect to socially recognized goals in the water sector. In a second step we refine the analysis of goals in the water sector with a specific ethical conception based on the capabilities approach and the theory of strong sustainability.

1.4 SOCIAL ENTREPRENEURSHIP AND WATER CHALLENGES

We have come to refer to the Earth as the blue planet. Water is fundamental to the life process. It is therefore of little surprise that water is a central target within MDG 7; in fact, access to water is the most widely reported target of MDG 7 (UNDP 2006, p. 26) and a 2003 Ashoka survey among its fellows ranked water as the top priority (Ashoka Concept Note Water Farming, 1).

One way to study water challenges is to look at freshwater availability, distribution and use. Only some 2.5 per cent of the blue planet's water is freshwater; of that, three-quarters is stored as ice and glaciers and about one-quarter as ground water. Only 1 per cent of freshwater is stored in lakes, rivers and soils. Freshwater is a 'blue gold' (Barlow and Clarke 2002), a precious resource not only for corporations but for all of life.

About 10 per cent of freshwater use is for private consumption including drinking water and hygiene; that is the drinking water and sanitation targets of the MDG 7 really only focus on a relatively small yet unevenly distributed quantity as far as the overall use of freshwater is concerned. Agriculture and industry are by far the largest users of freshwater, with agriculture accounting for about 70 per cent of global freshwater use and industry about 20 per cent (Mauser 2007). We thus draw a subcategory in relation to agriculture and industry as an important domain in freshwater usage. Issues here concern both the quantity of water used as well as the quality of its use, such as the pollution that may result from agricultural or industrial water use.

Finally and most fundamentally we focus on water in relation to ecosystems and its role for human beings and life as an interrelated whole. The politics and management of water within a watershed is a first category to delineate human activities as far as the role and use of freshwater on the land is concerned; this includes water for private consumption, industry and agriculture as well as water for animals and species within ecosystems that support all of life. River basin management and watershed development are well-known forms of engagement in this more general sense; these activities seek to bring together the diverse uses and functions of freshwater. Thus we can draw the following picture: a concern with watersheds and river basins as an overall, integrative concern that includes the spheres of agriculture, industry and private water use for drinking and sanitation.[8] We can then ask where SEI are active in relation to freshwater use and more specifically, watershed protection and its subcategories?

Maps 1.1 to 1.3 seek to visualize where SEI in the water sector have been accredited or promoted by recognized social entrepreneurship support organizations. The maps, which are located on pages 24–6, render visible SEI that are supported by one or more of the following organizations: Acumen, Ashoka, Echoing Green, Schwab and the Skoll Foundation, that is the leading global social entrepreneurship support organizations.[9] As these organizations tend to support a social innovation approach to social entrepreneurship, the fellow/support choices they make are of particular interest for our purposes. There is no way, especially for a single research group, to identify all SEI globally, not least because there are no established inventories from which one could draw. The support organizations effectively play the role of a discovery mechanism. Thus the maps below visualize SEI so discovered and promoted, but not all SEI. The maps are a conservative estimate that under- rather than overestimate the activity in relation to water challenges. The maps locate the SEI in terms of their respective headquarters.

By the end of October 2011 the search led to 13 SEI with a primary focus on drinking water and water consumption, and 28 SEI with a focus on drinking water and sanitation, that is, a total of 41 initiatives. Map 1.1 shows the state of MDG improvement with respect to the drinking water goal and positions SEI with respect to this issue of MDG 7. The estimate is that in 2011, 768 million people remained without access to an improved source of drinking water; 40 per cent of those people are in Sub-Saharan Africa. The map offers a first perspective on the claim that social entrepreneurs tackle 'society's most pressing social problems' (see the Ashoka approach introduced above), that is, where such SEI are promoted. It shows a relatively high number of social entrepreneurs on the Indian subcontinent; however, not so for India's neighbouring country China or for Sub-Saharan Africa, the area with the most pressing issues (according to the MDG).

Map 1.2 shows improvements with respect to the MDG 7 sanitation goal. In 2011 the UN estimated that over 2.5 billion people worldwide still lack access to improved sanitation facilities, with over 70 per cent living in rural areas and access problems on the rise in poor urban areas with rapid population growth. We found 12 SEI with a primary focus on sanitation and as noted above, 28 SEI with a focus on both drinking water and sanitation, making a total of 40 initiatives. Again there is a relatively high level of SEI activity in India, which responds to an urgent need; however, other urgent areas are not covered such as Mongolia and many countries in Sub-Saharan Africa.

Map 1.3 shows biodiversity threats to watersheds worldwide, thus highlighting the ecological dimension of watershed development (Vörösmarty et al. 2010). The problem areas here change somewhat to river basins that have a high population and are industrialized, such as many regions of Europe, the United States, India and China. With respect to different aspects of the management and politics of watersheds, we found 54 SEI. Again, India – here together with Indonesia – is a hotspot of SEI promotion, whereas there is less activity in Europe, the United States and in particular China.

Last but not least, in terms of our freshwater categories outlined above, we found 17 SEI in the category of water and industry and 36 SEI in the category of water and agriculture.[10]

Do SEI contribute solutions to the most urgent problems in the water sector? In conclusion, our mapping exercise revealed an initial broadbrush answer regarding the promotion of SEI in various water-related fields. The contrast with global water-problem maps reveals that while SEI are frequently active in some areas with high urgency (in particular India), there is a lack of SEI promotion in many areas with very high urgency, in particular many countries of Sub-Saharan Africa, China and as far as river basin management is concerned, Europe and the United States.

1.5 GETTING THINGS DONE SUSTAINABLY – THE GETIDOS APPROACH

The goal of our approach is oriented towards sustainability – *getting things done sustainably*. As sustainable development is a contested concept, we need to specify our conception of sustainable development and its link to SEI as actors in socio-ecological environments. This involves evaluating both the internal organization and external impacts of SEI in their respective environments and includes other actors from government, business and civil society acting according to formal or informal norms within diverse physical environments.

Ethics

On the ethical level our approach draws on the capabilities approach. This approach emerged from a philosophical debate of justice. It highlights problematic aspects of traditional liberal and utilitarian perspectives while at the same time seeking to retain their insights. According to the capabilities approach, basic questions of equality, justice and development ought to be evaluated according to their impact on human capabilities. These are doings and beings – such as participating politically or being in good health – and the focus is on the effective opportunity to do and to be (as opposed to a merely formal opportunity). For example, not just the formal right to vote but also the cultural, economic and environmental preconditions that make it possible to exercise that right.

Our approach to the social is accordingly one that puts primary emphasis on human development as a matter of heterogeneous doings and beings such as education, health and participation. If there is no single, overarching good or single index of development, then which capabilities should be focused on? Philosopher Martha Nussbaum has worked out a list of central human capabilities (Nussbaum 2000 and 2006) that are meant to spell out what is required for leading a human life in dignity. While this does not offer a comprehensive account of the social, it does offer orientation regarding a key set of issues that are likely important no matter what else will be important in specific contexts.

Moreover, her account helps to formulate a threshold of basic justice not just worldwide but also across generations, that is, an absolute standard of basic justice between generations (Ott and Döring 2004, 2.3.4. ff.). According to this view, the responsibility we have towards future generations requires as a demand of basic justice that we do not compromise the equal opportunity of future generations to lead a life in dignity as spelled out by the list of central human capabilities.

With a view on the Brundtland definition of the WCED introduced above, the list provides us with a conception and specification of the needs that are of basic importance as a matter of dignity whatever other problems there may be. The focus on central capabilities in relation to dignity is one way to focus on needs rather than wants. The focus on central capabilities also adds a choice qualification: what is important is not so much that the capability is exercised by person X, but that X has an effective opportunity to do so. An example is the difference between fasting and starving.[11] Just as importantly, there is a space for the cultural variation of capabilities, or different realizations, as Nussbaum says, of capabilities. What it means to have adequate shelter varies culturally and geographically depending on climate, tradition, and so on. In short, the abstract list has to be specified for specific contexts.

BOX 1.3   THE CENTRAL HUMAN CAPABILITIES

1. Life
2. Bodily health
3. Bodily integrity
4. Sense, imagination and thought
5. Emotion
6. Practical reason
7. Affiliation
8. Other species
9. Play
10. Control over one's environment (political and material)

Source: Nussbaum (2006).

For the specification of sustainable development, we focus on basic or central capabilities. It follows that development here is primarily a question of individual development (whereas technical, industrial or economic developments are a means to be evaluated in relation to their contribution to basic capabilities). Because central capabilities are frequently not met and as there is a constant task of development in the unfolding of generations, development is an always-present and enduring challenge.

Meeting the threshold of central capabilities depends on adequate institutions – in particular, Nussbaum argues, an adequate constitution. Adopting a term used by Maude Barlow, beyond the constitution the issue is one of a larger *covenant* (Barlow 2008). For the very possibility of ensuring basic capabilities co-depends on the natural environment. For example, the human rights to water for which Barlow and others have advocated, and which was declared a human right in 2010 by the UN General Assembly, not only depends on legal frameworks, but also on the availability of sufficient and clean freshwater for drinking and sanitation. If we pollute freshwater or over-deplete it for irrigation in agriculture, if we destroy forests and wetlands that purify water, then the implementation of the right will be very costly and in some regions impossible.

To generalize this point, basic capabilities co-depend on the natural environment.[12] Consequently, sustainability calls for a concern with the natural environment, its ecosystems and their relations to human capabilities. As the focus on the natural environment here is one in terms of its relation to us, specifically the benefits for needs and capabilities, sustainability research frequently frames this discussion in terms of natural capital. Generically, a capital is an X that yields a flow of benefits X. The benefits that we are primarily interested in are benefits for central human capabilities; however, what else can be said about natural capital and, more specifically, water as a natural capital?[13]

Natural capital comprises stocks and funds as seen from a human time perspective. A stock is depleted when used and in principle can be used up immediately. A fund yields a flow of benefits and is able to regenerate or reproduce itself. For example, oil is a stock that humans can use but that stock is likely to be used up at some point, and forests are a fund that inter alia offers timber for humans over time. Accordingly, the famous origin of sustainability in forestry science is associated with the maxim to only cut as much timber as can be re-grown. Not only can animals and plants reproduce as living funds, likewise water and soil can regenerate as non-living funds. Water flows in water cycles that have the capacity to regenerate; to the extent that this capacity is respected, there is the possibility of using water sustainably.

Water is a fundamental element of life and a medium of complex, interactive ecosystem-services that functions as an irreplaceable natural capital. It is the 'bloodstream of the earth' (Ripl 2003) with a finely tuned system of arteries and veins. In relation to the criterion of strong sustainability, freshwater as a regenerating fund must be sustained for present and future generations. Environmentally sustainable behaviour does not negatively affect the capacity of freshwater to regenerate itself nor does it negatively affect its multifunctional role in ecosystem services (Lodemann et al. 2010, p. 431; see also Box 1.4 for a list of the role of water in ecosystem services).

Central capabilities and environmental sustainability are the main ethical focus of our evaluation of getting things done sustainably; they provide a space of orientation to specify the ethical aspect of the social. In regards to SEI, this perspective implies a design challenge: is the product or service designed in a capabilities-sensitive way? Is it designed in a sustainability-sensitive way? For example, the inclusion of toilets for the disabled in the Ikotoilets (discussed below) is from our evaluative perspective a difference that makes a difference. It is an instance of capabilities-sensitive design; on the level of environmental sustainability, so is the installation of water-saving taps. Such design features help the target group (which, as the example shows, ought not to be considered as a homogeneous mass) to convert the resource into a capability. In the language of the capabilities approach, these are *conversion factors*.

Internal Organizational Responsibility

This space of ethical orientation is not only a matter of the impact of an organization on its target group – for example, whether social entrepreneur

---

BOX 1.4 EXAMPLES OF THE ROLE OF WATER IN HUMAN ECOSYSTEM SERVICES

Ecosystem services	*Examples of the role of water*
Supporting	
Soil formation	transport of nutrient matter
Primary production	photosynthesis
Regulating	
Climate	local cooling by evaporative processes
Disease control	hygiene and waste treatment
Provisioning	
Nutrition	drinking water, farming, industrial processes
Biochemicals	growth of medicinal plants
Cultural	
Heritage	settlement by lakes and rivers, sense of place
Education	understanding of complexity
Aesthetics	beauty and integrity of water bodies
Spirituality	wild rivers and groves

X in country Y helps improve access to drinking water and sanitation, and so on – it is also an issue for the internal management and external partnerships of an organization in the process of producing a product or service. On the one hand, this question concerns social standards within the organization and the way it engages with those affected by it (stakeholder participation). As is well known, organizations that do good things for others may put pressure on their employees to work harder and for less compensation precisely because it is for a larger good. On the other hand, there is a question of environmental standards in production: is the good or service produced in a way that does not negatively affect environmental sustainability?

These questions, often associated with the international dimension of corporate social responsibility (CSR) of companies, are also relevant for SEI (Gebauer and Ziegler 2013). They are of intrinsic importance because an organization that seeks to promote social dignity for a target group but violates requirements of social dignity in its own production process runs into problems of consistency and integrity. These questions are also of strategic importance. For a start-up in its early stage, the question of environmental sustainability may not seem relevant simply because the

---

BOX 1.5   A SPECIFICATION OF THE SOCIAL

Environmental sustainability: Social entrepreneurship initiatives contribute to environmental sustainability in the water sector.

Human capabilities: Social entrepreneurship initiatives contribute to human capabilities of their target group.

Internal organizational responsibility: Social entrepreneurship initiatives respect human capabilities of their staff and respect environmentally sustainable standards of production.

---

production may be very small or non-existent; however, for SEI who want to scale and achieve large-scale impact, these management questions are likely to be raised as questions concerning the responsibility and legitimacy of the organization in light of its increasing impact. CSR research even speaks of the iron law of responsibility. While SEI tend to be endowed with a start-up capital of trust owing to their focus on direct needs rather than profit-making opportunities, this capital may run out or become insufficient with the increasing visibility of the SEI. Based on our ethical conception we can state further theses for the study of social entrepreneurship (Box 1.5).

Politics

The discussion of the MDG highlights the political nature of the water issues discussed here. While governments agree on these goals, they may fail to deliver on these goals, let alone more demanding ones such as the human right to water for all and not just for a proportion. Likewise markets may fail to provide the goods and services required to meet such goals. Consequently there is ample space for SEI and others to work on goals and means, thereby exercising various forms of power.

The classic locus for power turned into legitimate authority is democratic government. Like other actors from civil society and business, even with a social mission SEI are not elected (input legitimacy) and their goals (output legitimacy) and processes (throughput legitimacy) require further scrutiny, as we noted above when we discussed the social side of SEI. If actors delegate power to agents, then we need to investigate the legitimizing reasons that turn the exercise of power into authority, that is, legitimate power.

We posit that the main source of legitimacy is the innovation of the SEI.

Their innovations can give them *output-oriented legitimacy* (Partzsch and Ziegler 2011, p. 68 ff.). This output must be a social one. Unlike business products, there is no established measure of success for the product or service such as profit or revenue, nor is there an established accountability mechanism. In the theory and practice of social entrepreneurship there has accordingly been much discussion of the social impact of social entrepreneurs and reporting practices, standards, and so on. From the point of view of a sustainability-oriented evaluation, we posit that the ethical clarification of this social impact is particularly important and the discussion of capabilities and environmental sustainability helps specify the output legitimacy.

Second, to the extent that SEI are locally embedded at least in the beginning of their initiatives, they have a good grasp of their respective local context. Close ties with affected communities introduce an informal accountability. The accountability of a person for a product that is used where she lives is different from that of a person or organization that produces a product for somewhere else or only comes to install the product and then leaves it to the community. This challenge of international development cooperation and the hand-out mentality it has been criticized of fostering is closely linked to expert power. Outside experts design and control what is right and good; by contrast, there is a civic quality to persons and organizations who work within a community to do what is urgent and important. This direct democratic aspect no doubt reduces the pressure on legitimacy to the extent that it can be seen as simply a form of direct democratic empowerment. Consider the difference between local entrepreneur X offering a solution to his community and multinational Y extending a product developed elsewhere with the aim of making profit in that same community. We thus propose to speak of *social accountability* as a second potential source of authority.

Third, SEI seem to indicate a distinct form of changemaking. Precisely because the goal is to solve a social problem, we find the phenomenon of SEI speaking of themselves as catalysts or of them being called transformation agents by others. They seek societal change and may no longer be needed when this change is achieved. In such cases, there is no power for power's sake and no growth for growth's sake. To the contrary, SEI frequently aim for more transparency and the empowerment of affected people (vis-à-vis state administration in particular). The SEI only have a *mediating role* by advocating for the affected communities and fostering participation. This participatory goal offers a third potential source of legitimacy.

Fourth, in practice 'social entrepreneur' is an outside distinction. It indicates that outsiders take an interest and recognize the idea as valuable.

BOX 1.6   THESES ON LEGITIMACY

Social entrepreneurship initiatives are legitimate agents. This legitimacy depends on their:

   a) output
   b) social accountability
   c) intermediate authority and respective success at empowerment
   d) outside recognition.

Consider by analogy the Amnesty International strategy of asking people from country X to write letters on behalf of people in country Y, referring to international norms. The authority of this outside recognition is partly owing to the fact that those outsiders will usually not be in any evident way related to conflicts of interest within the respective context. Their perspective as outsiders can endow the work with additional ethical objectivity (Sen 2009). Likewise, recognition as a SEI from organizations outside the specific sector and linked to international NGOs – such as Ashoka, Schwab or Skoll, which all take a global outlook – can serve as a distinction. This increases the local and regional recognition of the agent vis-à-vis other agents, makes it harder to ridicule new ideas and protects and promotes ideas changing minds. In short, we posit that *outside recognition* and the distinction as SEI may itself be a further source of authority.

These sources of legitimacy are possibilities. How these sources are played out, and to what extent, is a question to be studied in detail below. Hence we can again formulate theses for our investigation (Box 1.6).

Summing Up

Figure 1.1 visualizes our approach in terms of a capability conversion function (drawing on Robeyns 2005, modified). The capability set and environmental sustainability are the primary goals in this approach to sustainable development. Achieving these goals depends on access to the respective resources and goods, as well as the ability to convert these into capabilities. The classic role of the entrepreneur is the provision of new goods and services (circled in the graph). Owing to the social mission claimed by the SEI, we ask if and how they contribute to basic capabilities and environmental sustainability. This is a question concerning both the effect of the good or service and the process of production. Specifically with a view on capabili-

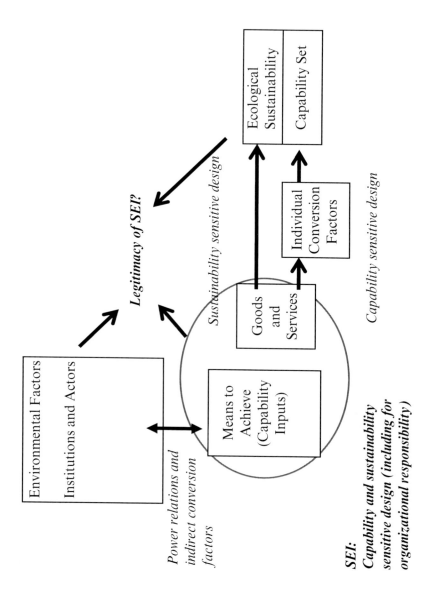

Figure 1.1 *GETIDOS approach in terms of capability conversion function*

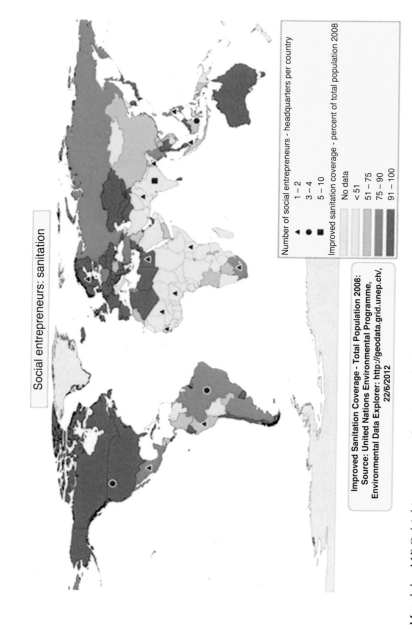

Social entrepreneurs: sanitation

Number of social entrepreneurs - headquarters per country

▲ 1 – 2
● 3 – 4
■ 5 – 10

Improved sanitation coverage - percent of total population 2008

No data
<51
51 – 75
75 – 90
91 – 100

Improved Sanitation Coverage - Total Population 2008:
Source: United Nations Environmental Programme,
Environmental Data Explorer: http://geodata.grid.unep.ch/,
22/6/2012

Map 1.1   MDG drinking water goal and accredited social entrepreneurs

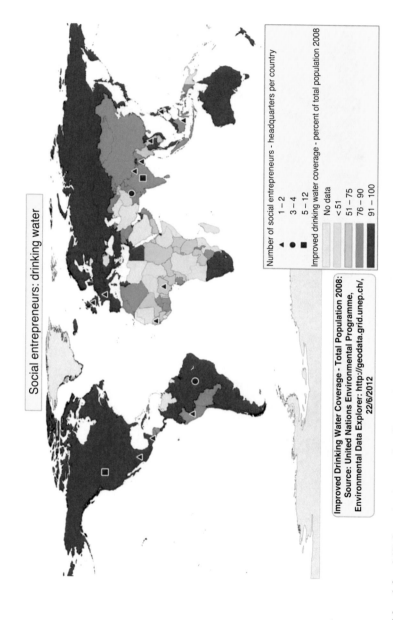

Map 1.2   MDG sanitation goal and accredited social entrepreneurs

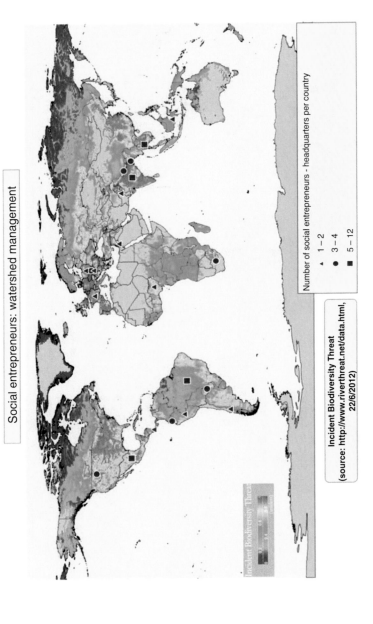

Map 1.3   Biodiversity threats to watersheds and accredited social entrepreneurs

ties, we can ask whether the design of the good and service is such that it is sensitive to the difference between individuals and groups so that they not only have a good or service but also are enabled to use it (for example not only a toilet for 'normal' people but also one that is accessible to people with physical handicaps). In parallel, we ask whether the process is such that it not only makes a product available but also does so in a way that takes environmental sustainability into account (for example not only a tap but one that saves water and energy). The graph of capability conversions also indicates the important role of social and environmental contexts for the production and reproduction of goods and services, of power relations and the indirect conversion factors that are important to stably produce a good or service. Where such a production has become possible, we can investigate the legitimacy of this production – for a pilot project or for a project in the process of being scaled or even institutionalized. We look at its innovation as output, the process aspects of its accountability and the nature of the power sought (intermediary and empowering others), as well as the outside recognition of this approach.

1.6   GETTING THINGS DONE SUSTAINABLY – AS A TASK OF RESEARCH FOR SUSTAINABLE DEVELOPMENT

This work is part of a larger research programme of science for sustainable development, now often called *sustainability science*. This research programme has emerged in the last two decades and remains internally heterogeneous.[14] The key terms of sustainability and sustainable development indicate a general concern (to sustain something). In this section we seek to briefly delineate central demands regarding the quality of such research and how we have attempted to deal with it.

Sustainability science typically involves: 1) cooperation with non-academic partners, 2) interdisciplinary approaches, 3) acceptance of the urgency of issues, which leads to the requirement of new ways of thinking where stakes are high but facts disputed, and 4) concerns with a normative challenge regarding our responsibility for the future and future generations, as well as the legitimate development expectations of people worldwide, especially of those whose basic needs still have not been met (Ziegler and Ott 2011).

In what sense then is the approach outlined above an attempt to do sustainability science? We can sketch an answer in relation to the four categories just mentioned.

Urgency

The MDG set targets for 2015; framing our questions against the background of these goals thus introduces an explicit temporal framework. The challenges are undoubtedly urgent, yet there is reason to worry that the MDG (minimal as they are) will not be fully reached. Accordingly there are questions not only of how established actors in development cooperation should work towards these goals (and of what they have achieved so far) but also whether alternative or complementary actors may have something to contribute to the MDG and to the post-2015 MDG discussions (which have already begun). It is with this broad framing here that we study the role of social entrepreneurs via selected case studies.

In the European context, MDG 7 with respect to water points to the European Union's Water Framework Directive (WFD), which also specifies goals for 2015. One of our case studies seeks to strengthen the participatory dimension of the WFD and we have chosen here to directly participate, not just studying an idea but also replicating it and performing it ourselves (Chapter 9). As is indirectly so in the other case studies, here there is a constant renegotiation of observing and participating. Such a renegotiation is just what we have to accept and live with in sustainable development research. The task is to make the presuppositions and consequences of such research explicit and transparent.

Normativity

As we have already seen, research for sustainable development involves normative questions and contestations. While normative questioning can initially draw on a vague concept, it then requires a more specific conception of sustainable development. Here we draw on the capabilities approach and strong sustainability to spell out our conception and to orient the subsequent case studies as far as ethical concerns. The verb 'to orient' is important. Normative analysis in the first place has the task to illuminate the normative dimension and the values and obligations at issue, to bring them into the discussion. This work is prior to specific judgments and prescriptions of what to do in a specific situation and the numerous contextual considerations such judgments depend on. The primary goal here is illumination in this first sense.

Sustainable development and sustainability are not exclusively normative concepts. To the contrary, they involve numerous descriptive, empirical aspects. Sustainable development is not only a contested concept, but also a thick concept in the sense that doing work on sustainability involves evaluative and descriptive tasks concerning societies and their natural environment (a point that we will return to below when addressing interdisciplinarity).

Justified Inclusion of Non-academics

Our non-academic partners in this project were SEI. Their ideas were explored via detailed change studies based on the approach outlined above. From this perspective we thought through the missions and approaches of our partners. This led to change reports, which we presented back to our partners in 2012 as critical feedback for them and for us. Three goals were associated with these reports and the subsequent discussion meetings: to offer helpful feedback to our partners from a perspective of sustainability, to hear their view of our work and finally, to discuss together the potential of social entrepreneurship for sustainable development. These discussions have co-shaped the final versions of the following chapters.

The epistemic and normative role of our partners for our research project is very important. Their inclusion was based on the following ideas. 1) *Local and tacit knowledge*: the SEI help us in the analysis of their respective cases, they help us understand in what sense they view themselves as entrepreneurs or innovators, and they especially help us see how their work is embedded in a historical context. Such qualitative understanding emerges from interviews and participant observation. 2) *Bias*: feedback from the SEI on our work provides criticism and questions beyond the lenses of academic work and its disciplinary biases. 3) *Care*: discussions with those who will be directly affected by practical implications of these conclusions, hence caring about them in a way academics might not, is incredibly valuable. 4) *Normativity*: because there are no experts in ethics with final authority, it is important to discuss ethical conceptions, disagreements and the reasons for them with the people involved. 5) *New conjectures*: including a selection of SEI introduces a variety of proposals for new ideas about doing things and ways of being, from the level of goal conception to the specifics of how to achieve those goals.

Interdisciplinarity

The team working on this project is interdisciplinary with backgrounds in environmental engineering and environmental science, management, philosophy and political science. Accordingly, we started with work on disciplinary interfaces that helped build the approach outlined above. We also engaged in a joint-work process on case studies. In 2009 we made a comprehensive overview of SEI in relation to major water challenges. In a second step, we selected change studies again for a joint-work process. To do justice to social entrepreneurship as a putatively global phenomenon, we wanted to include case studies from Africa, the Americas, Asia and Europe. This resulted in the following in-depth change studies:

Africa: Ecotact (Kenya)
Asia: WOTR (India)
Europe: People and Water (Slovakia), ERN (France/Europe), Viva con Agua (Germany)
Americas: Ecodecision (Ecuador)

This selection is based on actors selected as SEI by support organizations or otherwise externally recognized as innovators. There are many more individuals, organizations and networks who see themselves as SEI. The discovery and selection of SEI worldwide is real work in itself. Several large foundations have put their resources into this; they served for us the role of a discovery mechanism. More subtly, we thereby included initiatives that accepted the accreditation *as* SEI.

This selection created the space for further research. As anyone familiar with social entrepreneurship knows, there is a huge difference between the online profile of a given SEI, typically made available by the support organizations, and an in-depth case study of this SEI. Moreover, there is still a relative absence of in-depth, theme-specific approaches to social entrepreneurship research; in fact, we do not know of any in-depth, long-term sustainability-oriented research study in general, let alone specifically with a focus on water. There are learning possibilities here in regards to the idea and image of social entrepreneurship promoted via the support organizations and to the diversity of innovations SEI implement on the ground.

Case studies, in the original sense of learning and thinking about a complex reality, are practised for example in law, medicine and management (Krohn 2009). Here we bring a case study approach to the theme of social entrepreneurship and water challenges. We aim to learn about each case specifically and based on our conception draw conclusions from the cases to orient the role of SEI for sustainable development.

Outlook

The following chapters will accordingly present our change studies (Chapters 2 to 7). The final part of the book will draw conclusions from these change studies; this part is divided into two chapters. In our synthesis (Chapter 8) we will present the conclusions from our case studies with respect to the theses and will analyse the implication of these results for our conception of social entrepreneurship as well as for the role of SEI in sustainable development. In Chapter 9 we will discuss collaboration and cooperation, including an in-depth discussion of a collaborative project that we co-initiated during the project, the *Big Jump Challenge*.

NOTES

1. http://www.skollfoundation.org/about/ (accessed 20 July 2011).
2. http://www.ashoka.org/support/criteria (accessed 20 July 2011).
3. http://www.ashoka.org/social_entrepreneur (accessed 20 July 2011).
4. http://www.ashoka.org/support/criteria (accessed 20 July 2011).
5. https://www.se-alliance.org/what-is-social-enterprise (accessed 20 July 2011).
6. An overview of arguments advanced for the schools helps to better see this point (see Gebauer and Ziegler 2013). In support of the earned income school it has been argued that: 1) an earned income strategy promotes financial viability in the long term; 2) earned income creates independence and increases the space in which resources can be invested; 3) earned income encourages discipline via market activity and a business plan; 4) earned income helps the SEI to grow; 5) a focus on earned income resonates well with linguistic conventions, at least in capitalist societies, which tend to identify enterprise with market-based activity; 6) earned income also seems to have a close fit with market-liberal ideologies that tend to view social problems as market externalities; social enterprise is a way of internalizing problems and thus extending and perfecting markets. There are also a number of objections to the earned income school: 1) market income does not necessarily promote or even introduce financial viability and independence; what increases financial viability and financial sustainability is a contextual issue that depends on the problem (Dees and Anderson 2006); 2) the focus on earned income and business methods tends to require a focus on management and administration. Thereby the classic distinction between entrepreneurship and management/administration is blurred, and 'crazy' ideas may be at a disadvantage; 3) Making earned income an essential aspect of social entrepreneurship is to promote (knowingly or not) a selection bias in favour of dealing with problems that are marketable (Defourny and Nyseens 2010, p. 49), while many social issues cannot be dealt with by markets and there is hence a danger of confusing means and ends; 4) on the level of the theory of society and our conceptualization of it, there has been the worry that this approach is yet another form of market imperialism extending market questions to all domains of life. For example, policy questions tend to become a question of how to improve conditions for SEI and not of how to change policy for a specific social problem. The presence of an arguably radical edge – thinking outside the market or transforming capitalism – tends to disappear.
    There are also arguments in favour and ones against the social innovation school. In favour: 1) the focus on innovation resonates well with key practice players such as Ashoka and their popularisers (Bornstein 2004) – a view towards the power of ideas to change the world is very much in the centre of this community of practice; 2) the focus on innovation preserves the distinction between entrepreneurship and management/administration, which may be fruitful for theoretical purposes (such as the explanation of change) and also for practice (as in the well-known view that the skills of the entrepreneur are not those of the manager maintaining and sustaining an already established organization); 3) the focus on innovation and the carrying out of ideas leaves it open whether the carrying out is best a matter for market production, policy, civil society or some mixture. Therefore, here means and ends are kept distinct; 4) just as there are

market-liberal theories and ideologies, there are also theories that emphasize the need to transform markets and to introduce disruptive change, and social innovation is in principle open to such views. In objection: 1) the advantage of analysing entrepreneurship in terms of innovation (in contrast to management) turns out to be a weakness to the extent that the concept of innovation remains elusive and vague; 2) the focus on ideas changing the world tends to focus on an ideal outcome and not on what those entrepreneurs have already achieved and as a result practitioners may be discouraged and research focuses on questions with only limited links to practice; 3) with a view on the frequent emphasis on individuals in this model, it has been objected that this approach misunderstands the nature of societal change as a complex process involving structures and organizations in a dynamic, and therefore cannot *explain* change.

7. What about the social as a question of actor type? In particular, can we not co-define SEI as actors from the third sector (Nicholls 2010, p. 16)? From a perspective of social enterprise (as defined above), this move is problematic as this view includes for-profit business actors. Thus, the question of actors is non-trivial too. From a perspective of social innovation, the type of organization is secondary as far as the categories of civil society, business or governmental actors are concerned. As Nicholls also notes, this view is 'agnostic about the role of business' (Nicholls 2010, p. 17). Thus a further argument would be required that third-sector actors are particularly innovative, perhaps because they are not so strongly influenced by the inertia of large public or business organizations. However, this move inherits the problem already present in the account of innovation (Schumpeter 1942) – why should large organizations not innovate (for example via research and development)? In fact, there is much evidence that they do. Finally, the clarification of actor types will hardly solve the kind of normative expectations that are part of the use of 'social' and 'social entrepreneurs' in the typical language games that suggests improving, tackling problems, and so on.

8. No doubt, this categorization of freshwater use is only one way of categorizing the complexity of water challenges. In addition, there is the water in the sea and the hydrological cycle as a whole. In particular, fisheries and their impact on marine ecosystems are an important global concern.

9. Further to the already reported Ashoka numbers, as of 2013 Acumens supports 63 fellows, Echoing Green supports 500 social entrepreneurs, the Schwab Foundation supports over 260 social entrepreneurs, and the Skoll Foundation 97 social entrepreneurs.

10. And for completion: we found 19 SEI beyond freshwater working on issues related to marine protection and coastal management.

11. Having an effective opportunity in many cases depends on participation and an effective say in decision-making (Henkel and Ziegler 2010). Participation is a matter of degrees: from a) nominal and passive forms of participation; via b) consultations and petitions; to c) participatory decision-making including bargaining or deliberation. Drawing on the discussion from deliberative democracy theory, we can examine the following indicators of the participatory quality of the process: 1) inclusiveness and political equality – who is included in agenda-setting, goal formulation and implementation? Are those directly affected by the initiative included in a way that gives them equal opportunity? 2) Publicity – is the initiative proposed and discussed in a public and transparent manner so that information is made available to all? 3) Reasoned debate – is there space for the exchange of arguments (that is a way to bring them forward and listen to them)?

12. According to the MEA, ecosystem services are the benefits that people obtain from ecosystems (MEA 2005). The MEA working-groups list ecosystem services directly linked to people's needs and wants as provisioning, regulating and cultural. In addition, it names supporting services that frame and maintain the former processes.

13. We here adopt a perspective of strong sustainability, a view that sees sustaining natural capital – in a wide sense – as a constitutive and distinct task of sustainable development (Ott and Döring 2004). Put differently, investments in overall capital – that is, sustaining the total of financial, technical, human, natural capital – is not sufficient; there is a need

to pay specific attention to natural capital and the specific, non-substitutable services it provides.

14. Important and frequently overlapping research communities contributing to sustainability science include resilience research, common-pool research, socio-ecological research, transitions research and vulnerability research. For a list of publications and journals as well as further resources, see http://sustainabilityscience.org/document. html?type=journal. The categories discussed in this section are introduced in more detail in Ziegler and Ott 2011.

2. Toilets before independence – David Kuria and Ecotact

Franziska Mohaupt and Rafael Ziegler

2.1 INTRODUCTION

We arrived in Nairobi early one January morning in 2011. It was raining. This was a disappointment coming from grey Berlin in the winter. Yet it was a disappointment only for us; we were quickly told that a little rain in this dry period of the year was much appreciated by Kenyans. Weather aside, the streets from the airport to the city centre at this early hour were already full with cars. We got stuck in a traffic jam. Many people walked past; going to work, looking for work, shopping? We were not sure, but certainly the average age of the public had dropped radically from Berlin, Germany to Nairobi, Kenya. Via an industrial zone near the airport, a slum and then the city centre, our taxi took us to our destination – Kilimani. Here in this leafy, residential district of Nairobi, David Kuria has set up the headquarters for his social entrepreneurship initiative, Ecotact.

This Kenyan organization focuses on innovation in general, but had come to our attention owing to its work on sustainable and environmentally friendly sanitation and drinking water for all. This environmental dimension is noteworthy. In 2011 at least 12.5 million people were threatened by drought in the Horn of Africa (OCHA 2011). The rainfall in the last years has been below average; nearly the whole region is affected by extreme water scarcity, declining water tables, and time and time again, long periods without rain.

Accordingly, an efficient and effective use of water is a key challenge for infrastructure, not least in large and growing urban centres such as Nairobi. The Kenyan population increased by more than 20 million people between 1989 and 2010, from 20.4 million to 42.8 million (Kenya National Bureau of Statistics 2010, WHO/UNICEF 2012) – a huge infrastructure for any urban planner. Who will build the infrastructure, and with what means? Take the example of drinking water and sanitation: according to UN statistics of the Joint Monitoring Programme,[1] the percentage of people who only have access to drinking water that poses a likely threat to health – or what the UN calls *unimproved water sources* – went down from 56 per cent in 1990 to 41 per cent in 2010. While this means that Kenya is on track for the MDG drinking water target, it still means that 41 per cent of a growing and young population do not have such access. Likewise, lack of access to improved sanitation was reduced from 54 per cent in 1990 to 41 per cent in 2010; however, in absolute numbers, the people with access to no or only unimproved sanitation facilities increased from 12.67 up to 16.61 million in 2010 (own calculation based on WHO/UNICEF 2012). This poses a special challenge to the urban centres, where population growth has gone up from an amazing 18.2 per cent in 1990 to 22.9 per cent in 2012.

The challenge of access to sanitation is both a private and a public challenge. Public access is a matter of sanitation in schools and in public buildings and spaces. Next to the unexpected rain, the most striking experience for us when arriving in Nairobi was the mere amount of time spent in public transportation simply getting to work or for errands such as shopping in a market – unlike the rain, this is a regular occurrence! Access to public toilets is therefore a matter of concern for a large number of Kenyan citizens and it is frequently overlooked owing to a prevailing international focus on sanitation at home.

This chapter presents one approach to dealing with this challenge – the work of David Kuria and Ecotact. We will first introduce their general approach to change (Section 2.2) and then introduce the Ikotoilets – Ecotact's flagship product so far (Section 2.3). In the next step, we evaluate this approach from a sustainability perspective (Section 2.4). Our key questions in this chapter are: What is Ecotact's innovation and has the organization been able to scale it? What is social about this innovation and how does it contribute to human capabilities and environmental sustainability? In light of these questions – and considering that the Kenyan constitution recognizes sanitation as a matter of right – what is the legitimacy of a private actor to provide access to public sanitation?

The work in this chapter draws on desktop research, a preparatory meeting with David Kuria in 2010 and two research trips to Nairobi in January–February 2011 and in July 2012. The field trips were used to conduct semi-structured interviews with Ecotact staff and stakeholders. The trip in 2011 was also used to set up a survey in a market place where an Ikotoilet was opened in February 2011. The survey was conducted in three waves – January 2011 (before the opening of the Ikotoilet), February 2011 (directly after the opening of the Ikotoilet) and June 2011.[2]

2.2 INVESTING IN INNOVATIONS – ECOTACT'S MISSION

David Kuria and Dr. Kamithi Nganga founded Ecotact in 2006; the former is current CEO and the latter, current chair of the board. Ecotact's mission is to 'develop innovative answers to the growing environmental sanitation cry in Africa and globally' (Ecotact Homepage 2011, last accessed 11 November 2011). As the organization's motto puts it, Ecotact is *investing in innovations*. So far Ecotact has sought to pursue this mission via four fields of work: public toilets called Ikotoilets (in city centres, schools and slums), the environmental magazine *Ecodigest*, consultancy work in development cooperation and the project Iko-Maji, which works towards improving access to water in peri-urban communities. The flagship project is the Ikotoilet approach; accordingly, this will be the focus in the following discussions (see next section).

Prior to founding Ecotact, David Kuria worked as an architect with the City Planning Division of the Nairobi City Council (NCC) and with the NGO Intermediate Technology Development Group (ITDG) on issues of urban environment, especially in slums. In retrospect, he now says that neither government nor NGOs are in a position to develop practical and sustainable solutions for urban sanitation problems. In his view, government programmes are hampered by corruption, inefficiencies and political power games; and NGOs depend on the agendas of donor agencies rather than on meeting the real needs of people with feasible projects (Karugu 2011, p. 3). In this context, Kuria references his Ikotoilets to explain how social entrepreneurship is a viable approach:

> I don't think the case of the Ikotoilet is purely a business case. To me it falls very clearly between the business and the missionary. And that's purely between the donors who are looking purely at market niche – market positioning. . . . And that's pure business. On the other side, there are the missionaries, who are looking purely at 'you are so poor, you need toilets – we come and do pit latrines, take the key and go. . . .'. Social entrepreneurs are purely a hybrid of that. They try to address the issues civil societies should be addressing or have been struggling to address, but in a more sustainable way. (Kuria, 2 February 2011, Nairobi)

Kuria's view of social entrepreneurship as a hybrid of business and social mission is a matter of innovation with a social goal. His view of innovation takes inspiration from the technological innovations of for-profit products. When presenting on sanitation, he likes to show some slides on the rapid change in telecommunication from the early dial phones to the smartphone (in this spirit, Ecotact currently presents its awards on their homepage on the display of a smartphone). Change in sanitation is possible, he suggests, and like change in telecommunication, it could be attractive and linked to general transformations in self-understanding and lifestyle.

Kuria, however, does not view himself or other social innovators as the 'Steve Jobs' of sanitation. The reason is his conception of innovator as catalyst: 'Our strategy for the Ikotoilet . . . was to demonstrate the transformative model. Our vision was not to go on scale. . . . Just to demonstrate that it works. And other people can pick it up and scale' (David Kuria, 29 October 2010, Greifswald). 'To us the task is how we catalyse the private sector to see they have a role in things they had not even thought about like hygiene' (David Kuria, 28 January 2011, Nairobi).

The catalyst approach in Kuria's understanding has a clear core, but a less clear implication for scaling. The catalyst is open to new ideas, making them visible or developing them when the mainstream is still invested in established technologies and ways of doing things. The catalyst develops pilots that should convince and inspire. For the Ikotoilet in urban centres, Kuria estimates that this took Ecotact about three to four years. In regards to such pilots, Ecotact views the development of a pilot itself as a continuous process, at least up to the point where the pilot is in such a state that it can be easily replicated. As Kuria puts it when talking about the Ikotoilets in urban centres, '[e]verything in five, ten steps and it is done' (David Kuria, 2 February 2011, Nairobi). Establishing partnerships in this pilot phase is very important; this brings in resources, knowledge and political support, on the one hand, for establishing the pilot and, on the other hand, for further implementing and developing the approach on a nationwide or even continental scale.

The social entrepreneur as catalyst plays the activating role: '*as a catalyst you are the one driving*' (David Kuria, 2 February 2011, Nairobi). The limits of this role as driver in the process of scaling are less clear. On the one hand, Ecotact as an organization seeks to bring its toilets to urban centres across Kenya and to other countries such as Ghana, Uganda and Tanzania. On the other hand, Kuria states that the goal remains that big actors will eventually take on the job – KfW Banking Group, the UN and 'the rest of the world' (David Kuria, 2 February 2011, Nairobi). Only if larger players take on the approach, says Kuria, will it be possible to really have an impact across East Africa. Figure 2.1 illustrates this approach schematically; the next section sets it out in detail with the example of Ikotoilets.

2.3 IKOTOILETS

The main language of communication in Kenya is Kiswahili, and in this language Ikotoilet means *there is a toilet*. Thus the name indicates a place.

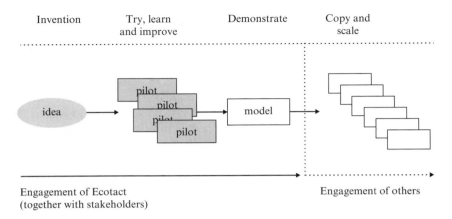

Source: Own illustration.

Figure 2.1   The Ecotact catalyst approach

Kuria aims to construct *toilet monuments*, as he says, that will serve in urban space as a landmark with recognition value. The Ikotoilet is to be perceived as a brand associated with high quality sanitation in public space. This goal is linked to the way in which Kuria situates his mission in Kenyan politics. Asserting Gandhi's slogan, *sanitation is more important than independence*, he argues that sanitary conditions are very poor and that improving sanitation might improve politics. There is a need, as the company slogan has it, 'to think beyond the toilet'.

In English, Ikotoilets connote ecological sanitation, a technical term for an approach to sanitation that is based on the principles of preventing pollution rather than attempting to control it after we pollute, of sanitizing the urine and the faeces, and of using the safe products for agricultural purposes. This sanitize-and-recycle system ideally approaches a closed loop, where urine is treated as a resource and the nutrients of both urine and excreta are reused in agriculture (SEI 2004). The technological design and construction according to these principles differs from place to place and depends on the socio-ecological context. As it has been very challenging so far to successfully promote ecological sanitation and to create acceptance for the fertilizer use, Ecotact has taken on board an important but difficult challenge.

Ecotact has explored the challenge of improving and providing sanitation in three different settings: urban centres, slums and schools.[3] In 2010 Ecotact reported 6.2 million users (up from 3.8 million in 2009) and invested over US$ 1.2 million in the construction of 40 facilities in

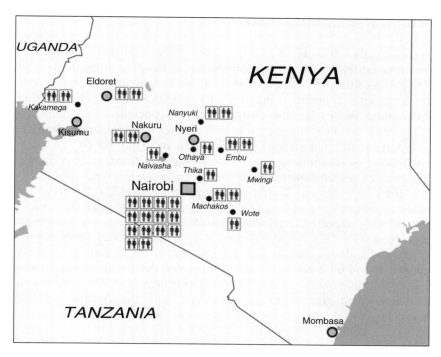

Note: The Ikotoilets indicated for Nairobi include all toilets in the wider metropolitan area and the nearby town of Limuru.

Source: Own source.

Figure 2.2   Ikotoilets in Kenya

20 municipalities.[4] As of early 2011, Ecotact has completed 31 Ikotoilets in Nairobi and 12 other Kenyan towns (see Figure 2.2). There are also two Ikotoilets in slums of Nairobi (Mathare and Kawangware) and ten Ikotoilets in schools in rural Kenya. Seven of those are in the process of construction, three of them have been finished and one of those three is in use so far. These figures show that Ecotact has so far developed a model for the urban centres in the catalyst sense outlined above. We will therefore outline this model in the urban centre first and in greater detail, and then turn to schools and slums respectively.

Ikotoilets in Formal Urban Settlements

In the capital of Nairobi, most public toilets were constructed before independence in 1963, with only a few built later in the 1970s and 1980s (WSP 2004, p. 2). After the construction of these toilets, however, very little has been done to maintain them. A survey by the Water and Sanitation Programme (WSP) for the city of Nairobi concluded the following: 'After 1980, the NCC appears to have lacked a clear policy regarding the development and maintenance of PTs [public toilets] in the city and only constructed or rehabilitated PTs in emergency situations, such as disease epidemics or special demands from central government' (WSP 2004, p. 2).

In 1995 the Water and Sanitation Department estimated that only a very small fraction of the costs required for renovating public toilets in Nairobi were actually allocated to rehabilitation (WSP 2004, p. 4). The challenges concerned both the physical infrastructure (maintenance of water supply, toilets, walls, doors, and so on) and the social aspects such as security (muggings and molestations made public toilets dangerous to access) and hygiene (cleanliness of toilets, hand-washing facilities). There have also been severe management problems observed within the responsible public body:

> At NCC's water and sanitation department 'W&SD', staff morale was low. There was lack of attention to supervision and quality control. Graft and corruption were widespread, leading to leakage of user payments and misuse of premises. Operations had lacked budgetary support and income due to inadequate pricing policies and inconsistent political support. (WSP 2004, p. 2)

In the early years of the new millennium, an initiative of the Nairobi Central Business District Association (NCBDA) appears to have been the first sustained attempt to improve public toilets in Nairobi; it aimed to address the issue and sought to identify private organizations for the renovation and operation of public toilets. With a more general perspective, the Government of Kenya's *Vision 2030* envisages that 'improved water and sanitation are available and accessible to all' (Government of Kenya 2007, p. 18) and stresses the importance of the 'commissioning of public–private partnerships for improved efficiency in water and sanitation delivery' (Government of Kenya 2007, p. 19). When Ecotact started its work in 2006, it did so in a situation of public need and the emerging public recognition of this need.

Ikotoilets are public toilets based on a public–private partnership of Ecotact with the respective municipality. The organization enters into a five-year contract with the given municipality to build and exclusively operate toilet facilities on publicly owned land, a build–operate–transfer

---

BOX 2.1   FINANCING AN IKOTOILET

In 2011, the construction of an Ikotoilet cost around 2 000 000 Kenyan shillings (Ksh.: roughly 17 600 euros), and operating costs for local staff and materials and repairs came to about 70 000 Ksh. per month (roughly 617 euros). Operating costs vary, as staff numbers vary between Ikotoilets. Ecotact generates revenue via user charges (5 Ksh. or a bit more than 4 euro cents for toilet use; 20 Ksh. or about 17 euro cents for a shower) and rental space in the toilet buildings. The monthly rent for a shop is between 5000 and 15 000 Ksh. (about 44 to 132 euros) and for a shoe-shine booth between 10 000 and 20 000 Ksh. (roughly 88 to 176 euros). Some additional revenue can be generated via advertising space in Ikotoilets. A key parameter is the number of users, which varies strongly amongst locations. As a result some Ikotoilets generate extra revenue while others run at a loss. Ecotact can respond to this variation to some extent by varying the number of staff in the respective toilet.

---

agreement (BOT). Ecotact holds operational rights for five years, at the end of which the contract is either renewed or the facility transferred to the municipality. Accordingly, Ecotact has five years to recover its construction expenditures (see Box 2.1).

Ecotact constructs its own public toilets because its goal is transformation in urban centres rather than rehabilitation (Ecotact Brochures 2010, 2010a). This transformation concerns both users and service providers in public space. As far as the users are concerned, the visually unusual and colourful buildings are to stand out as public landmarks – *toilet monuments* in Kuria's words – that may be confused with hotels and banks. According to Kuria, public sanitation has been too much of a taboo; therefore, there is a need to create buildings that are associated with success, which for many in Kenya means an association with business. He also speaks of *toilet malls* and actively encourages the media to report on the Ikotoilets via the opening of new facilities with politicians and celebrities. As shops and shoe-shiners are integrated into the building, he believes that users will be able to associate sanitation with something positive. The local staff provides clean, secure and convenient services inside the Ikotoilet mall. In this way Kuria aims at a double transformation of users and their hygiene behaviour and of urban centres and their architecture, where a basic need comes to be associated with an attractive, landmark meeting point.

On the side of service providers, Ecotact seeks to inspire others with attractive design and high service standards based on a business model that demonstrates how access to sanitation in public is not only a basic need but also an attractive business for the industry. Ecotact employs cleaning staff for the daily maintenance of the Ikotoilets as well as supervisors, who are in charge of several Ikotoilets, ensuring that local staff offers quality service and also dealing with unexpected technical or social issues. The Ikotoilet architecture allows shop operators to rent space for their small businesses, like shoe-shiners and M-Pesa facilities, for the Kenyan mobile-based money transfer services. Shop operators have an interest in keeping the toilets attractive for customers and thus increase pressure that toilets are cleaned on a regular basis.

This business case for sanitation as a toilet mall is complemented by the business case for sanitation as a resource conservation case. Low-flush toilets, waterless urinals, water-saving taps and tanks for rainwater harvesting and urine harvesting for fertilizer production are all elements of moving in the direction of ecological sanitation. As of 2011, toilets that are not connected to the sewage system have been equipped with bio-digester systems for turning human waste into biogas and compost ready for using, for example, in urban gardening activities.

The use of urine as fertilizer is underdevelopment (as part of a joint research project with Jomo Kenyatta University. David Kuria's vision of ecological sanitation relates to a notion of environmental sustainability based on a process of technical innovation: 'Not [that] we are coming up with the product and say[ing] this is now ecological – no! To us it's a continuous process. How do we make it continuously as ecological as possible?' (David Kuria, 2 February 2011, Nairobi). In this way, Ecotact aims at a double social and ecological transformation of public sanitation.

Already at the initial level of demonstrating this model in Nairobi's urban centres, this approach co-depends on stakeholders from politics, business, civil society and, at least in the medium term, science. As far as politics is concerned, the build-and-operate approach requires close cooperation with local authorities. In Nairobi this was the NCC, which is responsible for sanitation service delivery in the downtown area. In addition, the National Environment Management Authority (NEMA) plays an enabling role: it licenses all new projects in Kenya after ensuring that their environmental impacts will be acceptable. So far, NEMA has approved the construction of Ikotoilets without delay. What is also important is the support of members of parliament and ministries, not least given the possibility that a local authority may change plans and, for example, seek to collect revenue from an Ikotoilet itself. Hence it has been important that the Ministry of Public Health, which sets the regulatory framework for sanitation services in Kenya, has seen Ikotoilets in a favourable light and has collaborated with Ecotact. The Minister of Health as well as some members of parliament have on different occasions opened Ikotoilets.

Business partners are important for the operation and financial viability of the approach. The small shops within the Ikotoilet structure pay rent and play their role in demonstrating the toilet mall concept, and they have an interest that the toilet monument stays clean, affordable and hence attractive. Ecotact works with larger companies for the provision of construction and maintenance materials; some of these companies have in turn used the Ikotoilet to rent advertisement space.

Civil society – in the form of internationally operating foundations for the support of social entrepreneurship – has played an important role for providing finance and network resources for Ecotact. Kuria could not gain access to regular credit from banks; he did not have sufficient equity and toilets were not generally considered a promising area of business for banks. In 2008 Ecotact received a patient capital loan of 757 000 US$ from the social investor Acumen Fund. *Patient capital* means that the loan is assigned with a grace period where no interest has to be repaid and the payback mechanism is held flexible in order to be affordable for the borrower (in this case, Ecotact). Wendy Mukuru from Acumen Fund puts it like this: 'Ecotact was not a proven concept and Kuria was not a businessman. There was no balance sheet, no income statement. But he was compelling!' (Ebrahim and Rangan 2010, p. 7). In addition, the social entrepreneurship support organizations Ashoka and Schwab have included David Kuria in their networks; this provides invitations to international network conferences and provides international visibility. Finally, Ecotact partners with NGOs that do parallel and complementary work in the field of sanitation. For instance, Ecotact partnered with an NGO specializing in female hygiene education to distribute sanitary pads and underwear to girls who were not coming to school or who were not using the school Ikotoilets during their period of menstruation.

Last but not least, the ecological-sanitation dimension is knowledge intensive. Ecotact cooperates with the Jomo Kenyatta University in terms of developing, testing and adjusting ecosanitation technologies for the Ikotoilets. A research group at the JKUAT is currently developing a technique for the production of fertilizers from urine. Figure 2.3 shows the relationship between Ecotact and its stakeholders in the setting up of the pilot of Ikotoilets in urban centres.

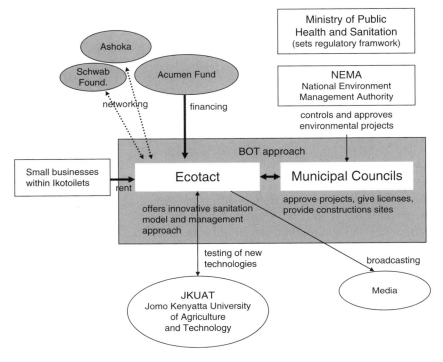

Source: Own illustration.

Figure 2.3   Ecotact's main partners, their relations and roles for setting up the pilot

Ikotoilets in Schools

The sanitation infrastructure in public schools has long been a problem. In addition to the high population growth of the last 20 years, the government's decision in 2003 to make primary school education free for every child increased classroom numbers and, with this, put added pressure on schools. Overcrowded classes and a student–toilet ratio of 50:1 are common (the recommended ration is 25:1, Ministry of Education 2008).

The Ikotoilet School Initiative aims to improve access to sanitation in schools. Started in 2009, the first school Ikotoilet opened in 2010 at Thirime Primary School. Another seven toilets were under construction on behalf of the programme when we visited Ecotact in 2010. The construction of two other toilets was complete but they are not yet in use. The Ikotoilet approach to school sanitation differs from the urban centre approach. After completion, the Ikotoilets are handed over to the schools, which are responsible for maintenance of the toilets. The main goal in the school context is to initiate a change in sanitation habits. Hygiene promotion is going to be fostered by a *talking wall* (walls with information about hand-washing), a *talking toilet* (interactive audio simulations in the school) and hygiene clubs, where the children can discuss about hygiene behaviour and then teach other kids. Accompanying activities such as tree planting and the technology lab, where pupils will learn about ecological sanitation technologies, supplement the approach so as to go beyond basic sanitation, as Ecotact promotes. There is a plan to produce biogas in digesters connected to the Ikotoilets and use it in the school kitchens in order to supplement other cooking fuel. The construction follows the toilet monument idea, but the mall concept is not and likely cannot be realized. Accordingly, there is no local source of income for the toilet.

The initiative so far has been financed via the Constituency Development Fund and H2O, an American NGO. Danone has agreed to provide soap and paint in exchange for one of their products being advertised on the walls of the Ikotoilet. The initiative is also supported by the Global Water Challenge. Ecotact faced several problems while implementing the toilets; these included enhanced construction costs as well as sudden withdrawal from national financial support, severe difficulties of water availability and high water supply costs, and finally the construction in the remaining seven schools stopped in 2011.

Ikotoilets in Informal Urban Settlements

Ecotact has also tested Ikotoilets in two informal urban settlements of Nairobi (Mathare and Kawangware). Again the architecture follows the toilet monument approach; however, like the schools, there are also significant differences owing to context. A key difference is the status of slums as informal settlements, which in Kenyan history implied the non-recognition of the area as part of the city. Accordingly, the infrastructure is poor (usually no public drinking water or sewage system) and it is difficult to maintain formal business relations. This increases the transaction and construction costs of Ikotoilets in the slums. In Mathare, Ecotact has worked with a local youth network, appointed by the community council of the respective part of the settlement to operate the Ikotoilet, but has found it difficult to maintain stable relationships and to recover revenue.[5] It is therefore not clear how Ecotact could recover its investment. Most importantly, the target groups in the informal settlements are in much more dire need than in the urban centre. In response, Ecotact has introduced a 'family mega card', which charges a monthly fee for using the Ikotoilet;

however, it has not been able to put this model into practice with its local partners in such a way that it generates revenue for Ecotact.

The family mega card indicates the radically changed context: the Ikotoilets in the urban centres serve as public toilets to be used during work hours, in transport, and so on; the Ikotoilet in the slum effectively offers a place for sanitation (including showers) for people who have only poor or no access to private sanitation and washing options. Accordingly, the peak use hours of the Ikotoilet in the slums has been early in the morning (before going to work) and in the evening (after work). Accordingly, the very rationale for the toilets changes: the provision of access here is substituting for an insufficient household or household unit infrastructure. Kuria admits, unlike in the urban centre, Ecotact has not yet been able to find a workable model for the Ikotoilets in the slums.[6]

Ecotact as a Catalyst of Public Sanitation

Is Ecotact a social entrepreneurship initiative that carries out a new idea relative to its temporal and/or spatial context of action (our innovation thesis)? Ecotact is a social innovator primarily owing to the Ikotoilets *in urban centres*. These Ikotoilets improve the existing public toilet infrastructure and they are clearly novel in their context. The transformative goals Ecotact associates with the Ikotoilets aim to impact at the national level and ultimately East Africa and beyond (our scaling thesis). However, Ecotact does not see itself as the organization that will carry out this transformation on the national level. Rather, it seeks to scale out its innovation by acting as a catalyst that attracts other actors from politics and business to cooperate on high-quality public toilets on the national level.

Ecotact currently receives invitations from municipalities regarding the construction of Ikotoilets. Possibly even more important, the model demonstrates that high quality and affordable public sanitation is possible and hence may invite imitation by other companies. As a model for urban centres, the Ikotoilet has the potential to be replicated by other companies in urban centres across Kenya and possibly beyond. There is already some evidence for this: an NCC employee stated in an interview that the city council receives applications on a monthly basis from small companies aiming to establish their own businesses in public sanitation. All in all, the role as a catalyst with national impact is at an early stage. As Kuria reflected in 2012:

> I am not sure for how long you can play a role of a catalyst. We have now been in this for the last four years and we are almost now drifting. What I thought primarily was that there were different stages involved. So I gave it a period of ten

years. But to me I think the way I have broken it down in terms of role strategy. The first one is what I call monitoring or sustainability monitoring. . . . For me that was very rapid, taking three [to] four years to provide a sustainable model and to prove to the world that you have this sustainable model. The next step is the scale. I think that's where we are now. (David Kuria, 5 July 2012, Nairobi)

Ecotact has done much to improve the conditions of scaling out as far as cultural acceptance of public sanitation is concerned. Its model demonstrates that there is economic space for public sanitation and that it is possible to use this space in cooperation with actors from the political space in Kenya. However, Ecotact does not yet have a medium or long-term model of how to cooperate with stakeholders on a national or even East-African scaling strategy. The visibility and the intention are there, but a clear partner strategy is still called for.

> We are trying to scale in Kenya and Uganda and Ghana. But I also see [this] as perhaps taking us another three years to do that. To prove that it works in three, five, ten countries . . . I would see [our role] in the final stage as being there as the catalyst. . . . We want to influence the KfWs to pump millions of dollars into this model. Influence the UN system. . . . You don't have to do fifty countries. Other people can do it but they need this amount of millions of dollars to do that. And these are the partnerships that are needed to make it sustainable so that the whole framework is clear. Might take ten years, might take more. (David Kuria, 5 July 2012, Nairobi)

2.4 SUSTAINABILITY EVALUATION

Our sustainability evaluation of Ecotact as a social innovator is based on the conceptual perspective and empirical work outlined in the first part of this book. The evaluation focuses on Ikotoilets in 'formal' urban space, which is the instance where Ecotact has successfully demonstrated a model. We will turn to the reasons for the difficulties encountered in other contexts by Ecotact later in this book.

For empirical evidence we draw on an Ikotoilet that was opened in February 2011 in Dagoretti, a marketplace for vegetables and fruits as well as for clothing and household equipment with about 600 merchants. The marketplace is located next to Nairobi's biggest meat market and serves as an instance of a well-frequented and busy urban centre in the Nairobi metropolitan area.

Prior to the opening of the Ikotoilet, the marketplace was already equipped with a public toilet, which offers free, gender-separated access to sanitation. Accordingly, there was an opportunity to compare the relative use and perception of an old public toilet with that of an Ikotoilet. We conducted surveys based on: a) a standardized questionnaire during market days as well as b) observations of toilet use prior to the opening of the toilet, right after the opening of the toilet and about four months later (26/29 January 2011; 19/23 February 2011; 15/18 June 2011). The surveys focused on the permanent main users of the Ikotoilets, that is, the roughly 600 merchants selling in the marketplace. For each survey, 280 merchants were interviewed; this selection was done in a way that systematically covered the entire marketplace in terms of a grid.

Environmental Sustainability

Environmental sustainability with respect to public sanitation in Kenya concerns water conservation and specifically the reuse of urine and faecal matter according to the ecological sanitation principles spelled out above.[7] Kuria's vision of ecological sanitation relates to a notion of environmental sustainability based on his already noted focus on the process of technical innovation. In this spirit, Ecotact is trying to figure out and develop the most appropriate ecological sanitation solutions for the Kenyan context. Visits to the various operating Ikotoilets show that each toilet, depending on the date and location of construction, differs somewhat in its external and interior design and equipment; there is a trial-and-error approach, with some features introduced or possibly dropped if they are not workable.

Public toilets in Kenya typically use water to regularly flush urine, whereas the Ikotoilets use imported waterless urinals, which use a special foam that does not mix with urine but floats. Furthermore, Ecotact aims to introduce an automated low-flush system with two litres per flush (as compared to the conventional nine litres). At present, customers have to flush manually using a jug after defecation. Ecotact tried out a dry toilet system in one Ikotoilet; however, the authorities refused to agree to the technical requirements for it. Thus at the moment, there is only a plan to introduce such a system. Rainwater harvesting on the same site was tried out, but proved not to be viable owing to insufficient rainfall.

Ecotact has begun to connect bio-digesters when it opens new Ikotoilets that do not have a connection to the sewage system (Ikotoilets in Dagoreti and Wangige, Spring 2011). The reuse of resources, that is, urine and faecal matter, has not yet passed the initial stage. In collaboration with the Jomo Kenyatta University, Ecotact is running urine-fertiliser tests. The goal is to manufacture fertiliser as liquid or pellets.

Finally, ecological sanitation offers an opportunity to learn about and use environmentally friendly technology (or what Ecotact calls *the transformation of social behaviour*, Ecotact 2010a and b). This opportunity is so far hardly used. Even one of the high-ranking members from the Ministry of Public Health, who was generally very favourable of the Ikotoilets, was hardly aware of the environmental dimensions and its technological features. In the Dagoretti marketplace, only 15 per cent of people surveyed thought that a bio-digester is connected to the toilet (as opposed to a sewage system or septic tank), and this number slightly decreased to 12 per cent four months later. As Ecotact makes no efforts with its Ikotoilets to inform users about its approach to environmental sustainability, these results are not surprising. Environmental education and learning are themes that bring us to the role of human capabilities in the provision and use of Ikotoilets.

Meeting Central Human Capabilities

Further to education, public sanitation in urban centres is directly relevant for the following central human capabilities.[8]

- *Social basis of self-respect and non-humiliation*: Ecotact seeks to restore 'social dignity in ever growing urban populations' (Ecotact 2011). The toilet monuments seek to transform public sanitation from a matter of cultural taboo and humiliation into a widely recognized and talked-about feature of urban centres – to make you 'proud to be Kenyan', as one visitor put it in an Ikotoilet guestbook. This character of a monument to be proud of is closely linked to bodily health, bodily integrity and economic participation.
- *Bodily health*: the option to use clean toilets, wash one's hands and take showers is very important in a place like Nairobi, where people, especially those with low income, spend much time in public space (marketplaces, transportation, and so on). In such a context, the public toilet is just as important as the private or household toilet, although the latter tends to receive much more attention in development discussions.[9]
- *Bodily integrity*: run-down public toilets or a lack of any toilet are a threat to bodily integrity, especially for women. Public toilets in Kenya were places notorious for drug trafficking and muggings. The presence of maintenance staff in Ikotoilets is thus an important feature for increasing safety and perceived safety. In 2010, three women gave birth in Ikotoilets.
- *Economic participation*: public toilets must be affordable to users. In addition, the diverse income streams of the Ikotoilets create the revenue to pay for the jobs of the cashiers, cleaners and managers supervising the running of the toilets. In the capitalist culture of

*Table 2.1   Results from Dagoretti surveys: satisfaction of merchants on a
scale of 1 (very dissatisfied) to 4 (very satisfied)*

Capability	Indicator	Old public toilet (1st survey)	Ikotoilet (2nd survey)	Ikotoilet (3rd survey)
Social	Privacy	1.26	3.97	3.87
bases	Courtesy of staff	n/a	3.97	3.95
of self-	Smell	1.1	3.88	3.6
respect	Charge	n/a	3.36	3.27
Bodily health	Cleanliness	1.25	3.96	3.89
Bodily integrity	Security	1.35	3.98	3.95

mainstream urban Kenya, the mall aspect further contributes to the transformation of sanitation from a taboo, or at any rate a non-topic, into something exciting and to be talked about. It is 'a real business', as a street vendor in Uhuru Park put it when we talked with him about the Ikotoilets.

The surveys in Dagoretti allow us to track the impact in comparison to the old public toilet in terms of user satisfaction. Users were surveyed on aspects of these above capabilities and asked to assess them on a scale of 1 (very dissatisfied) to 4 (very satisfied). Table 2.1 shows the results.

Table 2.1 shows a clear preference for the Ikotoilets in comparison to the old public toilet (which remained open and accessible free of charge).[10] Even though satisfaction generally reduces after the initial novelty effect, it remains at a very high level. With respect to health, we can add that while in the old public toilet there is no opportunity to wash one's hands, 92.5 per cent of women and 78.8 per cent of men (second survey) and 87.3 per cent and 63.5 per cent (third survey), respectively, used this opportunity in the Ikotoilets. While the overall hand-washing rate decreased between the last two surveys, the overall use of soap increased from 38.2 per cent to 47.9 per cent, with 31.5 per cent of men using soap and 43.7 per cent of women in the second survey, and 39.4 per cent of men using soap and 53.6 per cent of women in the third survey. Regular and frequent users of the Ikotoilet increased from 60.5 per cent in the second survey to about 72.6 per cent in the third survey. A possible reason for this is that some potential users initially did not feel entitled to use the toilet precisely because the toilet is cleaned and even has tiles; it may be that the toilet monument and toilet mall approach is an initial obstacle to users.

The lowest rated indicator in the survey was for the charge in the Ikotoilet; as for the affordability, the charge was still rated above satisfactory. Accordingly, it is interesting to compare user numbers. The absolute user numbers of the Ikotoilet are roughly comparable to those of the old public toilet even though the Ikotoilet has a charge and the free toilet remained open (and is located around the corner from the Ikotoilet). During the first survey, 424 persons used the old toilets between 8 a.m. and 4 p.m. Directly after the opening of the Ikotoilet, 352 users used the new toilet (during the same times); four months later, the number was up again and slightly above the old level, with 447 users of the Ikotoilet between 8 a.m. and 4 p.m. What is noteworthy is an increase in the use by women: the first survey reported 36.7 per cent of users were women, the second survey 56 per cent and the third 57 per cent.

This takes us to a further capability-relevant aspect of the Ikotoilets – their sensitivity to differences amongst users.

- Ikotoilets include toilets for the physically disabled; as with the other technical features, this feature varies from facility to facility.
- All the toilets are gendered; the toilets for women include sanitary bins as well as changing tables for babies. This is a possible part of the explanation for the increase in use by women noted above.

Finally, a note on political participation. Kuria puts Gandhi into the post-colonial Kenyan context by saying that sanitation is more important than independence. What use is independence without decent access to toilets and what possibility for real independence is there without such access? If citizens see and experience the possibility of safe, clean and affordable public toilets, they may also come to demand such standards as a matter of right, in sanitation and beyond. Kuria's approach with toilet malls and monuments is arguably most comprehensive once Ecotact's dimension of *thinking beyond the toilet* is appreciated. In 2010 in the town of Nanyuki, people staged a demonstration when the municipality closed down an Ikotoilet; the Ikotoilet was eventually reopened.

Internal Organizational Responsibility

Participation, however, concerns both politics and business. The evaluation of capabilities is not limited to external effects on users but also concerns the effects on the employees of Ecotact. A key issue here concerns the quality of the work offered.[11] Ecotact provides work for some 70 employees, out of which 14 work in the Ecotact office. The office staff consists of eight men and six women from different ethnic groups

(Kikuyu, Kamba, Meru and one Pakistani). Apart from the office staff, 54 employees work as cleaners, cashiers and supervisors in the Ikotoilets. The weekly working time of the Ikotoilet staff is 40 hours. Ecotact pays 15 per cent above the minimum wage for casual workers of 6743 Ksh. (about 60 euros) per month stipulated by the Kenyan Employment Act (KEA) as of February 2011. Ikotoilet supervisors earn between 12000 Ksh. (about 105 euros) and 22000 Ksh. (about 194 euros) per month, depending on their qualifications.

The contracts with the Ikotoilet staff are for a period of two months. According to the KEA, employees who work for longer than three months are entitled to health and old-age benefits, the right to form a trade union, 30 days of vacation with full pay and pregnancy leave. Even though Ecotact pays above the minimum wage, the two months labour contract policy is clearly not a favourable employment condition; it seems to contrast with Ecotact's ambitious goals, in particular the transformation of the sanitation industry (see Ecotact Brochure 2010a).

Ecotact as a Political Actor

Ecotact has demonstrated its ability to build and operate public toilets in urban municipalities. In the preceding parts we analysed this ability with a focus on environmental sustainability and capabilities. In this final part, we turn to the legitimacy of Ecotact as an organization providing a public good. As of 2010, section 43 of the Kenyan constitution recognizes the right of every person to 'reasonable standards of sanitation'. The importance of sanitation is now constitutionally recognized; the issue arises when this right is met by a non-governmental organization, which moreover charges users. Should a non-governmental actor provide public sanitation? In the following, we turn to the legitimacy of Ecotact (for our approach to legitimacy see earlier in this book).

Output legitimacy as innovation
If we look at the Ikotoilet approach with a focus on sanitation-related human capabilities, then there is a reasonable argument for ouput-oriented legitimacy. The above focus on sanitation-related human capabilities provides a qualified case for the legitimacy of Ikotoilets' sanitation output.

Notably, the focus on public toilets fits particularly well with the Kenyan concern to focus on access to sanitation in both public and private spheres and not solely in the household.

> You know, that's a big argument we have. We are not even just talking about private facilities. One thing we are talking about [is] that people in slums like

Kibera and Mathare don't have private facilities. If you provide an Ikotoilet there, it will be the only toilet. And if you are providing that, people can stop open defecation. (John Karioki, 8 February 2011, Nairobi)

This point by no means only speaks to the slums. Public spaces, such as marketplaces and bus stops, are also sites of public sanitation and many people from the slums will work in such public spaces or pass through them (transportation time taking a lot of time for many citizens of Nairobi). Likewise, schools are another public place with evident need of adequate access to sanitation.

Karioki's point, however, does speak mainly about slums. As the need for access to sanitation is greatest here, so is the potential recognition for genuine social achievement. As we have seen, Ecotact does not provide a model for public sanitation in slums (nor for schools). At the very least, Ecotact needs to further clarify its focus, where it sees its achievements and where it will invest its energies; otherwise, at least in the medium run, the output legitimacy is at risk.

This point is reinforced by the observation that internally Ecotact does not live up to Kenyan labour standards. In the short term this may be perceived as acceptable initial problems of a young organization. In the medium term, however, output innovation will no doubt be judged by both the output and how the output has been achieved.

Social accountability

A second source of legitimacy for non-elected organizations is their ability to respond to and hence be accountable to the needs of those they provide goods for. An indicator of this ability is the local expertise of staff, who can be expected to have a better grip of needs than distant or even foreign experts, who may leave the region as soon as the project implementation phase is over. Ecotact employs local people, including people from the informal settlements, according to the ethnicity of the respective region. The headquarter staff is from Kenya, it is not an external expert project.

Ecotact can also improve its accountability to users by formalizing the learning from the target group. Hence, it is notable that Ecotact has introduced guestbooks in two downtown Nairobi toilets, thereby offering users the possibility of feedback; however, these guestbooks have not been evaluated by Ecotact and they are also not available in all Ikotoilets. While the local origin of Ecotact staff contributes to its social accountability, and while Ecotact arguably has made a first step in the direction of formally introducing a learning system via the guestbook, there is much further potential here.[12]

Mediating role: transitional authority and empowerment
A further source of legitimacy involves advocating for the affected communities and fostering participation. The goal here is a contribution to the empowerment of the target group. As empowerment is the goal, the organization's authority is transitional even if it takes the initiative. There is empowerment in the public–private partnership entered by Ecotact: the toilet is handed over to the municipality after five years and the community, via its elected representatives, is in principle *empowered* to continue the provision.

Moreover, this empowerment goal is reflected in self-understanding as catalyst. Ecotact's goal is not its own growth as an organization, running as many Ikotoilets as possible. Rather, what is essential is the focus on results and achieving those results with others. The hope is that good sanitation will serve as a trigger for democratic politics by helping people to experience and then demand high-quality public goods.

There is one important qualification to this source of legitimacy. At the time of writing this chapter, no Ikotoilets have yet been handed over to the municipalities in urban centres. The successful handover of Ikotoilets will be an important test for the sustainability of the empowerment.

Outside recognition
The judgment of distant others with no direct interest and involvement in local resource distributions does not directly confer democratic legitimacy, but no doubt indirectly contributes to authority. Ecotact and David Kuria have received plenty of private and public recognition as innovators in sanitation. Private recognition include Ashoka, Lemelson and Schwab fellowships (2007, 2009), a citation by the Clinton Initiative (2009), Africa Social Enterprise of the Year (2009) by the World Economic Forum and inclusion in the World Toilet Organization Hall of Fame (2008). Public recognition includes the UN Dubai Best Practice Award (2010). Ecotact displays these awards in its communications with others (homepage, brochure) and the Kenyan media has reported these awards; we have found no evidence for negative responses to these outside awards. Outside recognition is thus a further source of legitimacy for Ecotact. However, we also would like to note that this outside recognition frequently focuses on Ecotact as a provider of public sanitation in slums. As this focus does not correspond to the core of the main activities of Ecotact, there is a potential risk here to the legitimacy of outside recognition.

2.5 CONCLUSION – GETTING THINGS DONE SUSTAINABLY?

Do Ikotoilets contribute to human capabilities (our capabilities thesis)? Ikotoilets increase the opportunity for socially dignified, hygienic and safe access to public sanitation in urban centres. Ecotact has succeeded in turning a basic human need into the talk of the town – a monument that is an object of discussion, a real business; in short, something that many Kenyans are proud to have. Our survey showed that users perceive this opportunity as such, with high comparative approval rates and high user rates (even in the presence of a free public toilet).

Nevertheless, this capabilities contribution has to be qualified with respect to the employment conditions at Ecotact. While they meet the minimum wage standard, in view of the short-term nature of their contracts, they have only made a halfway satisfactory contribution to the economic participation opportunities. Environmental education and concern for the environment is a conspicuous but not actualized opportunity of the Ikotoilet.

Does Ecotact – via its Ikotoilets – contribute to environmental sustainability in the water sector (our environmental sustainability thesis)? Ecotact demonstrates a will to try out numerous possibilities and new ideas for water conservation and resource use; the focus is mainly on technical possibilities. It is too early at this point to speak of a systematic and full implementation of ecological sanitation partly because Ecotact does not yet have nor endorse a specific model or concept of ecological sanitation and partly because some of the technical devices are at an early stage or not yet working. Finally, Ecotact – like other initiatives who are fostering the closed-loop approach to ecological sanitation – will be confronted with the challenge of generating acceptance for their fertilizer products. The business model will only work out well when people are willing to buy and use both urine-based fertilizer and composted faecal matter.

This evaluation in terms of the human capabilities and environmental sustainability has implications for the legitimacy of Ecotact as a social entrepreneurship initiative for the common good. We find the Ikotoilets in urban centres to be a source of output legitimacy for Ecotact, with the local origin of staff and the gained outside recognition adding further sources of legitimacy. However, at least in the medium term, this perceived legitimacy is at risk. Social entrepreneurs are expected to be active for those who need it most, yet not even 5 per cent of the Ikotoilets are located in slums; social entrepreneurs are expected to do good things well, especially if they want to transform an industry, yet labour standards at Ecotact clearly could be improved. Finally, they are expected to do good things sustainably – a point that takes us to innovation and scaling. Ecotact is an innovator owing to the Ikotoilets in urban centres. These public toilets improve the existing infrastructure and they are clearly novel in their context. The transformative goals Ecotact associates with the Ikotoilets aim at the national level (and ultimately at East Africa and beyond). However, Ecotact does not see itself as the organization that will carry out this transformation on the national level. Rather, it seeks to act as a catalyst that attracts other business actors and municipalities to cooperate nation-wide on high-quality public toilets. It remains to be seen whether this function as a catalyst will be successful. Moreover, it raises the question of what it means to be a catalyst for scaling social innovations. Ecotact has not yet been able to develop viable models for other contexts of high importance for public sanitation, that is, schools and slums. The scaling of innovation is very sensitive to institutional differences that promote or hinder whether innovators and their target groups are able to convert resources into real opportunities for people. We will turn to these points later in this book, also comparing them with the experiences of other innovators.

When our Kenyan colleague Benson Karanja came to visit us in fall 2010, the sun was shining – somewhat unusual for grey Berlin. We were late to pick him up not least because one of us had a train ticket that was valid only up to one stop before the airport and the controller came before the last stop and charged us 40 euros, or the equivalent of some 140 Ikotoilet visits. After we picked Benson up, the subway train arrived at 6.15 p.m. – as announced – and as we sat down to ride back into town, Benson remarked, 'This infrastructure does you a lot of good, doesn't it?'

NOTES

1. The information on water and sanitation situations in Kenya in this paragraph is from the WHO/UNICEF Joint Monitoring Program (JMP). Their homepage (http://www. wssinfo.org/) provides regularly updated information.
2. Interviews and survey work were conducted together with our colleague Benson Karanja from the Jomo Kenyatta University of Agriculture and Technology, Kenya, whose student team also helped with the survey. The 2011 trip was prepared and conducted together with our colleague Dr. Christian Dietsche; the 2012 trip was prepared and conducted together with Danica Straith.
3. The small amount of literature on Ecotact does not necessarily draw this distinction of settings (Karugu 2011) or comment on the very different success in these two settings (Maweu 2012, p. 81, where Ikotoilets in slums are listed as evidence for the morality of making money from sanitation) and this risks contributing to a misleading perception of the Ikotoilet approach, its successes and its failures.
4. Numbers based on personal communication with Ecotact, 29 July 2011.
5. An aside: The Mathare youth group, which was responsible for the Ikotoilet in 2011, is called River Jump. The reason for the name is not the poor quality of the water in the stream running through Mathare (though that could be a reason too, see Chapter 3) but

rather the ethnic divide in the informal settlement. 'River Jump' here stands for different ethnic groups working together.

6. More successful in this respect appears to be the Umande Trust, which also runs a public toilet model and has built over 50 public toilets in slums.

7. This section has strongly benefited from an interview with Ecotact engineer Jeremiah Kiragu Wanjohi in Nairobi (9 February 2011).

8. For a list of all central human capabilities see Nussbaum 2006 as well as the introduction of this book. For reasons of space, we focus here on what we view as the most important capabilities in our case, which is not to say that there are no further impacts. For a more detailed analysis of capabilities and their conversion factors see Ziegler, Dietsche and Karanja 2012.

9. John Karioki, Deputy Director of Environmental Health at the Ministry of Public Health, who is involved in the sanitation strategy of the country, says that he and colleagues from other East African countries have a 'big argument' here with the MDG methodology because it does not sufficiently recognize the importance of public toilets (interview conducted 8 February 2011).

10. A note on charge: we compared charges for toilet use in all public toilets in central Nairobi in February 2011. We found 5 Ksh. to be the standard charge, with only one toilet charging 10 Ksh. and one asking for a voluntary donation (a former Ikotoilet now run by the Catholic Church).

11. Gender and ethnicity are further issues that we at least want to mention. 1) *Gender*: of the 57 non-headquarter employees, 31 are women and 26 male (February 2011). The Ecotact leaders (CEO and Chairman) are male (in the headquarters, eight are male and six female). Ecotact reports to have hired a female engineer for its headquarter staff but encountered the difficulty that the women engineers had troubles working outside Nairobi (for fixing Ikotoilets) owing to family constraints. In our judgment, the Ecotact staff is at the moment still too small to make any general judgments about gender equality within Ecotact. 2) *Ethnicity*: a similar comment pertains to ethnicity, a major source of division and even conflict in Kenya. Judging by its leadership, Ecotact is a Kikuyu company (and says it has been perceived as such when operating in informal settlements). However, owing to its operation of Ikotoilets across Kenya, the company effectively has to be open to all ethnicities in the respective areas. This fact is reflected in the ethnicity of staff: six Embu, eight Kamba, 24 Kikuyu, one Kisi, four Lunyas, two Luos, 11 Meru and one Pakistani (Acumen fellow); in the headquarters there are nine Kikuyu, three Kamba, one Meru and one Pakistani. For issues of ethnicity and gender, Kuria endorses a policy of equal opportunity; however, Ecotact is at the moment too small to evaluate this policy in practice.

12. It could be argued that there is a user-feedback mechanism via the pay-per-use system: users signal satisfaction via their willingness to pay for the product on offer. If they do not like the product, they will not pay; in the extreme case, the business goes bust. Thus, there is a built-in accountability, or so the argument goes. In our view, there are two significant limitations to this argument as far as sanitation is concerned. 1) Sanitation is not just a market product but also a constitutional right. The price mechanism is notoriously insensitive to the equality consideration this implies – everyone has the right, not just those with the ability to pay. This point especially pertains to the slum context, where this equality consideration is especially relevant. 2) The Ikotoilet is a *thick* innovation: it addresses mindsets, health, social dignity and even potentially environmental education. To achieve this full impact, a good understanding of users and their ways of using and learning from the Ikotoilets is required. The price mechanism is only a very limited, non-discursive means to learn for such thick impact.

3. Roberto Epple – Reconcile with your river!

Lena Partzsch, Justus Lodemann and Léa Bigot[1]

3.1 INTRODUCTION

We first met Roberto Epple when he came to visit us in Greifswald in 2010. Immediately upon arrival, he wanted to see *our* river, the River Ryck, which runs through Greifswald with a length of only 28 kilometres. At the beginning of this change study we did not identify very much with the Ryck, nor did we conceive the river to be *ours* (we did not even know how to pronounce its name properly). Our research on Epple developed into a socio-ecological experiment, which became our own story of *reconciliation* with the river we had dreadfully neglected in the past. Like any other water body in the European Union (EU), the Ryck is subject to the Water Framework Directive (WFD) adopted in December 2000 (European Commission 2012). Article 14 of the WFD states that 'the success of the Directive relies on . . . information, consultation and involvement of the public'. In practice, however, public participation is a difficult process. People in Europe hardly identify with their rivers and there are no defined rules describing when and how public participation should happen.

Roberto Epple promotes public participation in river basin management and advocates an approach adapted to the natural river flow, allowing seasonal flooding and denying channels and dams (including dismantling old ones and denying new installations). Ashoka assigned Epple as a senior social entrepreneur in 2007 for his innovative approach to the conservation of rivers in Europe and the creation of a bottom-up network. His network encompasses local and national citizen organizations dedicated to the preservation of more than 50 river basins in Europe. In the last 30 years, Epple participated in several major anti-dam and river protection campaigns at the Danube, Loire, Elbe and many other European rivers.

This chapter will mainly focus on the Big Jump, the major innovation that made Epple famous in the European environmentalist scene.

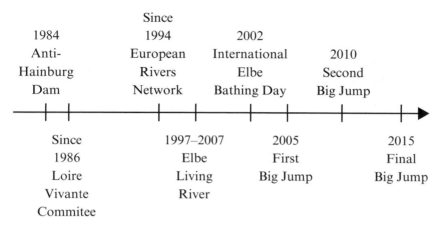

Figure 3.1   Time line of Epple's entrepreneurial journey

Big Jump refers to an event where people all over Europe jump in their rivers at exactly the same moment. The objective is two-fold: to purely enjoy the rivers communally and to demonstrate for clean water bodies vis-à-vis the public and political authorities. Epple coordinates these annual events and highlights the role of these jumps in promoting the implementation of the WFD. Following Epple's guidelines, GETIDOS organized two Jump events at the Ryck, the local river in Greifswald, on 11 July 2010 and 10 July 2011. These two *Ryck Jumps* were designed as socio-ecological experiments in order to investigate their impact. We conducted participatory observations, media analyses and surveys (in addition to qualitative, semi-structured interviews with people familiar with Epple's campaigns).

In this chapter we will first introduce Epple's entrepreneurial journey – from SOS Loire Vivante, the European Rivers Network and the Living Elbe project to the Big Jump (see Figure 3.1). We offer this overview as a glimpse of Epple's theory of change, which will subsequently be explained in more detail. Furthermore, we will evaluate Epple's management approach and his role as a political actor. We will focus on the Big Jump, Epple's major innovation, and our socio-ecological experiment to spot the impact of the innovation implemented in practice.

3.2   ROBERTO EPPLE – EUROPEAN WATER INNOVATOR

The first time we visited Roberto Epple we arrived at his house near Le Puy-en-Velay on a late August afternoon in 2011. While approaching the house we became aware of a big eye made of metal and coloured glass that stood on the roof of the barn. Epple explained to us that the eye was a present he had received when he bought the house around two decades ago after the anti-dam protests took place in the valley of the Haute Loire. The property is located on a slope of land that has a panoramic view over a part of the valley with a significant past – the site where the protest concentrated its occupation for several years. The colourful eye was handed over to Epple to function as a guardian of the area, even in times when he would be abroad.

Before we could settle down and relax so as to enjoy this view after our long travel from Greifswald, we were asked to grab our bathing suits and experience taking a bathe in the Loire so that we would know what we were talking about afterwards.

Epple's commitment for river conservation started in 1984 at the Hainburg Dam, part of the River Danube in Austria (see Figure 3.1). The World Wide Fund for Nature International (WWF) asked Epple to support the campaign to dismantle the dam. When he and his co-combatants succeeded, WWF sent Epple to the River Loire in France, where an opposition movement had emerged against the construction of four dams. Activists blocked a construction site in Le Puy-en-Velay for five years from 1986 until 1991, and Epple participated in this the whole time.

From the Loire Campaign to SOS Loire Vivante

In the course of the protests against further dam constructions at the Loire, Epple and other activists founded the *Loire Vivante committee*. A central idea of Loire Vivante is the *Living Loire* concept (*vivante* means living or alive), seeing the water system as complex entity that needs to be treated as such. Activists protested against the construction of four large reservoir dams in the towns of Le Veurdre, Naussac, Chambonchard and Serre de la Fare, fighting the French authorities' plans to regulate, and hence *kill*, the natural flow of these rivers.

The main pro-dam arguments put forward by the French authorities were flood management, development of tourism and support of farming activities, the Loire Basin being one of the main cereal production areas in France. The Loire Vivante committee, created with the support of the

WWF and France Nature Environnement, united several local groups based in Tours, Angers, Nantes (Estuaire), Nièvre-Allier-Cher and Le Puy-en-Velay. The most active of these groups was in Le Puy-en-Velay, where they obtained an official associative status in 1989, calling themselves *SOS Loire Vivante*. SOS Loire Vivante focused its contestation on the dam planning in Serre de la Farre through the occupation of the site and other local groups of the Loire Vivante committee developed a scientific counter-argumentation in dialogue with the French authorities.

The campaign resulted in the cancellation of the first two dams in 1991 and of the whole project in 1994. The government launched instead a ten-year initiative called *Plan Loire Grandeur Nature*, implementing many of the alternatives suggested by the Loire Vivante committee.

The Loire Vivante committee that had united several local groups almost disappeared at the end of their campaign success. Nevertheless, SOS Loire Vivante, which had become an association, managed to survive the post-victory crisis by restructuring itself; this was particularly owing to the commitment of Roberto Epple and Martin Arnould from the WWF. The WWF ceased its financial support because the ecological objectives of the campaign had been achieved and they did not want to continue the funding for only social reasons. The SOS Loire Vivante association progressively took over the coordinating role of the different Loire Vivante groups located along the Loire.

Most of our interviewees who had accompanied Epple's campaigns qualified the subsequent transformation of Loire Vivante – the *anti*-dam campaign's movement into a *pro*-active environmental NGO proposing new ideas for river management – as the association's key strength. The new ideas included concepts of how the natural flow of rivers can be conserved while still allowing infrastructural development along the river. The core concept is complying to, rather than fighting against, nature. This is the first sense of reconciliation for Epple's theory of change. An additional sense of reconciliation became obvious after the success of the Loire campaign – the reconciliation of actors and interests that were previously antagonistic, in this case, between farmers who had supported the Loire dam projects and environmentalists who had opposed them.

SOS Loire Vivante continues the fight against dams and is currently conducting several activities and projects, for instance their campaign against the French dam of Poutes. A new, more pro-active focus is the development of standards for sustainable hydropower. Most important for the association is the implementation of activities that raise educational awareness. Epple is actively involved in every project.

The European Rivers Network (ERN)

The work pioneered by the Loire Vivante committee has been replicated at the European level by the non-profit organization (NGO) European Rivers Network (ERN), which was created by Epple in 1994. ERN receives financial support from the WWF and the International Rivers Network. ERN is a bottom-up network of organizations and individuals who collaborate and share information based on personal contacts. Epple calls the network a *river parliament*. ERN uses collaboration to create new forces and synergies across different levels and scales of communities; this is where Epple's third sense of reconciliation shines through (see below). The network is not limited to environmental objectives; it also covers the fields of culture, human rights and education. In 2007 ERN joined the European Environmental Bureau and with them co-founded the Aquanet Europe Foundation, an NGO network created in order to apply for EU funding.

ERN is mainly a virtual network; *think camps* are occasionally organized in order to gather members and develop new strategies. It is unclear whether ERN could survive without Epple's commitment, in particular because the network does not have any permanent staff members. Epple uses ERN to implement several activities at the European and international level, including his major innovation, the Big Jump.

The Living Elbe Project

In parallel to his Loire activities Epple conceptually ran activities for the restoration of the Elbe. The European Big Jump originates from the *Living Elbe Project*. The Living Elbe Project was launched in 1997 by the Deutsche Umwelthilfe (DUH), a German environmental NGO, with support from the German publishing house Gruner + Jahr. The main objective of the project was to change the former frontier river – one of the dirtiest rivers in Europe at the time – into a *river of life, reconciliation and collaboration*. The fact that the Elbe project brought together people from both sides of the former Iron Curtain added a third dimension of reconciliation to Epple's theory of change – the reconciliation of people across borders (see below).

The project supported several grassroots initiatives developing cultural and educational activities in the field of nature protection. Between 1997 and 2007 more than 345 000 € was spent in order to support 400 environmental organizations located along the river. From 1989 to 2007 the river's pollution was reduced by 60–70 per cent (Deutsche Umwelthilfe 2007). It is likely these organizations contributed to this reduction; however, the causality between the initiatives and the environmental outcome is unclear. Several further incidents were major factors in this *Glücksfall Elbe* (stroke of luck), most notably the fall of the Iron Curtain and the EU enlargement to the East, including the adoption of EU environmental legislation by the upper river countries.

As the water quality of the Elbe improved, it became possible again to bathe in the river. In 2002 Epple decided to organize, along with several environmental NGOs, the Elbe International Bathing Day, which was to become the first Big Jump of many. There were 55 communities in Germany and the Czech Republic that participated in the event; 5000 people jumped in the Elbe that day and 90000 visited the event. Epple remained the director of the Living Elbe until the project ended in 2007 as funding was cut owing to the closure of Gruner + Jahr.

The Big Jump

With the ERN, Epple has continued to feature the Big Jump beyond the Living Elbe campaign. *Big Jump* means that people all over Europe jump in their rivers at the same time. The Big Jump 'aims at reconciling people with their rivers' and works on gaining 'people's support to the big European restoration effort for rivers and wetlands'.[2] Epple coordinates these annual events and highlights the role of these jumps in promoting the implementation of the WFD. The four central claims associated to the Big Jump are: 1) implementation of the WFD, 2) citizen participation in decisions related to river basin management, 3) citizen reconciliation with the rivers and 4) solidarity with other European rivers.[3]

After the first Elbe International Bathing Day in 2002, Epple organized another Big Jump in 2005 and again in 2010. These subsequent jumps were European-wide; in each, 2005 and 2010, 300000 people participated in the Big Jump. As the event became so popular, local associations have organized individual jumps each year since 2005, again, at the same time and across Europe. This means that they implement the Jump independently; sometimes local governments participate in the Jump's organization and put the event on a permanent basis. ERN is planning a third, final Big Jump for 2015; according to the WFD, European waters should have reached ecological good status by this year.

Epple's idea of *The Big Jump* has gained high popularity. It appears to be an impressive tool in order to communicate the objectives of the unwieldy WFD. The Big Jump has been particularly successful so far in Germany, France and Belgium, and progressively so in Southern and Eastern Europe (see Map 3.1). A Euro-Mediterranean Jump has been organized on an annual basis since 2005 with a collective jump in the Jordan River.

Epple has scaled out his objective of reconciliation and has accomplished this via collaboration. He not only helps people to reconcile with

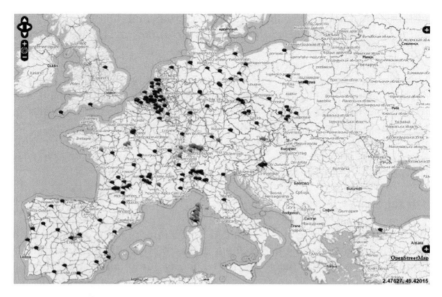

Source: Rivernet 2012.

Map 3.1   Big Jump locations 2010

their rivers by bathing in the water, he also successfully promotes the participation of local organizations with different backgrounds (not only the usual suspects, the environmentalists). Actors with different interests regarding the rivers bathe together. Furthermore, the European dimension adds to a reconciliation of people across nation-states, east and west, north and south.

In regards to scaling out, Epple was well aware of the need to set the conditions specific to his innovation. This meant creating the knowledge space as well as the environmental space needed to support the innovation, specifically by scaling the basic concept of *living rivers*, that is, the idea to advance infrastructural development in accordance with nature. He also created political space to support the Big Jump by advocating the adoption of the living river concept into policy documents, such as the Plan Loire Grandeur Nature and the WFD.

The Jump's participation increased from 90 000 participants in 2002 (Elbe Bathing Day) to 300 000 in 2005 and again in 2010 (Big Jumps). Moreover, the concept was replicated in different contexts; notably, a Big Jump in the River Jordan was organized simultaneously in Israel, Palestine and Jordan. The objective for 2015 is to reach 1000 Jumps. In some places, however, it is difficult to maintain people's interest in the Jump from one year to another. For example, many people along the Elbe in Germany still participate in the event, but the overall number of localities and people involved decreased considerably compared to 2002. The main reason might be the cessation of the publishing house Gruner + Jahr in 2007, which resulted in the reduction of DUH's financial means.

The fact that there were more participants in 2005 and 2010 when Epple announced the Big Jump event demonstrates his relevance, compared to the minor Jumps in the years in between. Epple is not present at each location nor does he have any financial control over the local events, hence his innovation has clearly developed dynamics independent of him. While Epple has set basic principles for organizing the Big Jumps, including practical advice such as safety issues and online registration processes, local organizers are free to adapt the Jump to their context as they please (both for the annual and five-year ones). In this way, Epple has an open-source scaling strategy that encourages mutability and seeks rapid diffusion through the transformation of beneficiaries into co-creators. This approach keeps the communities at the centre of the innovation.

Epple's major resource may be his ability to create smart networks; he is able to leverage groups across networks in ways that are greater than the sum of their parts so as to further the social impact. He motivates a large number of people to engage in environmental concerns as well as to express and share values together. In his political integration of the Big Jump into the WFD and the Plan Loire Grandeur Nature, he has further activated the network by encouraging mechanisms for members to put pressure on each other to deliver. Furthermore, he has used a piggy-backing strategy to leverage the scale of others through collaborations with the WWF, SOS Loire Vivante and the European Environmental Bureau. Epple may, for instance, inform local organizers about the time and further details of a Jump; his central role is being a networker.

In sum, what makes Epple special is his ability to mobilize a large number of people to engage in smart networks for environmental concerns, usually on a volunteer basis. He coordinates people without necessarily being a formal (top-down) leader. Though not the founder, Epple played a major role in the Loire Vivante campaign. He did found ERN and has been the president of the network since its conception; this organization would not work without his commitment.

The objective of most of the projects conducted by Epple, particularly the Big Jump, is to revive the links that bind people with their rivers and lakes (for instance, by communally bathing in the rivers' water). Epple finds it most important to change people's mindsets. Epple considers making people more aware of the need to live in harmony with nature as a precondition for developing technological alternatives (for example decentralized technologies instead of large-scale dams that massively interfere with the natural flow of rivers). He is convinced we do not lack particular technologies or alternative know-how; rather alternatives are simply not applied because of a lack of awareness for their need vis-à-vis nature.

Epple's theory of change is based on the assumption that reconciliation of citizens with their rivers and lakes is a necessary step for freshwater protection and restoration of rivers. The term reconciliation played a central theme for Epple when he worked on the Elbe, and reconciliation was the major issue at the previous frontier river between East and West. Epple realized here that his former projects, like at the Loire, were also about reconciliation: the reconciliation of citizens with their rivers and the reconciliation of actors and interests that were previously antagonistic (for example farmers who often support dam projects and environmentalists who oppose them). Moreover, trans-boundary projects also aim for a reconciliation of people across borders, creating a third dimension to reconciliation in Epple's approach to change. In the following evaluation we understand 'reconciliation' as a complex generic term that can be separated into cultural, economic, political and ecological dimensions.

3.3   EVALUATION OF THE INITIATIVE – GETTING THINGS DONE SUSTAINABLY?

Roberto Epple's theory of change is based on a paradigm shift in value, which gives priority to environmental considerations over economic ones. Presuming a complementarity of economic, environmental and social development, he goes even further than the strong sustainability approach by giving priority to environmental objectives. This means that he rejects economic development at the expense of river degradation. At the same time, Epple admits that constant change is natural and he supports the coexistence of urban (human) and river (ecological) systems. *Living rivers* are rivers where life is present inside and outside the rivers. The Big Jump symbolizes Epple's conception of sustainability, where the ecological system (in the case of the river) and humans can coexist. It is a communicative tool with the objective to support the implementation of the WFD.

Rather than evaluating his efforts in hard ecological data, we acknowledge Epple's main influence to be on intermediary factors such as public opinion and individual attitudes. Hence his contribution is to human capabilities. A quick glance at the Big Jump shows that this initiative aims to reconcile people with their rivers. It is thus possible to link the Big Jump to the human capability of 'being able to live with concern for and in relation to animals, plants and the world of nature' (Nussbaum 2006). Reconciliation with rivers is seen by Epple as an essential element to gain people's support for the WFD, and thus to increase public participation in water-related decision-making. This is directly related to Nussbaum's (2006) capability to 'participate effectively in political choices that govern one's life'. The Big Jump is also a festive and playful event that creates social connections between citizens. The initiative contributes to the capabilities related to justice and friendship and the ability to 'engage in various forms of social interaction' as well as the capability to 'laugh, play and enjoy recreational activities' (Nussbaum 2006). Finally, there is a very close link between the quality of rivers and people's health. The Big Jump supports the restoration of rivers, which enables people to bathe again without risking diseases. The initiative is therefore directly linked to bodily health (Nussbaum 2006). In Section 3.4, which deals specifically with the Ryck Jumps, we will return to this topic of capabilities.

Internal Organizational Responsibility

Environmental sustainability and a dignified life are not only a matter of a programme's effects on its target group but also of the organizations internal activities. Epple tries his best to sustainably manage SOS Loire Vivante and ERN. He contracted a renewable energy provider and also installed solar panels himself. In case of events when catering is needed, it is usually based on local organic products. Finally, Epple favours telephone conferences over greenhouse gas-intensive travelling.

Providing good working conditions for his employees is important to Epple; flexibility and well-being are central. Epple has very close relationships to the numerous volunteers and sympathisers, and he organizes regular team building activities, for example cycling trips, nature weekends, and so on. The farm of Bonnefont, a cottage in the countryside that belongs to SOS Loire Vivante, is open to all members of Loire Vivante and ERN.

Nonetheless, the limited duration of particular projects and their respective financial basis often cause awkward employment conditions. When activists blocked the dam construction site in Le Puy-en-Velay for five years, many of them lost their regular jobs. While Epple cares for his co-combatants, in the end each activist is self-dependent. Although Epple employs people for SOS Loire Vivante and ERN, earned income is not essential to these projects and his *river parliament* is no conventional employer.

Epple as a Political Actor

Civil society groups like SOS Loire Vivante and ERN partner with political authorities and hence come to share their power. Particularly owing to Article 14 of the WFD, water politics are increasingly exercised horizontally. Epple participates in negotiating standards of sustainable hydroelectricity with the French government. When Epple makes some hundred thousand people demonstrate for cleaner rivers, he exercises massive power. His political legitimacy in such processes can be evaluated along the criteria of output-oriented legitimacy, social accountability, his mediating role and outside recognition (Partzsch and Ziegler 2011).

Output legitimacy
We acknowledge that Epple's main contribution is to human capabilities, rather than changing hard ecological data. Nonetheless, SOS Loire Vivante achieved the cancellation of four hydropower dam projects at the Loire and motivated the implementation of a publically accepted alternative. Some of Epple's co-combatants who we interviewed spoke of an 'expost recognition'.

Social accountability
Epple is very well known and highly respected at the Loire. The headquarters of SOS Loire Vivante and ERN is in Le Puy-en-Velay at the Loire's spring. Epple was amongst the 300 000 people who participated in the Big Jumps both in 2005 and 2010. He travels a lot and involves himself with people, both advocates and opponents. He himself can be considered to be socially accountable to the affected people. Despite Epple's personal communication skills, however, the ERN website is not regularly updated (and lacks information; for instance the Greifswald jumps are missing in the maps). There is no systematic archive in place. This deficient documentation results in a lack of transparency that makes it difficult to hold anyone accountable, including Epple.

Mediating role
With the development of alternatives to new dam projects, SOS Loire Vivante antedated to some extent the EU water policy reform of the WFD. For the WFD to succeed, we need people like Epple who promote a scaling of basic principles. He plays the role of a *transition agent* who transfers ideas and knowledge through his networks. The increasing number of Big Jump events demonstrates how his innovation has developed a life of its own.

Outside recognition

The selection of Epple to the Ashoka fellowship in 2007 is a main example of his outside recognition. Along with this he received various other awards, often in the name of SOS Loire Vivante and ERN, including the French award Le Prix des Héros de l'Eau 2010 from WWF France and the French environmental ministry.

3.4 THE RYCK JUMP – A SOCIO-ECOLOGICAL EXPERIMENT

GETIDOS conducted a socio-ecological experiment in order to study the impact of the Big Jump beyond theoretical considerations. Following Epple's guidelines (checklist available at ERN homepage), we organized Jump events at the River Ryck in Greifswald on 11 July 2010 and 10 July 2011 (at the same moment like all other jumps across Europe). Rather than focus on an immediate measure of improved water quality after the Jumps, we concentrated instead on intermediary factors of civil society matters. Following Dieter Rucht (1999, see also Kolb 2002), we explored the influence on public opinion and individual attitudes. Alongside our participatory observations of the Jumps in 2010 and 2011, we conducted surveys with participants and visitors in Greifswald to measure the influence of the Jumps on individual attitudes; and for the effect on public opinion, we conducted a media analysis.

The research objective of the Ryck Jumps was to obtain a better understanding of the impact of the Big Jump as an implemented innovation. It was therefore necessary to apply the ERN approach and objectives to the specific context of Greifswald. We found a draft management plan online that provided some information on the implementation of the WFD at the Ryck, including basic deficits and development targets (StAUN 2006), which was prepared by the local authority Staatliches Amt für Landwirtschaft und Umwelt (StAUN). StAUN considers the intensive drainage of the river basin for agricultural purposes as the biggest challenge to achieve the objectives of the WFD. Authorities have not taken any steps in order to address water problems at the Ryck; local authorities assumed from the very beginning that the Ryck and several other regional bodies would not be able to comply with the targets set by the WFD (StAUN 2006).

Article 14 calls upon the EU member states to encourage all parties to actively participate in the implementation of the WFD. Accordingly, the local authorities discussed their plans with a selected group, including the local farmers, who are responsible for the major pollution of the river

(StAUN 2006). Yet a public discussion that included a broad range of citizens did not take place. Neither did the plans take into account topics that would be of great interest for many citizens of Greifswald, such as bathing in the Ryck. For that reason GETIDOS organized such a public hearing at the University of Greifswald on 4 May 2011 preceding the second Ryck Jump. With only a dozen participants, the response was moderate.

While a local jump appears to be a low-cost experience at first sight, we found that organizing such an event still binds some time and financial resources. For instance, as bathing in the Ryck is forbidden, we needed special permission to swim in the river. The German Lifeguard Association (DLRG) had to be on duty for both events and for the 2010 Jump, a sailing club provided changing and sanitation facilities. In 2011 a historic ship called *Atlantic* was used as a changing facility and a meeting place for the organizers. For both jump locations we chose the Museum Harbour, right next to the city centre and one of the most frequented places of Greifswald, especially in the summer.

GETIDOS asked people to act as patrons for each of the Ryck Jumps. In 2010 it was Konrad Ott, professor of environmental ethics at the University of Greifswald, and in 2011 it was the locally very well-known band Krach. These different kinds of patrons characterized the Jumps in each year. Konrad Ott gave a political speech about the WFD in 2010. To the contrary, in 2011 Krach did not engage politically; they just played some songs and watched the swimmers from the lawn while people jumped in the water. The more political character of the 2010 Jump was underlined by the fact that GETIDOS organized an exhibition on the WFD at the venue. In both years, however, ERN leaflets were distributed that were of a political character. On the GETIDOS homepage, interested people could watch a 45-second movie and download a fact-sheet about the implementation of the WFD at the Ryck as well as a press release. Moreover, we announced the Ryck Jump with 30 posters in various places such as cafés and university buildings and distributed 300 flyers in Greifswald in both years.

One week before the Ryck Jump in both years, GETIDOS sent out a press release and contacted local journalists. Both press releases on the Ryck Jumps contained a description of the project, the patrons and the four demands of the ERN adapted to the local context of Greifswald. The latter of which is as follows:

- implementation of the WFD at the Ryck, including an immediate examination of alternative concepts for land and water use;
- public hearing on the environmental condition of the Ryck and consolidation of Greifswald residents in decision-making processes (people's participation in decisions concerning their rivers);

- creation of bathing zone at the Museum Harbour (for citizens reclaiming their river);
- solidarity with other European rivers.

GETIDOS aimed to communicate these demands to the participants and visitors of the Ryck Jump. Participants were students and young people with an environmentalist background (that is, the usual suspects). A lot more people came to the Ryck Jump in 2011 (240 persons) than in 2010 (60 persons). With a temperature of 34°C, 10 July 2010 was the warmest day of the year. As there are no shady spots at the Museum Harbour, most of the participants came to the venue just before the Jump in 2010 and hardly anyone passed by incidentally to watch the Jump. Konrad Ott gave a short speech on the importance of the WFD before the 60 participants jumped in the Ryck at 3 p.m. shouting 'Für saubere Flüsse!' ('For clean rivers!'). After the jump, all participants quickly left the venue.

In 2011 we counted more than 240 people who came to the Museum Harbour to watch and listen to the concert; however, only 40 people actually jumped in the river. The band Krach started their concert at 2.40 p.m. before the Jump at 3 p.m. Unlike Konrad Ott, the band members did not swim in the Ryck themselves. Most people left after the concert at 3.30 p.m. In both years people were mainly present for the Jump itself and for the patrons' speech or concert, respectively. It is an ambivalent result that in spite of the higher number of attendants, fewer people actually jumped in 2011 than in 2010. Many visitors told us that they considered the Jump (and the concert) as a fun event, and that jumping in the Ryck would have been too much of an effort.

Ryck Jump Survey[4]

For a survey of individual relationships to the River Ryck, we first went through the central human capabilities (in the sense of Nussbaum 2006) to narrow down the focus to those capabilities that most pertain to the Big Jump. We concluded there were four central capabilities most pertinent to the Ryck context; these belong to the economic, environmental, cultural and political dimensions of capabilities in relation to the river. Specifically, this comprises the economic purposes such as transport and tourism, the environmental concern in the role of rivers for flora, fauna and ourselves, the cultural role of rivers as a place for recreation and recollection and finally, the political concern for river management.

On this conceptual basis we created a survey that asked people to evaluate both their actual relationships with respect to these dimensions, as well as how they evaluate these relationships as an ideal. Participants could respond on a scale from 1 (completely disagree) to 5 (completely agree). A key idea of the survey is that a discrepancy between the actual and ideal evaluation – for example between being informed de facto and how informed one would like to be – prima facie suggests a need for reconciliation along one of the four dimensions that the survey explored.

We aimed with the survey to learn about the following theses with respect to the ERN claim: 1) people are a) de facto not or not completely reconciled with the river; b) they ought to be reconciled with the river; 2) the river jump contributes to reconciliation; 3) reconciliation with the river is a necessary step for the participation of citizens in the implementation of the WFD.

Our first attempt to conduct a survey in 2010 with participants and visitors mainly failed due to the design of the questionnaire (our questions were too complex). The revised survey was conducted with river jump participants (jumpers and spectators) as well as a control group (cg) in the town (n=100) in summer 2011. A follow-up survey was conducted five months later. Table 3.1 shows the questions along with the results.

Based on the survey, we arrived at the following conclusions.

Thesis 1: Reconciliation with the Ryck
For the cultural dimension of being with and at the river (appreciation of the river during recreation), the survey did not indicate a significant difference between the de facto relation and the ideal. Participants already highly valued their cultural relation to the river (average rating [ar] 4.5) and only wished to improve it further (ar 4.7). However, there were differences between the de facto relation and the ideal for the political (items 11, 12 and 13), economic (items 2 and 4) and ecological dimensions (items 1, 3 and 13). People in the follow-up survey responded on average that they felt insufficiently informed about water quality (ar 2.6, as opposed to 4.2 as an ideal) and possibilities of participation (ar 1.8, as opposed to 4.2 as an ideal), that they were not engaged in water conservation (ar 1.8, as opposed to 3.6 an ideal) and that the economic use of the Ryck as a water street should be given less priority (ar 2.4, as opposed to 3.6 as an ideal).

Thesis 2: Reconciliation by means of the Big Jump/swimming in the river
The follow-up survey five months later did not suggest significant changes in the participants' personal relation to the river. Also additional survey questions on possible changes in water conservation related behaviour yielded no specific results.

Table 3.1 Results from the Ryck Jump Survey 2011

Themes [translated from German]	July 2011		December 2011	
	de facto	ideal	de facto	ideal
1. I am concerned about the pollution at the Ryck.	3,4	3,67	3,78	4,0
I ought to be concerned about the pollution at the Ryck.	*3,27*	*3,67*	*3,11*	*3,58*
2. The Ryck primarily is a federal water street for ships (for transport, tourism, and so on).	2,52	1,98	2,76	2,12
The Ryck ought to be used primarily as a federal water street for ships.	*2,53*	*2,11*	*2,05*	*1,79*
3. I am concerned about the heavily modified status of the Ryck (for example barrages).	2,66	3,1	3,24	3,52
I ought to be concerned about the heavily modified status of the Ryck.	*2,43*	*2,9*	*2,68*	*3,05*
4. The use of the river is primarily an economic one.	3,22	2,35	3,28	2,4
The use of the river primarily ought to be an economic one.	*2,98*	*2,22*	*2,84*	*1,95*
5. For me, the Ryck is a source of joy.	3,72	4,6	4,4	4,6
I would like to enjoy the Ryck as a source of joy.	*3,43*	*4,31*	*3,42*	*3,84*
6. I go for walks along the Ryck or use the Ryck for other recreational activities.	4,48	4,71	4,52	4,8
I would like to go for walks along the Ryck or use the Ryck for other recreational activities.	*3,69*	*4,41*	*3,37*	*3,68*
7. I spend time at the Ryck to relax.	4,22	4,69	4,44	4,72
I would like to spend time at the Ryck to relax.	*3,51*	*4,33*	*3,22*	*3,79*
8. I feel at home at the Ryck.	3,84	4,33	3,96	4,28
I would like to feel at home at the Ryck.	*3,21*	*4,02*	*3,21*	*3,94*
9. I enjoy spending time with others at the Ryck.	4,38	4,63	4,36	4,64
I would like to spend time with others at the Ryck.	*3,55*	*4,24*	*3,44*	*3,89*
10. I am informed about the water quality of the Ryck.	1,96	4,18	2,6	4,24
I ought to be informed about water quality at the Ryck.	*1,8*	*3,92*	*1,95*	*3,74*
11. I am informed about my participation possibilities regarding river management.	1,36	3,98	1,76	4,2
I should know my participation possibilities regarding river management.	*1,27*	*3,49*	*1,53*	*3,63*
12. I am active in river protection.	1,78	3,55	1,84	3,64
I should be active in river protection.	*1,69*	*3,22*	*1,39*	*3,42*
13. I am concerned about the detrimental living conditions for fish and plants at the Ryck.	3,22	3,9	3,64	4,12
I should be concerned about the detrimental living conditions for fish and plants at the Ryck.	*3,22*	*3,51*	*2,79*	*3,63*

Note: Numbers in italics = numbers from the control group.

Thesis 3: Reconciliation is a necessary step for participation of citizens in the implementation of the WFD
The survey indicated a low level of information regarding water politics and the WFD. In terms of items 10, 11 and 12, the evaluation of the de facto relation shows low averages. In general, as long as citizens are unaware of specific problems (in the case of the Ryck people were partly aware) as well as their rights and possibilities of participation, they will not be able to participate. Hence this thesis was supported by the case study.

Media Analyses of Ryck Jumps

A week before and after each Jump event, we searched for articles on the Internet with Google Alert and in the German speaking print press with Factiva (including German, Swiss and Austrian newspapers). We found 48 articles in total, 29 articles in 2010 and 19 articles in 2011. There were 14 printed and 15 online articles in 2010 and six printed and 13 online articles in 2011. While the online articles in 2010 were only announcing the event beforehand and copying the text of the GETIDOS press release, in 2011 there were 13 'proper' articles online. These 2011 articles also dealt with Jumps other than the Ryck Jump and contained more information than provided by the GETIDOS press release. We therefore decided to include them in the media analysis. So the total number of articles assessed in the media analysis in 2011 (19 articles) was even higher than in 2010 (14 articles).

The average length of the articles in 2010 was 459.5 words, whereas it was 267 words in 2011. With a length of 1021 words, one article stood out in 2010. In contrast to any other article in 2010, it covered several jumps at different rivers. In 2011 the longest article had only 615 words. In 2010 the shortest article contained 173 words, in 2011 only 53 words.

The articles evaluated in 2010 referred to the rivers Aare,[5] Danube, Havel, Isar, Main, Rhine, Ryck and Weser. In 2011, articles mentioned the rivers Aare, Danube, Elbe, Fulle, Leine, Main, Ryck, Spree, Weser and the Finow canal (but not the Havel, Isar or Rhine). There does not seem to be an immediate coherence between the number of participants and the extent of media coverage. For instance, eight articles issued in 2011 mentioned the Weser, although there were only 15 participants at this Jump location. Another example is the Danube: three articles mentioned this river in 2010 although only 12 participants actually jumped in it.

In our media analyses, we were interested to which extent the demands of the jumps were communicated via the media (WFD implementation; public participation in decision-making; river reclamation; solidarity with other European rivers). (We assessed the demand for solidarity with other

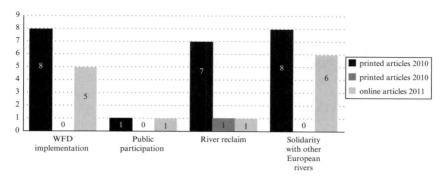

Figure 3.2   Number of demands mentioned in articles 2010 and 2011

European rivers by looking to see if an article mentioned other jumps or introduced the Big Jump as a European-wide event.) Figure 3.2 shows how many articles mentioned each of the four demands formulated in the press release in 2010 and 2011. Again, the total number of articles was 14 articles in 2010 and 19 articles in 2011. The possible optimum would hence be 14 or 19 articles, respectively, mentioning each demand. Our analysis shows that ERN did not achieve this optimum in any of the articles from 2010 or 2011. The articles mentioned some demands, but never all four.

Only one article in 2010 mentioned the demand for more public participation in decision-making, and this is an article about the Ryck Jump. At the same time, this article, which very much focused on the Jump-patron Konrad Ott, does not mention the European dimension to the Big Jump at all. The fact that alongside 60 participants jumping in the Ryck, 300 000 people all over Europe swam in their rivers was completely neglected. In 2011 the Greifswald Jump was even less successful in communicating the ERN demands.

Again, there does not seem to be an immediate coherence between number of participants and media coverage. The Ryck Jump in 2010 had a more political character and also gained more media attention. Rucht's model on the intermediary factors through which civil society matters (individual attitudes, public opinion) was thus approved in as much as our participatory observations on participants' individual attitudes were coherent with media reports and hence the potential influence on public opinion in 2010 and 2011.

The character of the Ryck Jump in 2011 was more fun-oriented (concert); however, the ERN demands for stronger efforts in river conservation were not communicated and hence the potential of influencing public opinion in that regard was rather low. While Epple clearly follows a political over a fun approach, as local jump events are organized in a decentralized way (we chose the patrons without having consulted Epple), it remains questionable if Epple and ERN can influence local priorities and hence the overall impact of the event.

3.5   CONCLUSIONS

Without the active commitment of people like Epple, the EU would probably not have adopted legislation as ambitious as the WFD. Epple's major resource is his networking capacities; he is able to inspire a large number of people to engage in environmental concerns. Most notably for our research, Epple helped us reconcile with the Ryck and become part of a larger movement for living rivers worldwide. Now we know for sure how to pronounce its name properly and where bathing in the river poses less risk to health. While the high participation in the Big Jumps of 2005 and 2010 demonstrates his continuing relevance for these events, his innovation clearly has developed dynamics independent from Epple himself. In theory, his innovation is system-changing in as much as it has the capacity to change people's mindset. In practice, jumpers tend to be environmentalists. In the case of the Ryck jump our survey indicates that the reconciliation in terms of *cultural* relation to the river was not deficient. People even seemed aware of some problematic issues concerning the Ryck, for example the matter of pollution. Nevertheless, only a few respondents were engaged in river protection. Most people feel insufficiently informed about the actual water quality and the possibilities of political participation. To close this gap it might be helpful, for example, if ERN could give advice on how to become further involved politically.

The WFD has not been implemented yet in Greifswald or across Europe. While the Big Jump is to some extent an attractive tool to communicate the objectives of the WFD, in terms of hard ecological data and political outcome, the Jump's impact is doubtful. The ecological status of European waters is far from good. In 2010 the Federal Ministry for the Environment, Nature Conservation and Nuclear Safety, in cooperation with the Umweltbundesamt, published the following data for Germany: 9.5 per cent of surface water bodies are presently in a good status as demanded by the WFD; a further 8.5 per cent are calculated to reach this goal by 2015; for the remaining 82 per cent it is aimed to apply the exception rule corresponding to Article 4 of the WFD and not take any measure to improve the quality of the water bodies. Although campaigns were successful and people began to revalue living rivers, there are still many conflicts of interest regarding waterway projects and specifically on the European level, regarding the Common Agricultural Policy (CAP). An improved water quality essentially depends on a reduced use of fertilizers and pesticides in agricultural practice. The Greifswald survey reveals that even if people become interested in water politics owing to the Jump, they still do not know how to become politically involved on behalf of their rivers.

NOTES

1. Survey work was conducted together with several students: Markus Kather investigated the implementation of the WFD at the Ryck and helped with the 2010 media analysis. Rafael Ziegler and Julia Pohlers conducted the survey in 2011 and 2012, and produced the data we use here (see Ziegler 2012b).
2. www.rivernet.org/bigjump/bigjump.htm (accessed 20 June 2012).
3. See press release Big Jump 2010: www.rivernet.org/bigjump/pdf/bj10/20100711_pr_bigjump_deutsch_ern_eeb_wwf.pdf (accessed 20 June 2012).
4. This section and its data draws on Ziegler 2012b.
5. The Aare is a river in Switzerland; but as we assessed the German-speaking press, a Swiss river covered most articles.

4. A new water paradigm – Michal Kravčík and People and Water

Justus Lodemann and Rafael Ziegler

4.1 INTRODUCTION

At the Skoll World Forum for Social Entrepreneurship in 2009, in response to the financial and economic crisis, Michal Kravčík presented a 'Green New Deal Proposal for Slovakia and Beyond' (Kravčík 2009). Kravčík outlined his *New Water Paradigm* as a strategy for water retention and job creation, which was inspired by the American New Deal from the Roosevelt administration. Kravčík was not only thinking about his native Slovakia; he envisaged millions of jobs around the globe and aimed at nothing less than greening the deserts of the world, with a projected first implementation on the Arabian Peninsula. To this end, he invited all his contacts to join this global effort in restoring the water cycle.

Unfortunately, the Saudia Arabia proposal fell through and we never got to travel there to visit his efforts. We did, however, get to travel to Eastern Slovakia in 2010, visiting Kravčík's hometown Košice and then the village of Tichy Potok in the Levoča Mountains. In the 1990s there was a plan to construct a large dam for flood prevention and drinking water provision in Tichy Potok, which is in the upper part of the Torysa River. The dam was projected to flood approximately 123 hectares of the Upper Torysa River Valley area, including Tichy Potok village and other small villages so that a resettlement of the inhabitants would have been necessary. According to the mayor of Tichy Potok, Lubica Dzuganova: 'We were told that there would be an apartment block in Košice for us, carrying the name of our village' (Dzuganova, interview on 23 July 2010).

Kravčík and his organization *Ľudia a voda* (People and Water) successfully supported villagers in their protest against the dam. In their anti-dam struggle they formulated the *Blue Alternative*, a system of small dams and water holdings meant to offer the same level of security against floods as well as an increase in the drinking water supply. From these efforts, the New Water Paradigm (NWP) emerged.

In Section 4.2 of this chapter we will first introduce the mission and work of Michal Kravčík and People and Water (PW) in its socio-ecological context, then in Section 4.3 turn to the novel aspect of this work and the approach to scaling. In Section 4.4 we evaluate this approach from a sustainability perspective. Accordingly our key questions are: What is PW's innovation and how has the organization been able to scale? What is 'social' about this innovation and how does it contribute to human capabilities and environmental sustainability? In light of these questions, what is the legitimacy of this non-governmental organization (NGO) to seek the implementation of a new water paradigm? As we will see, legitimacy is particularly controversial in this case owing to shifting Slovakian politics.

Against the conceptual background described in Chapter 1, this chapter has been written based on desktop research, semi-structured interviews with leading actors and affected people conducted in July 2010 and February/March 2012, and a survey conducted in 2011 and 2012. The first field trip was prepared in cooperation with our Slovakian colleague Pavol Varga; the second field trip and the survey described below were worked on in cooperation with our colleague Dr. Michal Gažovič. Translations, where necessary, were made by our Slovakian colleagues.

4.2   A NEW WATER PARADIGM – PEOPLE AND WATER'S MISSION AND ITS CONTEXT

Before we turn to the mission of Kravčík and PW, some history and socio-ecological context is necessary. During the 1940s in Slovakia, with industrialization and increased economic development, the demand for water by industry, agriculture and private households began to exceed the technical capacity of the water supply (Szolgay et al. 2009). These factors also increased the demand for energy. Large dams were built in an effort to improve the water supply and energy production. The Slovak National Committee on Large Dams now registers 50 large dams in total (SNCLD 2010); almost half of these dams (42 per cent) were built during the 1950s and 1960s. In parallel to these developments, there was an increase in the conversion of meadows, forests and wetlands into arable land for agriculture in the Eastern Slovakian Lowland. The so-called melioration programme was accompanied by a sustained effort to drain agricultural land for the production of crops such as wheat, barley and maize. Slovakia's system of drainage channels now has a length of 15 154 km, a third of which are artificially regulated rivers (MASR 2000).

Kravčík was born into this period of post-war melioration. 'I was born in February 1956 under the sign of Aquarius, and as it looks now, I was predestined to deal with water most of my life' (Kravčík 2009, p. 25[1]). Half a century later he was given a sculpture of the *waterman* (a mythological figure in Slovakia), which became the logo of the organization PW. Kravčík studied water management in Bratislava (1975–1980) and completed his studies with a thesis on computer methods for water management at the Gabčikovo Dam, a power station in the Danube and an important source of electricity in Slovakia. From 1981 until 1988 he worked for the Institute of Hydrology at the Slovak Academy of Science, where he focused on the Eastern Slovakian Lowland Basin. During these years he found his own understanding of water management in the lowlands to be different from the official policy of the institute. Following the publication of his views in a Czech journal, he was asked to leave the Institute of Hydrology; he then joined the Institute of Land Ecology, which was also part of the Slovak Academy of Science. There he continued to oppose the official water policy in the lowlands and what he saw as the unjustified draining of agricultural land; again, he was fired. He joined the Soil Management Institute, where he 'completed a project five times cheaper – the planned investment amounted to 10 million koruna, while my solution cost only 1.8 million koruna. My bosses, however, did not like that. They said that such a solution would not bring any money for the institute' (Kravčík 2009, p. 27). After leaking information about the drainage of a wetland project to a group of environmentalists, he lost his job again.

The *sametová revoluce* (Velvet Revolution) saw the overthrow of the communist government of Czechoslovakia in fall 1989. In June 1990 the first post-communist election was held. In January 1993 the *velvet divorce* left the Slovak and Czech Republics as independent neighbours. Kravčík reports that he experienced the period of *glasnost* (openness, transparency) at the end of the Cold War as very liberating: 'Our group of young ecologists was encouraged by this policy [of *glasnost*] and we were not afraid to speak out' (Kravčík 2009, p. 27). In 1993 he co-founded the NGO *Ľudia a voda* (PW) with Jaroslav Tesliar; Kravčík has remained its director up to the present. Slovakia's citizen sector is estimated to have grown from 11 citizen groups in 1989 to more than 10 000 in the first ten years after the fall of the Iron Curtain. The number of registered international citizens groups grew 650 per cent during the 1990s (Sen 2007, p. 538). The political change, along with funding flowing in from the United States and other Western countries, promoted the rapid growth of civil society. Notably, however, this growth also increased the competition amongst civil society organizations. According to Tesliar, who now works for an international organization, it is a sign of the strength of PW that they are among the groups that survived the initial period of the flourishing of NGOs despite these being some very difficult years (Tesliar, 28 July 2010, Košice).

A final political event is important to contextualize the work of PW. In

BOX 4.1   PW PROJECTS

1993: *Water for the Third Millennium* – an integrated water management concept for Slovakia's water policy in 1994.

1994–2001: *Blue Alternative* – an alternative water management programme for the Upper Torysa River in response to the construction of a dam, including pilot projects, summer camps and a regular publication.

1997–1999: *Village of the Third Millennium* – a conception for regional rural development in the Carpathian Euroregion, including pilot projects (family farming, biological water treatment, fish farming).

1998: *Village and Democracy* – the dissemination of materials and organisation of 14 discussion forums in the Levoča Mountains as part of a civil society campaign for fair parliamentary and municipal elections.

1999–present: *Blue Torysa Foundation* – a volunteer non-profit organization that supports local community activities through small grants.

2001: *We Live in One Basin* – a civic participation project based on stakeholder discussions.

2001–2003: *Crafts for Children* – children's camps for learning crafts.

2004–2005: *Košice Water Protocol* – a political framework approved by the Košice City Council for the mobilization of communities around the globe for water restoration in water cycles.

2005–2006: *Water Forest* – a project to decrease runoff and restore the forest area of the High Tatras in response to a storm.

2007–2008: *Water for Tatras Botanical Garden* – a water supply system for a botanical garden.

2007–2008: *People's University of Water* – an educational project regarding water management to build water capacity in municipalities.

2008: *Erosion treatment for Košice forest* – a water retention project.

2009–2010: *Water Without Borders* – a Slovak–Ukrainian project on water management.

October 2010–March 2012: Participation in the *Programme of Landscape Revitalization and Integrated River Basin Management* in the Slovak Republic (PLRIRB) – see main text.

2004 the Slovak Republic (SR) joined the EU – and with it, the various policy and funding mechanisms of the EU. This notably includes the European Water Framework Directive (WFD), a policy instrument that is generally considered to be the EU's approach to so-called integrated water resource management. With a view on the Millenium Development Goal 7 of environmental sustainability, the WFD is the key legal framework for environmental sustainability in the water sector for Europe. It promotes the adoption of river basin management plans with the goal to achieve good ecological and chemical status for European rivers and lakes by 2015 (Article 4).[2] According to the WFD, 'water is not a commercial product like any other, but, rather, a *heritage* which must be protected, defended and treated as such' (WFD, Preamble, italics added). Also, the WFD is to be implemented with the active involvement of the public (Article 14). We will return to this point about an ecological and socio-cultural framing of water as heritage below; we now turn to the mission of PW.

People and Water's Mission

Founded in 1993, PW states its mission is:

> To provide services to urban and rural communities, mostly within the Carpathian Euroregion. The goals are to solve the economic, social, cultural and environmental problems on a grassroots level by encouraging citizens to be proactive through development, renewal and promotion of the traditional culture and diversity of this region.[3]

The mission focuses on water management with water retention as a key aspect, specifically in rural Eastern Slovakia. There is also a goal to extend such water management to urban areas, as well as other parts of the Carpathian region (other parts of Slovakia, Ukraine, Poland and Hungary). As Kravčík puts it: 'The mission of our organization is to promote an alternative, integrated water management' (Kravčík 2009, p. 21).

The recognition abroad of the Blue Alternative and PW's relative success – Kravčík received the EU–US Democracy and Civil Society

Award in 1998 and the Goldman Environmental Prize in 1999 – resulted in as many problems as opportunities. In Kravčík's experience, other NGOs did not want to acknowledge his international success and in reaction tried to make it more difficult for him to receive funding on the national and regional levels (Kravčík, 30 July 2010, Košice). As we noted above, in the early 2000s it became more difficult to obtain funding owing to the increase and maturation of civil society and the consequent increase in competition for resources. PW widened its spectrum of activities to areas such as regional development and handicraft, as well as the inclusion of ethnic minorities. The cooperation with outside partners also became more important owing to the limited possibilities of cooperation within Slovakia. During this period Kravčík and colleagues began formulating the Blue Alternative in a more theoretical fashion – and translating the information into English – leading to the publication of the book 'Water for the Recovery of the Climate – A New Water Paradigm' in 2007. Kravčík summarizes the NWP as follows:

> The presence or absence of water is the key factor for the destiny of solar energy coming to the land. If water is present on the land, the solar energy is consumed in evaporation and it does not cause increase of temperature; vice versa, water vapour moderates temperature differences . . . In the New Water Paradigm, we elaborate the theoretical background of the water cycle mechanism, as well as the measures to be taken to get the benefits of plentiful good water quality, anti-flood and anti-erosion policy, increase of biodiversity . . . our New Water Paradigm still needs to be tested further, as is the case for any pioneering, eco-systemic, holistic approach. (Kravčík 2009, p. 30)

In order to strengthen the small water cycle, small-scale measures are promoted that improve water retention in the landscape.

An important aspect of PW is to implement water retention projects that are in direct contact with mayors and citizen groups. Along with working on education – workshops, information brochures, and so on – projects fostering water retention and its infiltration in the soil are implemented on a local level. There is a focus on regional development (again, especially in Eastern Slovakia) and on ways to improve the economic and social livelihoods in villages, for example by fostering local craft (see Box 4.1).

When we travelled to visit Kravčík in Slovakia in summer 2010, Kravčík and PW had conducted a number of small projects in Eastern Slovakia and had made numerous educational efforts. However, it had not been possible yet to implement the NWP approach on a regional level, let alone a national one. To the contrary, when we visited Tichy Potok in 2010 the discussion over the dam had reappeared and Mayor Dzuganova was worried that the dam would be built after all.

A Summer of Creative Confusion

In fall 2010, following both a change in government and a period of major floods, an opportunity opened up to implement the PW approach on a much larger scale. The new prime minister was Iveta Radičová, who Kravčík knew from civil society work in the early days of the Velvet Revolution. Radičová's government, the SDKU-DS (Slovak Democratic and Christian Union – Democratic Party), initiated the *Programme of landscape revitalization and integrated river basin management in the Slovak Republic* (PLRIRB) in close cooperation with Kravčík, creating a special office under the prime minister headed by Martin Kováč (co-author of the NWP and also an Ashoka fellow). The following is an outline of the implementation phases of the PLRIRB.

- A **pilot project** was launched in 2010 with 23 municipalities in the catchments of the Ondava, Torysa, Váh, Kysuca and Hornád rivers; it had a budget of 580 000 € from the SR Prime Minister's reserve. The aim was to gain practical knowledge about the construction of water holdings. Over a period of three months, 341 people were employed and a water retention capacity of over 140 000 m³ was installed (Michal Kravčík et al. 2012).
- The **First Realization Programme** (1st RP) was approved by the government 9 March 2011 with 190 municipalities;[4] it had a budget of 24 million € from the SR government and the European Social Fund. It focused in particular on capacity building with local companies (knowledge for building catchments). The programme created 2500 jobs for a period of six months and a water retention capacity of 6.1 million m³ was installed (Michal Kravčík et al. 2012).
- The **Second Realization Programme** (2nd RP) was approved by the government in fall 2011 with 354 municipalities; it had a budget of 18.5 million € from the SR government and the European Social Fund. It focused in particular on including unemployed people from local rural areas and created 4200 jobs for a period of six months. A total water retention capacity of 3.9 million m³ was installed.
- The **Third Realization Programme** (3rd RP) had already been planned but was finally stopped owing to a change in the SR government in March 2012. The third round was supposed to include, for the first time, cities and their role in water retention.

Throughout both the 1990s and 2000s, including the large programme of the last few years, PW has remained a small NGO with a staff of around six members and a wider network of volunteers (around 50). The permanent staff consists of project managers and an accountant. Members view themselves as entrepreneurial and self-determined (Hronský, interview on 27 July 2010); nevertheless, for all the important decisions Kravčík is the key person of the organization. He is also the face of the organization for the larger regional, national and international audiences. The organization finances itself via grants from public and private sources; it has not yet developed an earned income strategy. In the next section, we turn to its specific approach to innovation and scaling.

4.3 INNOVATION AND SCALING

The idea of creating small water catchments is 'not new on [an] international level but in Slovakia it is innovative' (Kravčík, interview on 18 July 2012). In present-day Slovakia, the idea of building small dams is new in a temporal context; however, before the socialist time, farmers built wooden measures and barriers of a similar type. People and Water seeks to revive this *heritage* of water culture.

Kravčík aims to bring this small-dam idea on the national level and beyond. The idea is in conflict with the established water management techniques in Slovakia, such as the construction of large dams. The implementation of the idea mainly draws on local labour and delegates responsibility to the municipalities, whereas the construction of large dams requires (outside) experts for construction and maintenance. Hence the idea demands a change in the flow of resources and authority. This disruptive side is familiar from many innovations in general; Kravčík's track record with official Slovakian institutions indicates that he views resistance and dissidence as an aspect of his way of doing things (Kravčík 2009).

An analysis of PW's projects as well as interviews with members of the organization and stakeholders suggest at least five elements with which PW seeks to establish its approach against the established view.

1. *Identifying contact persons willing to take on responsibility for local project implementation, respectively fostering the sense of responsibility of decision makers on the local level and establishing close relationships to these decision makers.* In the case of Tichy Potok, Kravčík got in contact with all of the mayors in the Upper Torysa Region (five villages) in 1993 when the idea of constructing a huge dam came up. The mayors felt they had no power to avert the construction. Trainings, workshops and regional meetings took place; (re-)establishing responsibility on the local level by overcoming the feeling of powerlessness played a major role. Lubica Dzuganova, mayor of Tichy Potok since

1994, described the work of PW as follows: 'It has opened our eyes – we went beyond borders of our normal vision, they [PW] showed us what we can do' (Dzuganova, 23 July 2010, Tichy Potok).

2. *Proposing projects that are feasible on a local level.* The ideas for water holdings and dams fostered by Kravčík and PW are based on simple techniques and mainly use wood, stone and earth. These techniques need a certain know-how, which is established via workshops and training. The subsequent implementation by people in the village and small businesses promotes the experience of empowerment and responsibility.

3. *Anchoring projects and ideas in tradition.* In presentations, Kravčík and PW repeatedly emphasize the link between their approach and a traditional sense of home and place in Slovakia. For example, they present their approach as part of the healing of the scars and wounds of the homeland (Kravčík et al. 2012, Chapter 2). That water is a heritage thus receives a specific meaning here in relation to innovation: innovation is not positioned as the new that takes away from the old, but as a return and revival of tradition.[5]

> In our country we have sufficient evidence to date about how responsibly our ancestors looked after their home soil that fed them. If you travel around Slovakia with your eyes open and know what to look for, the land is like an open book offering the wisdom of old solutions. In Slovakia there are still the last remnants from the time of the Wallachian colonization that divided farming into small fields. This prevented rainwater from rapid draining into gullies and streams and avoided dramatic flash flooding. . . .
> (Kravčík 2012 et al., p. 71)

4. *Creating visibility by actively inviting the media and international partners to follow project implementation.* Kravčík runs a blog on a major national news portal, which he updates regularly. He uses the blog to make ideas and actions visible;[6] he also simply enjoys the communication. Even Vladimir Holčik, a staff member of the State Water Building Company in Bratislava, which seeks to construct large dams, described Kravčík as follows: 'He is an eloquent speaker at conferences . . . He can present himself perfectly in front of a camera' (Holčik, interview on 22 July 2010). Media visibility makes it more difficult for opponents to attack the proposal. Kravčík does not confine himself only to Slovakia but actively searches for international cooperation.

5. *Generating political support on the regional and national level.* As the project list above shows, PW has repeatedly made legislative proposals and protocols, which along with their publications, communicate the content of the NWP and seek to generate political will for its

implementation. In this context, PW also actively seeks support from abroad in order to communicate that the paradigm is part of a larger, international development. According to Jaroslav Tesliar, Kravčík's concept of water management would not have survived in Slovakia had it not been for this strong international support. Having a network of cooperation is thus very important, it 'gives faith to fight' (Tesliar, interview on 28 July 2012) and also provides financial support (for example Ashoka Fellowship, Goldman Environmental Prize).

The above five elements put together suggest the following approach to the *scaling* of the idea: to implement the NWP, Kravčík and PW focus on scaling out the idea via the identification and empowerment of people in villages (mayors and to some extent local businesses). The approach to water retention is low-tech, which makes it possible to adopt the techniques at a local level. To this end, the conditions for scaling out have to be created and promoted, which is done mainly via lobbying for change in legislation and applying for project grants. In view of the strong opposition to the project – not least by the state water construction company and water management company, which are in charge of construction and maintenance of large dams – PW tries to generate support via international networking and media visibility. Figure 4.1 represents the approach.

How has this approach been implemented so far? PW prevented the construction of the Tichy Potok Dam and proposed a Blue Alternative that

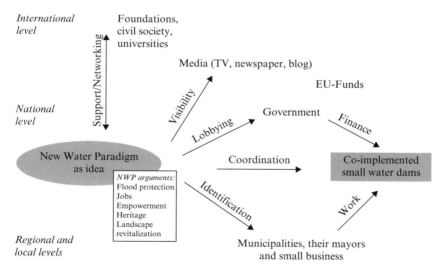

Figure 4.1   The PW approach to scaling

ultimately led to the formulation of the NWP. For a long time PW struggled to move from very few projects and publications to more on the regional and national level. With the PLRIRB, an opportunity arose for the first time to try out this paradigm on a large, national scale; PW was able to do so through a collaborative strategy with the government and in this way, *scaling out* was achieved rather suddenly. This temporarily turned Kravčík into a social intrapreneur – working for the government – who drew on the contacts, publications and experiences he had made over the prior two decades to rapidly come up with a programme for municipalities that is low-tech and can be implemented by municipalities and small businesses.

This collaborative strategy, however, proved not to be resilient with respect to changes in government (March 2012) – the programme was stopped by the new government. PW has a stable network of partners in municipalities and the coordinating ZMOS (Slovak Association of Towns and Villages) but it lacks a strategy that is independent of short-term changes in party-politics. Its very limited organizational capacity also means that much depends on Michal Kravčík personally.

4.4   SUSTAINABILITY EVALUATION

This section evaluates the work of Michal Kravčík and PW from a sustainability perspective based on the approach outlined in Chapter 1 of this book. It starts with the dimensions of environmental sustainability and human capabilities, and moves from there to management and politics. The empirical focus for this evaluation is on the PLRIRB as the major implementation so far of PW's vision.

Along with literature research and in-depth qualitative interviews during our field trips, we conducted a quantitative survey in fall 2011 and 2012 with a questionnaire that focused on participants' impressions of the PLRIRB. The questionnaire mainly consisted of statements to which the respondents could agree, disagree or stay neutral. Individual participants (n=687, workers employed in the project) were questioned on various aspects of the PLRIRB in regards to central capabilities. A second round of the questionnaire was conducted in late fall 2012 (n=139).[7]

Environmental Sustainability

Conceptually, the restoration of the water cycle is at the core of sustainability with respect to freshwater. The water cycle ensures the regeneration of available freshwater as a non-living fund, thereby providing a constant freshwater supply (along with all of its indirect benefits) to humans and nature.

This is only possible if human water management does not interfere with the regeneration process in such a way that freshwater quantity or quality is threatened. Such a threat is precisely what Kravčík and colleagues discuss as the *old water paradigm*, that is, a centralistic approach to water management that neglects the role of water retention for the small water cycle, resulting in increased risks of floods and droughts (Kravčík et al. 2007).

The NWP has two central management dimensions (Lodemann et al. 2010).

1. *Local water retention* (keeping water in landscapes and cities):
   a. The process of runoff is slowed down, which increases the volume of freshwater that infiltrates the soil, thereby supporting plant growth and replenishing groundwater aquifers. By guaranteeing water availability for plants as producers and other species within the ecosystem, functional diversity is held intact. In dry areas inhabited by only a few species, the introduction of water opens up opportunities for establishing more diverse communities, thereby increasing resilience.
   b. Loss of matter from the landscape to the oceans is reduced, including for example soil base cations that serve as essential nutrients for plants (Ripl and Hildmann 2000). By reducing the superficial runoff, less matter is washed out of the system.
   c. Water retention results in higher rates of evaporation and evapotranspiration, which have local – and maybe further reaching – cooling effects.

2. *Catchment-based perspective* (primary hydrological unit of rainwater harvesting and retention): in contexts where the fund has been endangered or reduced by past events and management practices, 'restoration' and 'recovery' are thus clarified in terms of working towards a water cycle as a non-living fund. This take on environmental sustainability primarily focuses on quantity (water availability in the water cycle) and not on quality (pollution may occur even with a restored water cycle).

We now examine how these management implications are respected in practice by the PLRIRB.

The PLRIRB and environmental sustainability

Local water retention   The PLRIRB sets a minimum volume of water retention to be reached as a grant requirement for villages (for example a minimum of 30 000 m³/municipality in the 1st RP). Improved water retention is a key goal of the PLRIRB.

Matter loss   The construction of small dams and water energy-dissipating measures in forest roads are effective ways to reduce erosion and matter loss. However, there are no specific grant requirements for this goal similar to the water retention goal. Also, the programme does not include a method of tracking how much matter has been effectively retained in the short term and in the long term. The long-term perspective seems particularly important owing to the open question of long-term maintenance for these dams and consequently their long-term capacity to prevent erosion.

Local cooling   Increased water availability increases the possibilities of evaporation and then evapo-transpiration, thus the potential for cooling. However, there are no specific grant requirements for this goal and the programme does not include a method for tracking the actual effect. The effect beyond the local level (that is on the regional or national one) thus remains an open question.

Catchment-based perspective   There is some evidence for a catchment-based perspective in the PLRIRB. In the selection criteria of the 1st RP, the PLRIRB considered municipalities in the upper part of the catchment so that the measures taken positively influence the municipalities in the lower part of the catchment; this criterion had a weight of 10 per cent. In the selection criteria of the 2nd RP, the PLRIRB considered for the same reason municipalities higher up in the catchment or neighbouring to one of the municipalities chosen for the 1st RP: this criterion had a weight of 30 per cent.

In conclusion, the NWP suggests a conceptual approach with specific policies to regenerate the water cycle and to take responsibility for human management practices that fail to do so. The approach yields management implications that are water-specific and focused on water retention, matter loss and local cooling in catchments. Evidence for these management implications can be found in the PLRIRB. The NWP conceptually and empirically contributes to environmental sustainability. This conclusion is subject to two main qualifications: 1) the so-far limited methods employed by the PLRIRB to track the impact of the programme, also in regard to unintended, environmentally destructive consequences; 2) the presently open long-term impact of the programme, particularly due to the open maintenance question – who will maintain the measures in the long run?

Meeting Central Human Capabilities

Our conceptual analysis of the NWP in terms of its importance for central human capabilities (see Chapter 1) suggests that in the Slovakian context special attention needs to be paid to the following capabilities (the other capabilities on Nussbaum's list being of indirect or marginal relevance only, see Lodemann et al. 2010):[8]

1. *control over one's environment* – the capability to have economic and political control over one's environment via the economic capability of having real opportunities to work and to hold property as well as the political capability to have a say in decision-making – in relation here to water management;
2. *leading a life of normal length and in good health* – in relation here to flood prevention;
3. *affiliation* – the capability of living with and for others – in relation here to the sense of community and working together (or lack thereof) at the village level;
4. *living in concern for other species* – the natural world, its plants and species – in relation here to the task of taking responsibility for the restoration of the water cycle;
5. *emotion* – the capability of having attachments to things and people outside ourselves – in relation here to fear caused by flood risks.

In the following we will analyse the PLRIRB in relation to each of these capabilites.

Economic and political control over one's environment

Employment   In this case the opportunity to find employment is a matter of job availability. The programme improved the opportunity space in the participating villages and hence the real opportunity to find employment in rural areas. The Organization for Economic Co-operation and Development (OECD) estimated unemployment (harmonized) for 2012 in Slovakia at 14 per cent, the fifth highest in Europe at the time, behind Spain, Greece, Portugal and Ireland. As mentioned above, the PLRIRB created 341 jobs for a period of three months in the pilot phase, 3500 jobs for a period of six months in the 1st RP and 4200 jobs for a period of six months in the 2nd RP.

As a contribution to economic participation possibilities in rural areas, however, two qualifications have to be made with a view to this increase in opportunity space.

a. *Short term versus long term*: at this point, the effect is limited to the short term as there are no provisions in place that would secure such employment and work once the government programme is over (so far the phases have a length of six months each and there is no guarantee for the phases to continue). Each municipality is supposed to employ (at least) ten long-term unemployed persons per project. The employees of each phase could only be employed for one phase, and then had to stop for at least three months before being employed again. Thus the programme did not create permanent jobs. Nevertheless, respondents to the survey were optimistic with respect to the long-term effects. In response to the proposition that skills gained during the programme will help them to find another job, 70 per cent agreed and 11 per cent disagreed.[9]

b. *Decent pay*: participants received 327 € per month plus health and social insurance as well as food tickets during the working time. The minimum wage in Slovakia is 317 € (as of January 2011); the average net monthly wage of forestry and related workers in 2012 was 484 €.[10] The payment is thus slightly above the minimum wage level, though still far from the average income for this field of work. In the first round of the survey many respondents commented on the low salary, often arguing that the jobs are hard physical labour and that payment should be according to skills. Also, during the interviews in 2012 some mayors reported difficulties in finding ten unemployed people owing to the small difference of the programme's salary compared to the money they get being unemployed. 'We had a problem to choose 10 unemployed people. Because, if you would employ them, they will lose [the] social subsidies they get. When they recalculate how much it is, it was not worth [it] for them to break their unemployment' (Orenicova, interview on 20 February 2012).

Property   High economic costs owing to floods are well known in Central Europe (Reinhardt et al. 2011). Flood prevention, one of the main goals of the PLRIRB, is important for the effective opportunity not only to have property but also to have property that is valuable and secure. Accordingly, this point depends on the flood prevention impact of the programme. An assessment of the programme's achievements in this respect is only possible following the next experience with major rainfalls in the participating regions.

The survey showed that property damage occured to respondents or people around them owing to floods before and after the PLRIRB. The year before the PLRIRB was implemented, ca. 67 per cent of the respondents agreed that they or people around them had suffered from damage of property, whereas 18 per cent disagreed with the statement. The data from the second round differs from that: 45 per cent agreed and 42 per cent disagreed. The conclusion that the programme helped to protect property cannot be drawn directly from the current data; as noted already, 2012 was a year with less flood-inducing weather extremes than the years before.

Natural resources   Another aspect of control over one's environment is the control over natural resources. In the case of the PLRIRB this control is not about the exploitation of natural resources but rather the control over them to prevent floods. Presently, flood prevention is mainly the responsibility of the regional and central government in Slovakia. Municipalities can apply for renting their streams in order to manage them, but flood prevention projects are normally expensive and the applications for government support are difficult. The PLRIRB improved the capacity of municipalities to take control over their environment. This should not be interpreted as an anti-technology stance. In the first round of the survey 85 per cent agreed with the statement that flood protection would require experts and their technologies (9 per cent disagreed). In the second round this ratio got stronger: 91 per cent agreed, only 4 per cent disagreed.

Political participation   The programme was a governmental programme and as such, a funding decision of a democratically elected government. We can still ask whether the programme was a) public (was information available and were decisions made in a transparent manner?), b) inclusive (who can participate in decision-making and implementation?) and c) open to reasoned debate (was there space to engage in debate regarding the goals and the means of the programme?).[11]

Publicity   The main information source was a governmental web page (www.krajina.gov.sk).[12] All materials about the pilot project, 1st RP and 2nd RP were gathered here, including a photogallery and a list of press releases regarding the programme. By now the material on the sub pages is not accessible any more, the only residue being the sentence 'It works good!' on the main page.[13] Prior to its implementation, Kravčík helped the government organize regional meetings with mayors to discuss the programme. The programme was also reported and discussed on television and in newspapers.[14] Kravčík runs a blog on a major national newsportal,[15] which he directly used during the programme to send regular updates to all the mayors involved.

Inclusiveness   The programme was open to all villages in Slovakia and as such was linked to the local political structure of Slovakian villages and their mayors. In the spirit of a Green New Deal job creation programme, there was a requirement regarding the inclusion of unemployed people (see above). There were no specific provisions regarding gender or ethnicity.

Reasoned debate   Regional meetings before and during the programme offered information and space for discussion. There was also intensive scrutiny of the pilot; notably, the Ministry of Agriculture and Rural Development made four objections and the Ministry of Environment made nine. These objections were discussed and publicly posted;[16] they resulted in the 'involvement' of both ministries in the 2nd RP. 'Involvement' is in quotation marks as there appeared to be a struggle between the different ministries and the programme over who should receive the programme resources. In this situation, Kravčík preferred a speedy implementation of the programme out of fear that debate may de facto be the attempt to gain control over the resources or even to stop the programme. This sense of urgency was confirmed with the change of government in March 2012 when the programme was stopped.

Normal life, health and shelter
Floods are a risk to life, health and shelter. According to the SR government, the effects of floods on humans in the last two major floods have been as follows.[17]

The risk from floods for leading a life of normal length and health is real. In addition to physical injury, as Kravčík highlighted to us in conversation, there is psychological damage to health (Kravčík, conversation on 9 January 2012). This point was also made in the PLRIRB outline that spoke of 'traumatized citizens' (Government of Slovakia 2011, p. 6). Psychological damage may be owing to the risk to both health and property. In the first round of the survey 38 per cent of the respondents agreed with the statement that they or people around them suffered a health damage caused by floods the year before, 31 per cent disagreed. The

Table 4.1   Effects of floods on humans in Slovakia in 2009 and 2010

	2009 Flood	2010 Flood
People affected	6889	33 080
People evacuated	271	7729
People saved	39	1697
People injured	2	12
People killed	3	2

results from the second round differed: 25 per cent agreed and 57 per cent disagreed. As in the case of property above, the impact of the PLRIRB remains an open question, which can only be assessed after there are major flood-inducing events in the areas that have participated in the programme.

Affiliation
This category concerns the capability to live with and towards others and to have a basis of social respect and non-humiliation. The background issue here is Kravčík's claim that water management during Soviet times (the old water paradigm) provoked a crisis of community and responsibility, that it was part of a technocracy corrosive to community and subsidiarity. If the persistence of top-down, centrally-planned water management implemented by outside experts, along with the high rates of unemployment in post-communist rural Slovakia, are detrimental to a sense of community, then we can ask whether the programme contributed structurally to the possibility of improved living with and towards others.

The concern for others is structurally expressed in the programme via the social and environmental selection criteria. The 1st RP focused on areas in the upper catchment with high flood risk and it took the rate of unemployment in the applying villages into account as a selection factor. The 2nd RP included flood risk, position in catchment and unemployment as selection criteria.

If the possibility to work – subject to the two qualifications discussed under the capabilities category 'economic and political control over one's environment' – is an important structural feature for affiliation in a society, then the inclusion of unemployed people is an indicator for affiliation in the project. The PLRIRB created jobs that were partly handed to unemployed people:

- Pilot project (three-month period): 341 jobs, of which 165 people were previously unemployed.
- 1st RP (six-month period): 3500 jobs, of which 2500 are estimated to have been previously unemployed.
- 2nd RP (six-month period): 4200 jobs (the proportion of previously unemployed participants was not known to us at the time of writing).

This point is strengthened by the observation that the programme had an inclusive approach to technology. In contrast to the construction of large dams, the villagers were fully involved in the construction of small dams according to their creative ideas and materials (see Kravčík et al. 2012 for many photographs of the diversity of dams that have been built).

As already noted above, the NWP should not be interpreted as an anti-technology and anti-expert stance.

Recognition and responsibility for the work are strongly embedded in the respective villages owing to the local involvement. In both rounds of the survey, the majority of respondents agreed with the statement that the villagers agreed with what they were doing (86 per cent in the first round and 90 per cent in the second), that the respondents' participation has been valued by the villagers (86 per cent in the first and 88 per cent in the second) and that there were other people who would like to join a programme like the PLRIRB (80 per cent in the first and 90 per cent in the second).

This point about inclusion is subject to the qualification that the programme did not include any explicit requirements regarding gender or ethnicity. The PLRIRB did contribute to an improved community perception with regards to ethnicity in one sense: seven of the construction teams were mainly Roma groups (one of these teams was visited by a minister). The news image generated of Roma working for a societal task went against the expectation of non-working Roma dependent on unemployment money; it remains doubtful, though, if the perception of the Roma communities has undergone a major change (Kravčík, conversation on 9 January 2012).

Other species
This category concerns the human capability to live with concern for other species and nature as a whole. A variety of comments made in the survey suggest that the programme may contribute to a concern for other species and nature as a whole. Comments exhibit a range from cognitive and enlightened self-interest to possibly biocentric or even holistic claims familiar to environmental ethics. In reply to the question of how the programme may have changed their attitude towards nature protection, comments in the survey ranged from learning ('I got to know more healing plants', 'I think differently about the importance of water and I am thinking of why the streams are drying', 'I understand more about the importance of water in the landscape'), an increased sense of awareness ('I am more conscious of nature'), enlightened self-interest ('It is good for me and my village') to an increased respect ('I respect nature and the forest more') and a sense of responsibility ('We have to protect it more'). The statement that the programme changed their attitude towards nature protection was agreed upon by 74 per cent in the first round of the survey (12 per cent disagreed); in the second round the answering scheme differs: 93 per cent agreed upon the statement, only 1 per cent disagreed.

Table 4.2 Selected statements from the survey

Statement	Agree [%]	Disagree [%]
1. Q1 Skills I have gained during the programme will help me to find a next job.	70,45	11,35
Q2 Skills gained during the programme helped me (or will help me) to find a new job.	79,86	6,47
2. Q1 Last year, I or people around me suffered a property damage caused by floods.	66,52	18,34
Q2 This year, I or people around me suffered a property damage caused by floods.	45,32	41,73
3. Q1 Flood protection requires experts and their technologies.	85,01	8,88
Q2 Flood protection requires experts and their technologies.	91,37	3,60
4. Q1 Last year, I or people around me suffered a health damage caused by floods.	38,28	31,44
Q2 This year, I or people around me suffered a health damage caused by floods.	25,18	56,83
5. Q1 People in the village agree with what we are doing.	86,32	4,37
Q2 People in the village agree with what we were doing.	89,93	0,72
6. Q1 The inhabitants in the village think positively about me joining the work in the project.	86,46	2,77
Q2 The other inhabitants in the village value my participation in the project.	87,77	0,72
7. Q1 I know of other people in the village who would like to join the project or a similar one in the future.	80,20	3,93
Q2 I know of other people in the village who would like to join the project or a similar one in the future.	89,93	0,72
8. Q1 During the programme, I have changed my attitude toward nature protection.	74,38	12,08
Q2 The programme has changed my attitude toward nature protection.	92,81	1,44
9. Q1 Since the construction of dams and water holdings, the flooding of our village after heavy rainfall decreased.	84,72	3,93
Q2 Since the construction of dams and water holdings, the flooding of our village after heavy rainfall decreased.	92,09	2,88
10. Q1 Dams and water holdings made our community safer.	91,56	3,64
Q2 Dams and water holdings made our community safer.	95,68	2,88

Note: Q1: first round, Q2: second round of the survey.

Emotions

Anxiety and fear are obstacles to a healthy emotional development, so is the absence of associations and communities that allow the development of attachments to other people. Childhood development is important for nurturing this capability along with a communal life able to sustain such attachments.

As noted above, the risk of flood (and of drought) can be an existential threat to health and economic security (destruction and damage of shelter, forced migration). Depending on this risk and how it is experienced, floods can become an obstacle to a healthy emotional development. The government's outline of the 1st RP speaks of 'traumatized inhabitants' caused by the experience of floods (SR government 2011, p. 6).

The results of the first and second round of the survey indicate that the respondents have a huge amount of trust for the functionality of the implemented measures of the PLRIRB. They have experienced the post-programme period as less flooding-extensive after heavy rainfalls; again this is subject to the qualification that there was a lesser amount and severity of flood-inducing events in 2012.

In conclusion to our discussion on the human capabilities of the target groups in the villages, our evaluation highlights the creation of jobs, particularly for the unemployed in rural areas. The programme structurally included the unemployed with respect to work that has a direct community goal; the source of recognition and respect such work may offer is indicated in the survey. Likewise, the programme appears to have led to an increase in a sense of concern for the environment, the sense of concern hereby having different meanings such as learning about, enlightened self-interest in or respect for the environment. In regards to emotions, the programme has seemingly led to an increase in a feeling of safety. Evidently, all these points depend on further developments of the approach and its impact on villages and their environments in the coming years.

Internal Organizational Responsibility

Capabilities and environmental sustainability not only affect the target group of a programme but also concern the internal management of organizations, its partners and suppliers. This is a point that is well known from the discussion of corporate social responsibility. PW has not yet developed an integrated policy in the sense of social and ecological work and production standards. Such a policy that dealt with environmental management and production, wage levels, types of contracts and other social issues such as gender and ethnicity policies would allow the internal assessment of whether these goals are well achieved.

People and Water is a very small organization, with a maximum of six employees at a time; questions of decent pay, gender equality or ethnic diversity can therefore only be addressed in a very limited way. Moreover, the major scaling effort to date did not depend on the organizational capability of PW in any significant way, but rather on Kravčík's role as social intrapreneur in the government. Consequently, we did not focus on management in our research in any depth and would therefore end this section with two short observations: 1) as with other organizations that we have studied, payment even for headquarters staff is hardly comparable to income in for-profit enterprises, and in the case of PW is subject to the uncertainty of obtaining grants; 2) PW does not produce something beyond the water projects already evaluated above, so the question of ecological standards of production *in the office* is relatively limited. When questioned in this respect, Kravčík says that for him what matters is not the green roof on his office for rainwater retention but rather the water in the system (Kravčík, interview on 18 July 2010). This system stance makes the focus on a green office a lesser priority and creates a tension with the call for taking responsibility in the community, rather than leaving water to technocracy. In fact, PW has installed a system of ecological sanitation in their community house in the Levoča Mountains. It seems plausible to assume that similar actions in their headquarters in Košice may set a positive example for others by demonstrating what can be done in cities.

Michal Kravčík and PW as a Political Actor[18]

Flood prevention is no doubt a key challenge of integrated water resource management and environmental sustainability. In the EU context, the WFD sets the standard for a catchment-based and participatory approach (see Section 4.2). In their conceptual approach, Kravčík and PW take on and endorse such an integrated and participatory approach, pushing it in the direction of flood prevention not just in the rivers but also on the land; a point that has not received much attention in the WFD (Grüne Liga 2004). With the PLRIRB, Kravčík found a way to implement his ideas on the national scale for the first time. Yet his approach is controversial and has met with resistance. Hence the issue of legitimacy arises, which we now turn to in accordance with the criteria introduced in Chapter 1 of this book.

Output legitimacy

A first source of legitimacy for social entrepreneurs is their innovation, that is output-oriented legitimacy. The NWP – its practical expression in the Tichy Potok protest and later in the PLRIRB – is not absolutely novel, but it is novel in Slovakia's post-communist context (see Section 4.3). The output legitimacy can be conceptually linked to the WFD and integrated water management. However, this output legitimacy will strongly depend on developments in the next years, that is the actual success or not of the PLRIRB with respect to its goals. In practice, the output legitimacy of the PLRIRB was hotly contested on the national level owing to the fact that the progamme was perceived as the fruit of the Radičová government; support was cut off as soon as the new government came to power. On the municipal level of the target group, however, our survey suggests a high level of output legitimacy – with due qualification.

In addition, the project also draws on input legitimacy: the programme was approved and discussed by a democratically elected government and was implemented by elected mayors. Quite independently of the output and outcomes, the PLRIRB and by implication Kravčík draw on this source of legitimacy – and its consequences! The new government stopped the programme in March 2012.

Social accountability

A second source of legitimacy for non-elected organizations is their ability to respond to and be accountable to the needs of those for whom they provide goods. This second source of legitimacy builds on a number of factors.

First, Kravčík and PW's collaborators are all from Slovakia. The office of PW is located downstream in Košice, the city for which the original Tichy Potok Dam proposal was elaborated. This existential fact, the contextual knowledge it implies and the personal significance it has for its protagonists ('I will also live here in the future!') fosters social accountability as compared to a project driven by outside experts who personally will not have to bear any local consequences. A further indicator for this claim is that Kravčík invested part of his Goldman Environmental Prize money to purchase a house for PW in the contested area, which serves as a community house for the NGO and is intended to become an information centre in the future.

Second, as part of their approach, Kravčík and PW emphasize the importance of subsidiarity. One of the key components of the approach is that natural resources are to be managed on the local level, for example by a local association of villages. The work needed in the realm of management should be done by locals if possible or should at least include locals. Moreover, Kravčík and his collaborators seek to recover the knowledge of local farmers in water harvesting and retention in order to form solutions. These techniques were neglected by the state's hydraulic mission, which favoured large-scale infrastructure dependent on the expert knowledge of outside engineers. The inclusion of local (traditional) knowledge as well as the process of seeking further knowledge may lead to a closer relationship amongst the locals, Kravčík and PW.

Third, PW included numerous educational efforts from the start. These efforts include the publication of a regional journal called *Blue Alternative* (from 1995–2001 with five to six issues per year), the organization of numerous water-related conferences in the region, the hosting of regular summer work camps in the Tichy Potok area (one each year from 1995–2001), the organization of a People's University of Water (2007–2008), the maintenance of an active blog as part of a national news portal and recently, the organization of regional conferences with mayors. In short, the history of PW exhibits a concern with education. Kravčík himself writes:

> The citizens of the disadvantaged villages grasped very quickly that they also had allies, and their self-confidence grew. They learnt how to present their views publicly; they could lead sound and assertive discussions. At the final public meetings held in the affected villages, the situation was such that the state officials and investors deputies' could not answer the citizens' well-complied and well-founded questions. (Kravčík 2009, p. 23)

This was also confirmed in an interview with the mayor of the most affected village, Tichy Potok, who described these efforts as an empowering experience for the community.[19]

Mediating role: transitional authority and empowerment

A further source of legitimacy is advocacy for affected communities and fostering their participation. Hence the goal is a contribution to the empowerment of the target group; even if the organization takes the initiative, its authority is transitional as empowerment is the goal.

Kravčík's educational efforts illustrate the aim of empowering affected people. On the conceptual level, local resource management requires a decentralization of power. Kravčík and PW thereby have a mediating role by advocating for the affected communities. They are transition agents who seek institutional change. However, it is precisely this goal that depends on the long-term success of the project. A serious obstacle to the goal of empowerment for the PLRIRB is the current short-term nature of the programme. This obstacle leaves two main questions open: economically speaking, what will happen to its participants after the six-month period? Environmentally speaking, who will maintain and further develop water retention once the programme is over?

Outside recognition

A further source of legitimacy is outside recognition. The judgement of distant others with no direct interest or involvement in local resource distribution does not directly confer democratic legitimacy but may indirectly contribute to legitimacy.

Along with an Ashoka fellowship in 1994 and the Goldman Environmental Prize in 1999, Kravčík received the EU–US Democracy and Civil Society Award in 1998. The NWP has also been recognized internationally; for instance, Maude Barlow, international human rights activist and senior advisor on water to the 63rd President of the United Nations General Assembly (October 2008–2009), made the NWP the ecological framework of her global water covenant (Barlow 2008). Kravčík has also featured in international documentaries such as Sam Bozo's 'Blue Gold – World Water Wars' (2008).

This outside recognition has not been as purely positive as might be expected. In particular, the Goldman Environmental Prize caused considerable resentment amongst other environmental NGOs in Slovakia at a time when the competitive pressure regarding financing was increasing (Kravčík, conversation on 31 July 2012).

It is too early at this point to speak conclusively of innovation as a source of output legitimacy for Kravčík and PW: this will depend on the outcome of the PLIRB as the major legitimacy test. Nonetheless, independently of actual outputs and outcomes, Kravčík and PW draw on input legitimacy and additionally on: a) an informal social accountability, primarily in view of the local and sustained educational efforts to include citizens from the villages directly in the discussion and implementation; b) the empowerment this offers to the villages; and c) the outside recognition Kravčík has received over the years.

4.5   GETTING THINGS DONE SUSTAINABLY?

In 1963 Ivan Klíma published a novel about people and water (Klíma 1963). Set just after WWII, engineer Martin Petr travels to rural villages of East Slovakia with a mission to improve the lives of the people via large dams that prevent flooding and thus help to move them out of their miserable poverty. Petr's intention is genuine and he promotes what he takes to be progress at great personal costs. However, Petr and his comrades never get around to listening to the people in the villages and hearing their desires. It is only when he meets with open resistance towards the end of the novel that Petr hears the silence of the villagers with respect to the plans for progress. The novel *Hour of Silence* was first published in 1963, banned by the Czechoslovakian censorship at the time and only republished in 2009.

In the 1990s the hydraulic engineer Kravčík was drawn from the city of

Košice to the countryside of Eastern Slovakia – to Tichy Potok, known as the *silent stream*. He listened to the people there and participated in the fight against the old paradigm of large dam construction for flood prevention and energy supply. Eventually he began to fight in the name of a new paradigm – not in the name of progress but in the name of the water cycle, and with it the renewal of a cultural heritage. So what is repetition here and what is new? And what is the contribution to sustainable development, the twenty-first-century child of progress?

The idea of creating small water catchments and thereby strengthening the small water cycle is novel in the contemporary Slovakian context. The innovation aims at ecological sustainability and secondarily at local empowerment. The PLRIRB has allowed Kravčík not only to aim for the national level, but to actually scale the NWP on this level via a governmental programme.

The primary sustainability goal is investment in water as a fund. On the conceptual level, the NWP suggests an approach with management policies and implementation measures to foster the regeneration of the small water cycle by way of retaining water. The PLRIRB is the main implementation so far of the NWP and provides the largest level of evidence for management implications. We conclude that the NWP conceptually and empirically contributes to environmental sustainability. With a view on promoting environmental sustainability, it seems necessary to put further emphasis on the monitoring of the water retention schemes for learning as well as increasing the possibility of support or imitation by others. Of particular interest are effects on erosion and biodiversity, and the actual impact in terms of local cooling and smoothing of weather events.

With a view to the goal of meeting central capabilities, our evaluation of the PLRIRB suggests that the programme appears to have had positive effects, especially in regard to the capability of economic and political control over one's environment. Here we have highlighted the creation of jobs and the inclusion of unemployed people, in particular the development of their skills and the indication of their work being a source of recognition and respect. Moreover, there seems to be an increase in the participants' sense of concern for the environment and an increased feeling of safety. Within the framework of the programme the municipalities gained control over the implementation and were empowered to make their own decisions (also in regards to the general decision whether to apply for the programme or not). Nonetheless, there are questions that remain about the long-term impact. The major limitation concerning the long-term viability of the approach chosen via the PLRIRB is clearly its dependence on the dynamics of Slovakia's national politics. This issue takes us to the question of legitimacy.

It is clearly not possible to speak of the innovation as a source of output legitimacy on the national level. The programme is deeply contested between political parties and ministries, resulting in the present impossibility of a medium-term (or longer) implementation of the programme via government. However, we also noted that independently of actual outputs and outcomes, the programme draws on input legitimacy and a) an informal social accountability primarily in view of the local and sustained educational efforts to include citizens from the villages directly in the discussion and implementation, b) the empowerment this offers to the villages and c) the outside recognition Kravčík has received over the years.

Owing to the domestically contested nature of the innovation process at the national Slovakian level, a key question is to what extent the NWP can further develop on the regional and international level. While the focus on flood prevention is important in the Slovakian context, it may be useful for Kravčík and PW to further develop ideas for arid geographies and the problems of drought and famine, and to link those respectively with the NWP approach (see Chapter 5). In the European context, the NWP focus on green water and the role of the small water cycle for flood prevention has much to contribute to the discussion of the European Water Framework Directive. The WFD will not meet its targets by 2015 and has only to a very limited extent so far considered the role of water in catchments as a whole (as opposed to the narrow focus on *blue water* in lakes and rivers). Increasing floods and droughts in Europe make the kind of inclusive view NWP promotes an important topic. A reassessment of the WFD, along with a discussion of landscape productivity and maintenance payments under the EU Common Agricultural Policy, could create a space for municipalities to create long-term work in relation to investment in a public good – restoring and maintaining water as a fund for people and ecosystems.

NOTES

1. The information in this section relies on Kravcik 2009 unless otherwise indicated.
2. See WFD Article 4.
3. http://www.ludiaavoda.sk/en/?page_id=4 (accessed 2 February 2011).
4. See map from PLRIRB.
5. This topic of different knowledges and their inclusion and authority is clearly a central theme for the discussion of new and old water paradigms. It is further discussed in Justus Lodemann's ongoing dissertation.
6. There is also a dissemination function to this: during field trips, if Kravčík sees water-retention constructions that interest him for various reasons – now mainly constructions that have been built during the PLRIRB – he takes pictures and writes brief summaries of the constructions for his blog. He then also sends these materials via email to his database of mayors across Slovakia.
7. The results of the second round have to be viewed with caution due to two reasons: a)

in 2012 Slovakia did not experience as many flood-inducing events as in former years, b) the return rate of answered questionnaires in the second round was low (n=139). The data presented is solely descriptive; the results are further discussed in Justus Lodemann's ongoing dissertation.

8. Note that the central capabilities here do not follow the order in Nussbaum 2006; rather they prioritize the capabilities that appear to be of most importance in relation to the PLRIRB.
9. These numbers and the ones reported below are taken from the survey mentioned above and shown in detail below in Table 4.2. The numbers in the text are rounded for better readability.
10. Source: Statistical Office of the Slovak Republic, 'Structure of earnings in the SR, 2012'.
11. These criteria are derived from deliberative democratic theory, so as to operationalize Nussbaum's category of control over the environment (see Henkel and Ziegler 2010 for a full discussion).
12. http://www.vlada.gov.sk/tlacova-konferencia-o-programmee-revitalizacie-krajiny-a-inte grovaneho-manazmentu-povodi-sr-protipovodnove-opatrenia/ (accessed 9 May 2012).
13. Accessed 4 July 2013.
14. http://novohrad.sme.sk/c/6046983/obce-sa-mozu-hlasit-do-projektu-revitalizacie-krajiny.html (accessed 9 May 2012).
15. http://kravcik.blog.sme.sk/ (accessed 9 September 2012).
16. http://www.vlada.gov.sk/ under http://www.rokovania.sk/File.aspx/ViewDocument Html/Mater-Dokum-129427?prefixFile=m_ (accessed 15 December 2011).
17. http://www.minzp.sk/sekcie/temy-oblasti/voda/ochrana-pred-povodnami/sprava-priebe hu-nasledkoch-povodni-uzemi-sr-roku-2009-01-08-2010.html (accessed 30 November 2011).
18. This section draws on the discussion in Partzsch and Ziegler 2011.
19. Interview with Lubica Dzuganova, 23 July 2010.

5. Fostering real social contracts – Hermann Bacher and WOTR

Rafael Ziegler and Marianne Henkel

5.1 INTRODUCTION

Visitors to India have to fill out a visa application. This application would be as unremarkable as any other visa form if it were not for the slogan on top – *welcome to incredible India* (and computer-savvy India, for good measure, also maintains an *incredible India* homepage run by the government). Readiness for the seemingly *incredible* is part of the subcontinent's meta-culture. Having passed through customs, new arrivals to cities like Mumbai and Pune are exposed not only to bustling roads, but also, every now and then, a holy tree in the middle of all the buzz.

For this case study, we travelled from Mumbai via Pune to the Ahmednagar district in the Indian state of Maharashtra, where the organization WOTR (Watershed Organisation Trust) first started working. Watershed development refers to the conservation and regeneration of water in its relation to land, vegetation, animals and humans within the draining basin of a river or lake. It concerns taking care of freshwater as a fund so that it can sustainably provide its key functions in the watershed, not least for livelihoods and income from agriculture.

Watershed development thereby raises many technical issues. Yet, WOTR posits that the social side is just as important. It has developed a complex participatory approach; in fact, something seemingly incredible: a real social contract.

The concept of 'social contract' in Western European and North American thought – think of Rousseau, Kant or Rawls – is usually associated with philosophical treatises that investigate the conditions and principles of a just way of living together in a state. What are the principles that people could agree to as just? How could this legitimize the state and its monopoly of power? These are important questions, yet also highly abstract and idealistic. In the shadow of the Indian holy trees – on the soil of the ideas of village democracy catalyzed by Gandhi – social innovators seem determined to accomplish the incredible in the practical; they aim for a real social contract between real people, not only as an intellectual exercise, but practically creating social contracts. Is this pursuit possible? How did it come about? What has been the impact and is it sustainable?

In this chapter we will study these questions in regards to the work of WOTR.[1] The next section introduces the history, mission and approach of WOTR, followed by its approach to scaling and replication (Section 5.3). We then evaluate this approach from a sustainability perspective (Section 5.4). Our key questions in this chapter are: What is WOTR's innovation and how has the organization been able to scale it? What is social about this innovation and how does it contribute to human capabilities and environmental sustainability? What is the legitimacy of a trust (a non-governmental organization) that seeks to facilitate and implement social change, including the set-up of institutions? On the basis of this questioning, we will return in the final section to the seemingly incredible: real social contracts for sustainability.

Against the background described in Chapter 1 of this book, this chapter has been written based on desktop research regarding the literature on and by WOTR, as well as field trips in Maharashtra in April and June 2011, and in February and June 2012. The field trips were used for semi-structured interviews with WOTR staff and stakeholders as well as for data collection. In addition, executive directors Marcella D'Souza and Crispino Lobo were available twice for interviews during trips to Germany, and founder Hermann Bacher for a telephone interview in April 2012.

5.2 EMPOWERMENT WITHIN THE WATERSHED – WOTR'S HISTORY, MISSION AND APPROACH

In 1948 the Jesuit Hermann Bacher, son of a Swiss farmer, arrived in India one year post-independence. Mumbai was still called Bombay; with roughly two million inhabitants, it was nine times smaller than it is today (presently, an estimated 18 million inhabitants make it over twice as large as Switzerland; the metropolitan area is growing so quickly that it seems to slowly merge in the east with the next city, Pune, with 'only' 5.5 million inhabitants). This rapid population growth might seem to make India an unlikely place for experiments in village democracy and real social contracts; however, about 70 per cent of India's (ever-growing) population live in rural areas. It was the rural areas where Bacher pursued his goals following a spiritual experience in the Alps, which yielded his decision that 'the measure of his life would be that he make a difference, for him the service for others was the measure of self-identity', as his pupil and WOTR co-founder Crispino Lobo put it (Crispino Lobo, 9 February 2012, Darewadi). In response to the rural poverty he saw, Bacher first developed a project to improve the income of farmer's with a lift-irrigation scheme, which pumped water from the river to the fields. In doing so, he 'jumped on the band-wagon' (ibid. Lobo) of modernizing agriculture. In collaboration with a sugarcane coop-eration and a cooperative bank, Bacher successfully co-created the first opportunity for lift-irrigation schemes for small farmers in the Ahmednagar district in Maharashtra. However, he had to realize that this success had limits and high costs. On the social side, the scheme left farmers indebted with loans for irrigation schemes and fertilizers. Moreover, the approach could not reach the poorest farmers, that is, those working in rain-fed areas with no access to lift-irrigation from rivers. On the ecological side, the success of lift-irrigation led to a massive over-extraction of water from the rivers. Water-lifting from the Pravara, a tributary of Godavari, reached such an extent that today the river does not deliver sufficient water down-stream and electricity has to be shutdown upstream at regular intervals by the police so that sufficient water can reach downstream.

To be sure, these developments have to be contextualized. For rain-fed farmers, water availability for personal use and for farming depends on the ability to harvest and retain rain in the land. Yet, over half of the Indian territory is degraded; wind and water erosion along with deforestation cause desertification (Ministry of Environment India 2001, p. 15 ff). Such challenges hold for Bacher's first region of work, the Ahmednagar district of Maharashtra, which lies in the rain shadow of the Western Ghats and has a semi-arid climate.

A major drought occurred in 1972 in the state of Maharashtra, in which an estimated 25 million people needed help. Subsequently, further droughts and drought-like situations followed. While these droughts are not reported to have caused famines, they did contribute to the poverty of the rural population in Maharashtra, including malnutrition, forced migra-tion, indebtedness and suicides. Notably, the Vidarbha region in the east of the state is notorious for suicides among cotton farmers during droughts. Migrant families find it hard to send their children to school, which lowers their chances of finding better work in the future. The political economy of the state has also made the situation more difficult. While the government does support drought-prone areas with a special Drought-Prone Area Programme (DPAP), it appears to be a strongly political decision which blocks are chosen; in practice, this programme does not necessarily favour those most in need.

Around 73% of sugarcane produced in the state [of Maharashtra] is grown in DPAP blocks! And sugar cane is about the most water-intensive crop you can get. Secondly, the area under irrigation in Maharashtra is pathetic. Just inching towards 15% of cropland. But in the DPAP blocks in one estimate, it is 22% – nearly 50% higher than the state average. (Sainath 1996, p. 319)

In Maharasthra, as in many places around the globe, decision-making in water policy is subject to strong pressures from lobbies. A further drought in 1987, along with experiences made along the way, provoked Bacher to rethink and practically change his approach. He adopted a *watershed perspective*. For that he coined the phrase '*Panlota shivay dushkarala pariyan nahi*' that means 'There is no solution to drought without watershed development'. It became a very famous slogan in Marathi and caught on like wild fire' (Lobo, 9 February 2012, Darewadi).

The specification of the drainage area and regeneration potential is a technical task, and typically watershed development therefore had been promoted by the government with a technical, top-down approach. Yet, there was some exception to this top-down approach. Thomas Palghadmal, who has known and worked with Bacher since the 1960s, explained to us how in the Ahmednagar district during the 1980s, Bacher, Anna Hazare[2] and others successfully pushed the importance of participation and the social mobilization of the community (Palghadmal, 6 February 2012, Ahmednagar). Bacher worked towards an approach to participatory watershed management that complements the technical dimension with the consistent inclusion of the community in the preparation and implementation of watershed development and ultimately village development. He successfully used a re-evaluation period of German Development Co-Operation to pitch for a large grant for participatory watershed development, which would become the Indo-German Watershed Development Programme (IGWDP). The IGWDP was established in 1989 as part of a bilateral agreement between the governments of India and Germany. Bacher was so successful, in fact, that the grant obtained in the end was much bigger than expected and the competence and resources were lacking to implement such a large-scale project. What was called for was a distinct approach, one that was both participatory and capable of being scaled; this provoked the foundation of WOTR – today an established organization headed by executive director Dr. Marcella D'Souza; while Bacher has been asked by his order to return for his old age to Switzerland. So let's have a closer look at WOTR.

Mission

WOTR aims 'to contribute to poverty reduction and improvement in the quality of life of rural communities in a manner that is upscaleable and replicable'.[3] WOTR contributes to participatory watershed development, rather than a top-down, technical approach; at the heart of its vision are the goals of equal participation and community ownership. Its vision is for 'communities, especially the poor within, [to] be empowered to live in dignity and secure their livelihoods in sustainable ecosystems' (ibid.).

WOTR is a non-governmental organization (NGO) with a head office in Pune, a project office in Ahmednagar (the old headquarters' location) and nine regional resource centres (in the Indian states of Maharashtra, Andhra Pradesh and Rajasthan), as well as a training centre in Darewadi (Maharashtra). Some work has been delegated to two sister organizations – the Sampada Trust, which is in charge of the microfinance dimension of watershed development, and the Sanjeevani Institute of Empowerment and Development (SIED), which focuses on project implementation in Maharashtra, especially in tribal areas. All three organizations together have a staff of 280, with WOTR having a staff of 150 (as of February 2012).

WOTR drew on its practical experiences over the last two decades[4] and has developed the *Wasundhara approach* so as to join the implementation of its approach to watershed development together with the villages' practical situations. *Wasundhara* is a Sanskrit term meaning 'flourishing earth' and for WOTR connotes compassion, caring, co-responsibility and harmony. More technically, it is used as an acronym – **WOTR A**ttentive to **S**ocial **U**nity for **N**ature **D**evelopment and **H**umanity in **R**ural **A**reas (Jewler 2011, p. 6, second a in bold added). We will now highlight the two phases to this watershed development approach.[5]

Watershed Development in the Village

Phase 1 (12–18 months): Providing the ground for participatory watershed development

In the first phase, WOTR prepares the grounds for establishing informed working together in a watershed. If a village indicates interest in the approach, WOTR will then offer audio and visual aids to further teach about the approach and will organize exposure visits to villages that have already participated in watershed development. Crucially, there is a *Shramadan*, a four-day watershed development workshop, in which the village population is required to participate. A woman and a man from each family must participate (for a detailed description, see Joshi and Huirem 2009) and the WOTR will only continue working with villages if at least 70 per cent of the population participates in these workshops. In short, the *Shramadan* provides a test to see if the villages not only live up to a formal agreement, but also are able to practically agree to work together on participatory watershed development. In addition, WOTR seeks to provide the conditions that foster real participation possibilities for families, and especially for women. Each family participates in *participatory net planning* that gives each family an improved understanding of their land and its watershed potential. Women are invited to join self-help groups (SHGs[6]), and these are united in a Joint Women's Commitee, a federation of women's self-help groups at the village level. The goal is to provide space for women to voice their views on village development, first in a group of women but eventually also in the village as a whole. Finally, WOTR also organizes a participatory wealth ranking:[7] the organization supplies four categories – very poor, poor, middle class and better off – and the villagers concretize the categories and classify the wealth distribution in the village.

All this can make your head spin – but it is only when these measures for informed and inclusive village action have been made that there is the formation of a Village Development Committee (VDC, formerly Watershed Development Committee). The formation of the VDC seeks to include the different geographical and wealth groups of the village based on the prior wealth-ranking exercise.

Phase 2 (3–4 years): Participatory implementation

In the second phase of the *Wasundhara* approach WOTR will tackle the main implementation of watershed development and socio-economic development. Again, this includes a *Shramadan* (required participation in four-day workshop). With the help of government as well as development cooperation funds, jobs are created for afforestation, pasture development, horticulture, agriculture, soil and water conservation measures and livelihood measures. Grants and loans are given to SHGs, activities. The work is accompanied by monitoring and evaluation that includes peer-group assessment (villages cross-examine each others' work). WOTR helps to set up a maintenance fund for the post-watershed development and assists with building relations, for example with government agencies. It also assists with making demands, for example, from the government when they have not lived up to infrastructure promises.

Training

In parallel to the watershed development works facilitated in villages, WOTR maintains a watershed development training centre in Darewadi, Maharashtra for NGOs, governmental officials, donors, villagers and international participants. As noted, WOTR was founded in a context where the knowledge for the implementation of participatory watershed development was not widely spread. Accordingly, the training of others has been a key feature of the WOTR mission from the beginning, and we will return to it again below.

Finance

WOTR is financed through donations and grants from governments, business and civil society institutions. Of special importance has been the initial, multi-year support from the IGWDP and the resource flow it made available from Germany via the Kreditanstalt für Wiederaufbau (KfW) and the Deutsche Gesellschaft für Internationale Zusammenarbeit (GIZ).

Corporate donations, however, only play a limited role. There is a tradition also in India of large enterprises donating money or in-kind support to philanthropic purposes.[8] While Indian companies for example like to fund hospitals that will bear their name, WOTR has persuaded some companies to fund parts of watershed development projects (Lobo, interview on 31 May 2011). For example one bank has sponsored toilets blocks (without the demand that those bear the name of the bank). Nevertheless, the organization feels that support from the private sector could be improved (Lobo, interview on 3 February 2012).

From an investment perspective, it is important to distinguish the income generated for a social entrepreneurship organization and the income generated for the respective community – not immediately, but in the medium or long term (Ziegler and Gebauer 2012). Integrated watershed development can increase water availability and, eventually, income from agriculture. The investors in a watershed invest in an ecological (and social) *fund* of water that regenerates once properly restored and managed. Such investments seem as important as – and are in fact a pre-condition of – investments in *stocks*, defined as the amount of water available at a given time for consumption or production. An organization may draw on water as a stock for drinking water, sanitation or agriculture and from this yield a financial return. However, you can only use a stock in the long run if there is a fund that regenerates it. Such a focus on funds is especially important in a context of poverty, where there is frequently no or little prospect of earning income without a prior investment in the resource base. In a comparative study of 23 villages 1999–2005, WOTR found a 57 per cent increase of employment months/per year in agriculture post watershed development in comparison to pre-watershed development (D'Souza, 12 September 2012, Frankfurt).

5.3   SCALING AND INNOVATION

WOTR has operated watershed development projects in five different Indian states (as of 2011) – Maharashtra, Andhra Pradesh, Madhya Pradesh, Rajasthan and Jharkhand. It has set itself the goal to operate in seven Indian states and three countries by 2020 (Lobo, 9 September 2012, Darewadi).

WOTR has been directly involved in watershed projects in 326 villages (impacting 348 009 people and 2 228 887 hectares of land) and it has provided capacity building and/or financial support to partner agencies for work in 756 villages (impacting 571 858 people and 429 035 hectares). It has promoted 8214 SHGs, which involved 103 823 women; of these WOTR has been directly involved in building up 4804 of these SHGs, directly impacting 58 966 women. So far, 11 547 loans have been provided via WOTR and Sampada to these groups with a total sum of 523 million Indian rupees (Rs), roughly 8.44 million €.

Scaling out is not just a matter of WOTR implementing projects; in fact, for WOTR, it is not even the main approach to scaling. WOTR has been able to offer training to NGOs and governmental agencies from 27 (out of 30) Indian states and 29 countries, training over 180 000 persons already by 2010 (WOTR 2010a). The implementation and training efforts have led to a network of 184 NGOs and governmental implementing agencies. As a result, more projects have been implemented by NGOs trained by WOTR than by WOTR themselves. Scaling out here is a collaborative process involving other NGOs and governmental agencies. As the numbers show, WOTR has been quite successful in scaling out its approach.

WOTR's approach to change thus rests on a double strategy: 1) a detailed participatory watershed development approach that is tested and revised over time; 2) training other NGOs and governmental agencies so that they have the know-how to promote and accompany the process. The key stakeholders in WOTR's approach are a) villages in arid rural areas with rain-fed agriculture, b) NGOs that adopt and implement the approach and c) government authorities that accompany the process (local government) and those that provide the funding for the approach (state and national government, as well as development cooperation groups). Figure 5.1 visualizes this multi-stakeholder scaling approach.

Three observations need to be made to properly appreciate this approach to scaling. First, the term 'replicable' has to be used with caution, as current executive director Marcella D'Souza points out.

> What we did find in these projects is the *replication of process*, not so much of this activity or that activity, and this methodology and that. It doesn't always work. Even in India, what we are doing in Maharashtra has to be adjusted to [the] Andhra Pradesh context or to Rajasthan. (D'Souza, 9 February 2012, Darewadi; italics added)

In WOTR's understanding, 'replication of process' requires a distinction between principles on the one hand, and adaption to context on the other hand. The principles D'Souza points out are not negotiable. They include physical principles of watershed development as well as social principles of

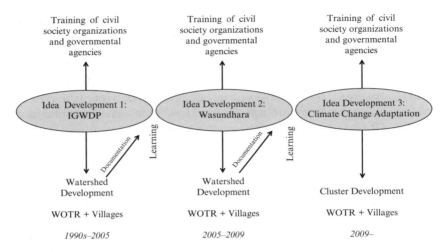

Figure 5.1   The WOTR approach to scaling

governance. We will turn to these in the next section. The important point here is that villages have to agree to these principles if they want to cooperate with WOTR.

Second, the scaling approach is part of a learning process that includes the modification of the approach itself. The documentation of village-level projects is very important for this. 'Basically what we do is we document how we do it. We find out what works and what doesn't work. We go back to our own project areas, with a different team to assess, is it really working or not?' (D'Souza, 9 September 2012, Darewadi).

For example, Mister Rajapure, a project manager, points out that experiences made in the first ten years taught WOTR that watershed development was a) insufficiently linked to the *Gram Panchayat* (the local self-government at the village level), b) lacked post-communication when the project was over, c) paid insufficient attention to other aspects than water (gender, wealth and caste), and d) did not benefit sufficiently those least well-off in the watershed (Rajapure, 6 February 2012, Ahmednagar).

In response to these challenges, WOTR has added a further element when developing the *Wasundhara* approach. WOTR seeks to pay better attention to those least well-off by insisting that the formation of the VDC must include at least 50 per cent women as well as representatives from all wealth groups based on an all-inclusive wealth ranking. Moreover, this wealth ranking is used to determine the differential contribution of villagers to various projects. For example, a wealthier household may have to contribute more to the purchasing of equipment than a poorer household.

WOTR seeks to strengthen the link to the existing political structure by making the VDC a sub-committee of the Gram Panchayat, that is, the local government at the village level. The socio-economic development of the village is given attention through the SHGs (which also can apply for micro-loans via the Sampada Trust) as well as activities on agriculture, horticulture, and so on. A maintenance fund is meant to ensure the long-term sustainability of the project.

Third, Figure 5.1 above is an over-simplification to the extent that it does not show WOTR's simultaneous work on the conditions of scaling out. Political advocacy and networking have been important from the beginning; Bacher helped to build a coalition between the German Development Cooperation, the government of India, the National Bank for Agricultural and Rural Development (NABARD), and the Ministry of Forestry, which resulted in the IGWDP.[9] Crispino Lobo, in his responsibility as a representative on a national planning commission for agriculture, was able to co-initiate the idea of a Watershed Development Fund (WDF), which was administered by NABARD and financed by the central government of India. According to the agricultural bank,

> the success of IGWDP-Maharashtra has led to [the] setting up of [a] Watershed Development Fund in NABARD with a corpus of Rs. 200 crore [= roughly 31 million euros] (GOI [Government of India] and NABARD each contributed Rs. 100 crore) with a broad objective of unification of multiplicity of watershed development programmes into a single national initiative through involvement of village level institutions and NGOs.[10]

The fund has taken on essential elements of the WOTR approach and as of today has supported 203 projects on a grant basis and 322 on a loan basis, covering 140 000 and 350 000 hectares, respectively, in Maharashtra. Likewise, the 2008 Common Guidelines for Watershed Development Projects of the Government of India (2008) adopt aspects of the WOTR approach to watershed development, such as the emphasis on a participatory approach (including a mandatory 10 per cent contribution to project implementation by the respective village).

These three observations finally take us to what is innovative about the WOTR approach. To be sure, participatory watershed development emerged as an idea in the 1980s, not least in reaction to the difficulties and unintended consequences of the green revolution and the commercially oriented introduction of high-yield crops and fertilizers along with large-scale irrigation and large-dam building, which were implemented with a top-down approach. Anna Hazare, also from Maharashtra, pioneered a participatory watershed approach in his village as part of a general village development (Hazare 2003), and Bacher was in close contact with him.

Other *watermen* – as they are called in the Indian media – developed participatory approaches for their villages. Examples include Rajinder Singh and Laxman Singh. What distinguishes Bacher from watermen such as Hazare is his intent and ability to move from the pioneer model of one village to an approach that includes scaling from the beginning, or to recall the goal, to an approach that can be 'upscaled and replicated'. Bacher and WOTR had to go against the conventional logic of first testing and prototyping an idea, moving to scale only when the model is well established. He did this for pragmatic and ethical reasons; the window of opportunity opened up by the IGWDP on the one hand and the urgency of poverty in rural areas on the other. Lacking an established prototype or proof of concept, learning was an imperative from the beginning.

The emphasis in innovation is not on the new idea as such (the invention) but on the *carrying out* of this idea (the innovation). WOTR is a learning organization that has repeatedly revised its approach since its foundation; the chief innovation of the WOTR approach[11] is found in its scaling out of participatory watershed management.

5.4   SUSTAINABILITY EVALUATION

WOTR's mission is to 'empower communities, and especially the poor within, to live in dignity and secure their livelihood in sustainable ecosystems'.[12] Dignity is a complex moral value and this difficulty only increases if human dignity is to be analysed in relation to ecosystems. In this section we draw on a conception of dignity as developed by the capabilities approach and the theory of strong sustainability (see Chapter 1).

Hermann Bacher was aware of the complexity of these issues:

> The health of the watershed fluctuates with the social health and tenor of the human community therein. For there is an intimate and symbiotic relationship between the environment and the human community in that living space which draws sustenance from it. Deterioration in the economic and social well-being of the community leads to over exploitation of the natural resource base and its degradation. (Bacher in WOTR 2005, p. 26)

WOTR has recently begun to view this dynamic as a nexus of natural, social, human, physical/manufactured and financial capital.[13] Drawing on this language of capitals, we can think of project implementation in a village as a matter of all five capitals (see also Figure 5.2). WOTR draws on financial capital (external to the village) to invest in education and economic and political participation. The human and social capital thereby created makes it subsequently possible to restore natural capital and

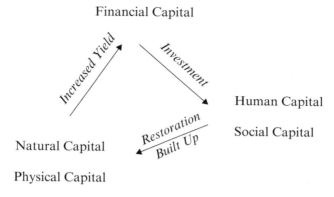

Figure 5.2   Closing a small cycle

build up physical capital (construction of trenches, bunds and dams). The work improves water as a natural capital in the sense that groundwater is recharged and water availability increased. Water as a non-living fund, and with it the moisture level of the soil, is thereby strengthened. This improvement in natural capital increases the agricultural yield (and with it the benefits from agricultural, physical capital) and also yields capability benefits for health and shelter owing to improved food security, as well as for education and life choices more generally. If more than one harvest is possible per year, forced seasonal migration is no longer necessary. Children have better options to obtain education and may opt to move elsewhere when they are adults out of choice rather than necessity. Material wealth increases and with it the available financial capital; villagers are able to pay into a maintenance fund that pays for the maintenance of the created structure. Ideally, a small socio-ecological water cycle has been closed. And in practice? A closer look is needed to evaluate if the people in a given context can move from a situation of deprivation to one of improved social dignity and environmental sustainability.

Environmental Sustainability

There are five principles of environmental sustainability that WOTR gives central space to so as to increase water availability and restore the natural environment:

1. *Ridge-to-valley principle*: Implement watershed development downhill from the steeper slopes to the valley[14] so as to improve the rainwater harvesting.

2. Ban on bore wells for agricultural irrigation so as to prevent ground-water over-extraction.
3. Ban on mono-cropping and water-intensive crops so as to avoid situations that may lead to an over-extraction of water and a reduction in soil quality.
4. Ban on felling of trees so as to prevent soil erosion and to improve water retention.
5. Ban on free grazing (at least during project implementation) so as to prevent soil erosion.

These five principles make for a distinct approach to natural capital restoration in terms of water availability. Empirically, the effect of these requirements should be indicated by increased water availability. Practical indicators are the number and the depth of wells (where a decrease in depth indicates an increased water table) as well as the irrigated area.

The village of Mhaswandi offers us an example of the impact these principles can have. In this case, watershed development started in 1994 and project implementation lasted until 2001. Table 5.1 shows the respective change before and after the project implementation.

Examples such as the Mhaswandi case show that the WOTR approach can contribute to the improvement and maintenance of water as a natural capital during the project phase. We will turn to the post-project phase in the subsequent section.

Capabilities

As a comprehensive approach to village development, the work of WOTR involves many capabilities. The main focus as stated by the mission is

Table 5.1   Mhaswandi I

	1994 [ex ante]	2001	2006	2011
Irrigated area perennial [hectares]	29	70	175	200
Irrigated area seasonally [hectares]	35	135	423	395
Number of wells	33	56	70	82
Depth of wells	90 feet deep	No data available	No data available	60–70 feet deep

Source: WOTR 2006, D'Souza 2008, p. 124 and own compilation.

empowering communities and securing livelihoods; they aim to foster the political and economic capabilities of what Martha Nussbaum calls 'control over one's environment'.[15] With a focus on these capabilities, we can study the emergence of a *real social contract*.

A brief contrast with philosophical, hypothetical social contracts is useful. *Received social contract* thinking is focused on the national level; it looks at the comprehensive impact of institutions on the lives of citizens and the rules that could govern such impact in a fair way (Rawls 1999). Real social contract, by contrast, is focused on a local level and a practical problem to be jointly solved. In the WOTR case it is thematically focused on improving the resource base and aims to achieve sufficiency for all in a dynamic way. The central social principle for WOTR is *community owner-ship*; a focus on this principle will help us to better understand WOTR's approach to facilitating a real social contract (Marcella D'Souza, 16 September 2012, Frankfurt). This is a complex and dynamic normative principle. It is therefore helpful to introduce it in a temporal way.

WOTR launches a test of consent and participation early on in a given project. The members of the village participate in four-day watershed development workshops; the process will only continue if at least 70 per cent of the households of the village have participated. WOTR then facilitates the creation of the village institutions, in particular the VDC, which is responsible for watershed development. Members of this committee are to be selected from each social group and geographical area of the village (D'Souza and Lobo 2008, p. 125, 131; Jewler 2011); geographical representation is ensured via a subdivision into territorial subgroups or wards. The committee must also be made up of 50 per cent women and include representatives from all wealth groups (based on the prior exercise in wealth ranking, see above). These formal requirements for participation in decision making are accompanied by material activities targeted to help people make informed decisions and to enable them to participate. Participatory net planning ensures that each household is informed regarding the characteristics and potential of its land. The early initiation of SHGs provides women a forum for discussion prior to the formation of the VDC and complements the VDC process when it is established. During project implementation, the VDC and the entire village have to meet at least once every three months. A qualitative impact matrix, which allows village members to track progress along various watershed development criteria, along with peer-review visits to see the work of others (including a regional award) seek to promote the flow of information about villages between villages. WOTR makes a concerted effort to give people in their respective villages a real opportunity, not only a formal possibility, to participate.

Table 5.2   Mhaswandi II

	1994	2001	2006	2011
Fodder production (tons/year)	950	1920	2500	2550
Employment in agriculture (months)	3	8	12	12
Migration	Primary migration	Primary migration	Observed reverse migration	Secondary migration only
Land value (agriculture) per hectare (Rs)	15 000	80 000	750 000	Data missing

Source: WOTR 2006, D'Souza 2008, p. 128 and own compilation.

The other side of the community ownership principle is the economic dimension of control over the environment. From a capabilities perspective, there is a difference between owning land and land that is valuable. The challenge in rain-fed agriculture in an arid zone is increasing the productive value of the land and reducing the risk to agriculture from drought or insufficient water availability. If it is not possible to live on the land throughout the year, stable political participation is clearly also not possible. The material value of land for livelihood is indicated by a variety of interlinking factors: the monetary value of land, the crop yield, the effective time during which agricultural employment is possible in the village, and primary migration (here understood as migration owing to lack of employment in the village). The Mhaswandi case gives evidence for WOTR's contribution to economic participation and suggests that the WOTR approach can dramatically contribute to this dimension of participation (see Table 5.2).

Summing up, we can unpack the community principle in terms of a) a voluntary and practical test of willingness to participate, b) the creation of (regularly meeting) institutions according to inclusive membership rules, c) accompanying efforts to make informed decisions and d) an approach to the natural resource base that makes it possible to live stably on the land. In this way a real social contract emerges over time as opposed to being hypothetically agreed on from the onset. The aspect of real agreement is also appreciated as such by the participants, or as VDC members put it in a feedback evaluation of the approach, 'consent of all is always the basis of obligation' (Joshi and Huirem 2009, p. 42). In cases such as Mhaswandi, this has led to improved political and economic participation possibilities; and also to a complementarity of these two aspects of participation. Political participation is appreciated as benefiting one's environment; in turn, the improvement in livelihood improves the possibility of a stable political village culture.

A qualification on inequality needs to be made in regards to the high demands on justice associated with social contract thinking. Working together on watershed development does not affect prior land-ownership patterns. The landless remain landless. They do gain more work opportunities in the village during the project implementation phase and so there is an absolute improvement in value; however, relative differences in wealth remain relatively stable (Kale 2011). Decision making is influenced by a patriarchal culture and a system of castes that limits the political and economic opportunity of women. WOTR seeks to counter these inequalities via its group-building activities, such as the economic empowerment created by the women's SHGs, and the formal project requirements, such as the requirement that a man and a woman from each household participate in the participatory net planning (Joshi and Huirem 2009) or that there must be a 50 per cent representation of women in the VDCs. Despite these attempts, a detailed study of the dynamics of inclusion and exclusion (Kale 2011) has demonstrated the relative persistence of the gender, caste and wealth divisions even within villages that go through the WOTR approach.[16] Thus the impact of the approach is more focused on a *sufficientarian lift* – enabling people to live in dignity above an absolute threshold of sufficiency: what is needed for a life in their ecosystems – rather than on inequality as such. We will now evaluate this sufficientarian lift in the medium and long term.

The Medium- and Long-term Perspectives

In 2012 we visited a village in the Sangamner Taluka of the Ahmednagar district, where a WOTR project had been completed in 2009. There we noted that the ban on free grazing was not enforced; in discussion with the secretary of the VDC, we also learnt that one farmer had constructed a borehole for irrigation purposes in agriculture and no penalty or ban was enforced in this case either. Particularly when rainfall is late or low, there is strong pressure to infringe on WOTR principles and the VDC in Sangamner Taluka found it difficult to enforce them.

We gathered data from ten villages in Ahmednagar (the WOTR home district) to get a more systematic overview. We selected villages from different parts of the district as well as its different rainfall zones (see Figure 5.3). The data gathering focused on environmental sustainability

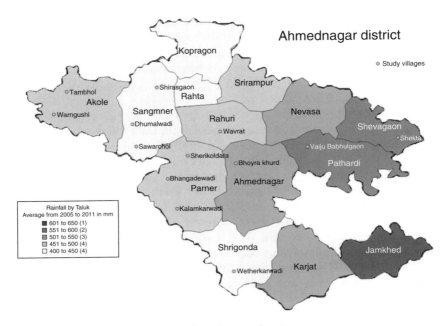

Map 5.1   Sample villages in Ahmednagar district

in regards to whether the WOTR principles (as outlined above) were being enforced, and on human capabilities in terms of the continued existence and sustained promotion of the institutional arrangements created during the project period.

We had the following results for the principles of environmental sustainability:[17]

1. Ban on bore wells: five out of ten villages had bore wells for irrigation.
2. Ban on mono-cropping[18] and water-intensive crops: four out of ten villages had mono-cropping and water-intensive crops.
3. Ban on felling of trees: not effective in nine out of ten villages.
4. Ban on grazing: not effective in nine out of ten villages.

In addition, three out of ten villages encountered problems with encroachment (turning forestry land into agricultural land). In short, we found persistent problems with the enforcement of the rules designed to ensure environmental sustainability.

We found the following results in regards to the institutional arrangements put into place for the promotion of political and economic participation in village and watershed development:

1. VDC meeting: four out of ten villages had no meetings at all and there were no regular meetings in the other six villages.
2. SHGs: effective in all villages.
3. Maintenance fund: in nine out of ten villages the maintenance fund played no role or had ceased to exist.

In short, we found that the participatory structure created to ensure and maintain long-term participation is under heavy strain. The Ahmednagar district is the WOTR home district for implementation and so especially intense and longstanding efforts have been made in this area; because of this, it seems fair to assume that our sample does not underestimate the post-project sustainability evaluation. The evidence suggests difficulties in maintaining sustainability rules and institutional arrangements in the medium term. If the WOTR principles are not maintained, then the natural-capital improvement and sustainable use is in danger, and in turn the economic and social benefits associated with it. If this is the case, the socio-ecological cycle can no longer be closed.

Dynamics of Real Social Contracts

Hypothetical, social contract theory typically builds on the assumption that though a sovereign state has relations to other states, it is for basic political and economic aspects more or less independent (Rawls 1999). For real, problem-focused social contracts this assumption does not hold (and to be sure, many are sceptical that it even holds for the nation state because of the effects of global economic systems as well as of colonial history, see Pogge 2001).

The individual watershed is subject to larger sociological and ecological trends beyond its power. In discussion with WOTR staff and stakeholders, there were three outside dynamics that repeatedly came up. 1) *Climate and extreme weather events*: The most widely discussed example is climate change. For the villages, this is an exogenous shock threatening increased variability in rainfall, more extreme weather events, and so on. 2) *The market and the threshold dynamic between poverty and growth*: The market is another exogenous trend. Suppose the WOTR approach successfully improves central capabilities and natural capital, and in turn the economic (agricultural) possibilities of people in the village. Accordingly, the possibilities of virtual trade in water would also be extended, such as the possibility to export goods out of the catchment in exchange for increased revenue. The threshold of having moved out of poverty turns into a jumping board for increased revenue via a focus on water-intensive cash-crops and mono-cropping (onion, wheat, sugar cane; compare the sample results on mono-cropping) and thus a loss in agricultural diversity (plants and livestock). The increased demand for water results in the risk of over-abstraction and reduced water availability downstream (see the sample results on water from boreholes used for irrigation). Fertilizers may be increasingly used to boost productivity, consequently leading to risks in water and soil quality as well as financial dependence owing to the cost of fertilizer. Next to the intensification of agriculture, extension may happen, that is, increased use of land that threatens biodiversity and ecosystem stability (see the sample results on encroachment). 3) *The City and 'people-leakage'*: Cities exert a strong pull in the villages; those especially with education and good grades are likely to move to the city. The improved education made possible by watershed development at least partly strengthens a people-drain from the villages (in the sample, all villages reported secondary migration). As this is migration by choice rather than forced migration (the primary migration of seasonal labour), this movement as such is unobjectionable from a capabilities perspective. Nevertheless, the majority of Indians live in the countryside and ensure the food supply of those in the urban centres. Moreover, in terms of the important dimensions to a sustainable lifestyle, such as energy consumption and waste production, the rural life is more sustainable. The ecological footprint of citizens without cars and air conditioning is a fraction of citizens' footprint in the city. If the city is dependent on the countryside and the countryside is more sustainable, the question arises whether the 'capacity to aspire' (Appadurai 2004) *in* the village has not been thwarted. Arjun Appadurai coined this term to highlight the expectation over the poor to subscribe to norms whose social effect is to diminish their dignity (Appadurai 2004, p. 66).

In sum, we found three trends that pose a severe challenge for the WOTR approach to real social contracts: extreme and erratic weather threatens the potential benefits of watershed development, the market dynamic puts pressure on water abstraction and creates financial dependence, and the city drains people from the village, thereby threatening the build-up and maintenance of local know-how and related organizations and institutions (see Figure 5.4).

Internal Organizational Responsibility

Capabilities and environmental sustainability not only affect the target group of a programme but also concern the internal management of organizations, their partners and suppliers. This is a point that is well known from the discussion of corporate social responsibility. However, at this point WOTR does not report on this aspect, and we have not been able to carry out such an assessment ourselves.

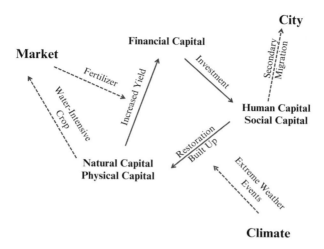

Figure 5.3   Challenges to the closing of the socio-ecological cycle

There is, however, one aspect of organizational structure that we would like to highlight here, which is unique with respect to the initiatives described in this book, and that is the learning facilitated via the organizational structure of the organization. 1) *Concept development*: WOTR has its own unit for documentation and systems thinking, which is also responsible for concept development. As human resource manager Keshor Telong points out, the goal is to be responsive to experiences in the practical work, and to develop new concepts and approaches in response to them (Telong, 10 February 2012, Pune). 2) *Leadership rotation*: During our fieldwork we did come across posters at the desks of WOTR staff with a picture of Bacher and under it the slogan *our inspiration*. Unlike many other social initiatives co-created by an entrepreneurial person, WOTR has succeeded in being independent from the founder. In fact it has introduced a principle of rotation and the executive director has to change at least every ten years. As Marcella D'Souza put it in correspondence, Bacher is a visionary who found Lobo to be the first director and to manage the organization with a view on effective functioning. The second executive director is the current director Marcella D'Souza, who is currently preparing her successor (D'Souza, 9 February 2012, Darewadi). 3) *Responsive team building*: D'Souza pursues the policy that WOTR project leaders are to train their juniors (within the organization and in the villages) in such a way that the juniors can take over and the leaders can 'make themselves redundant'. A priority for her is value learning and value regeneration of staff. To this end, WOTR organizes an annual mediation course, preparatory weeks with a focus on values and requires immersion of staff via direct experience in the villages (D'Souza, 12 September 2012, Frankfurt). 4) *Functional delegation*: WOTR has delegated some of its work to two sister organizations – the Sampada Trust and the Sanjeevani Institute of Empowerment and Development (SIED), which we introduced above (and of course in addition there is the indirect work achieved via the training efforts discussed above). As organizational learning, especially in response to practical needs, becomes more difficult with the increase in size of the organization, delegation is an important final element for an organizational approach that encourages learning. A missing further element may be a social-learning strategy that explicitly includes other organizations as co-responsible actors in watershed and village development. In discussion, D'Souza says that WOTR has recognized this point and in its current phase seeks to develop its capacity as an interface between universities, governmental agencies and villages (D'Souza, 12 September 2012, Frankfurt).

WOTR as a Political Actor

Like all civil-society actors, WOTR is not democratically elected and there is hence a question regarding the legitimacy of its power to influence the lives of people – indeed to facilitate real social contracts as a source of political obligation, which is traditionally associated with the legitimacy of the state. In this part of the fourth section we turn to the legitimacy of WOTR (for our approach to legitimacy see Chapter 1 of this book).

Output legitimacy and innovation
WOTR's goal to 'contribute to poverty reduction and improvement in the quality of life of rural communities in a manner that is up-scalable and replicable' (WOTR Brochure 2010b) has led the organization to develop an approach to watershed development that is innovative relative to its context. The goal of poverty reduction as part of sustainable ecosystems responds to MDG 1 and 7 (compare Section 1.2). More specifically, as described in the discussion of scaling above, participatory watershed development has been recognized in Indian national policy. Accordingly, the project output is a source of legitimacy for WOTR.

With the *Wasundhara* approach, WOTR moves to the dimension of input-legitimacy on the local level. Villages agree to implement the WOTR approach after being provided plenty of information. With the *Wasundhara* approach, the VDC has been made a subcommittee of the *Gram Panchayat*, the local structure for democratic decision-making.

Social accountability

A second source of legitimacy for non-elected organizations is their ability to respond to and hence be accountable to the needs of those for whom they provide goods and services. An indicator is the local expertise of staff, who can be expected to have a better grasp of needs than distant or even foreign experts, who may leave the region as soon as the project implementation phase is over. While co-founded by 'outside expert' Herman Bacher, WOTR has been directed and staffed since 1993 by Indian locals. 'Outside expert' is in quotation marks for the double reason that Bacher is not a water engineer or other technical expert and, as Marcella D'Souza points out, he has lived in India longer than anyone else working for WOTR (1947–2009).

Moreover, the watershed development is consistently participatory (see the instruments discussed mentioned in Section 5.3 above, such as participatory net planning). WOTR includes local labour and attempts to improve the inclusion of the poor and marginalized in the watershed development and hence give them a say in what happens, and what could be improved. In a related vain, WOTR puts a strong emphasis on education and has produced numerous handbooks and educational materials, which in turn improve the possibilities of social accountability.

Finally, WOTR's entrepreneurial journey shows the organization to be a learning organization. As one example among others, learning from its insufficient inclusion of the less powerful and wealthy in the village, WOTR included a participatory wealth ranking in the early stages of watershed development as part of its *Wasundhara* approach. Therefore, we conclude that social accountability is a further source of legitimacy.

Intermediate authority and empowerment

A further source of legitimacy involves advocating for the affected communities and fostering participation. The organization's authority is transitional even if it takes the initiative because the goal here is to contribute to the empowerment of the target group.

WOTR seeks 'transformation' (D'Souza and Lobo 2008, p. 123) but it does not seek permanent power over villages. It has clearly stated from the beginning that its goal is the empowerment of the villages: 'WOTR's watershed development approach is driven by the people who live in the area, and not by WOTR as an organization' (WOTR Drop by Drop 2005, p. 26). Evidence for this empowerment goal is the creation of water-related local institutions such as the VDC and the SHG. It is clear that this source of authority strongly depends on these institutions continuing to function in the medium and long term. Our sample data on post-watershed development suggests that this task has not been fully achieved.

Outside recognition

A further source of legitimacy is outside recognition. The judgment of distant others with no direct interest and involvement in local resource distribution does not directly confer democratic legitimacy but indirectly contributes to authority.

Bacher and WOTR have gained state-level and national recognition. In 1994 Bacher earned the Federal Cross of the Order of Merit (Germany) and later in the same year the Krishi Bushan agricultural award (Maharashtra State); in 1996 he received the *Vanashree* (Friends of Forests) Award (Maharashtra State). His first successor, Crispino Lobo, was a 2005 Schwab Foundation finalist and in 2009 Lobo's successor, Marcella D'Souza, received a Kyoto World Water Grand Prize during the 5th World Water Forum in Istanbul.[19] In 2010, WOTR was awarded the *Krushi Ratna*, Maharashtra's highest award for agriculture; this was for the work in reclaiming degraded lands and bringing water to drought prone villages.

Notably, villagers within the WOTR programme have also received awards. In 2010 the village Wankute was awarded the JSW-TOI Earth Care Award under the category 'Community Based Mitigation and Adaptation to Climate Change'.[20] In 2008 four villages that were mobilized by WOTR won the Clean Village Award from the Government of India. Thus we conclude that outside recognition is a source of legitimacy for WOTR.

5.5   CONCLUSION – GETTING THINGS DONE SUSTAINABLY?

WOTR has been *innovative* in proposing a way for the replication and scaling up of participatory watershed management and doing so as a learning organization. It has repeatedly revised its approach since its foundation. WOTR aims at the broad societal level, here the Indian states. It has been able to *scale* its mission in terms of scaling out via the facilitation and implementation of watershed projects and especially via the training of others to facilitate and implement such watershed projects.

The WOTR approach contributes to the improvement and maintenance of water as a regenerating fund. WOTR improves capabilities of political and economic participation via training and organizational arrangements (VDCs, SHGs) as well as via the economic benefits obtained from improved freshwater availability and use. However, the approach faces difficulties in the medium and long term in regards to the enforcement of water and land conservation principles as well as the maintenance of the participatory watershed organizations created during the project phase; in short, there are difficulties with the medium and long-term sustainability of the approach.

WOTR's legitimacy draws on scaling participatory watershed development as an innovative output, on its role as a locally embedded, learning organization for social accountability, on its training and institutional arrangements for the empowerment of citizens in poor, rain-fed agricultural villages and finally (and indirectly), on the national and international recognition of its work. The critical questions, both as far as the output and empowerment goals are concerned, are what is the medium and long-term impact, and who is responsible for this impact?

New arrivals to Mumbai, Maharashtra first witness what is hard to believe: the large slums of Mumbai directly next to a modern airport. Yet, anthropologist Arjun Appadurai has vividly described the creativity of movements in the slums of Mumbai and their aspiration for decent standards of sanitation and water supply (Appadurai 2004). Via WOTR we have been led to a further source of such creativity, not in the city but in the countryside: real social contracts, seemingly incredible and yet deeply linked to the Gandhian tradition of democracy and its focus on the village and a sufficientarian life. 'The world has enough for everyone's needs, but not everyone's greed' (Gandhi). Also the 'incredible' is closely linked to innovation and social entrepreneurship. New ideas are frequently seen as 'incredible' from the perspective of the old; and social entrepreneurs have therefore even been highlighted as 'unreasonable people' (Elkington and Hartigan 2008). Our discussion suggests that we should take real social contract seriously as a social innovation for sustainability worthy of more attention and further discussion, not least in the context of the call for a new social contract for sustainability (WGBU 2011). Real social contract as studied here takes the perspective of the poor and intimately links the social contract to the investment of the community in the resource base. It is an investment in a fund, and it requires a holistic perspective as manifest in our case via the focus on the watershed and the physical and social principles associated with participatory watershed development. The key to the question emerging above regarding the medium- and long-term viability of this approach is in our view the capacity of learning.

Recall the three large challenges to medium-term watershed sustainability in the rural, arid areas – climate change, external market forces and the people-drain to the city. WOTR has developed a Climate Change Adaption Project that is currently in its pilot phase in selected villages in the Ahmednagar District. The focus is on agriculture and biodiversity and coping mechanisms to deal with climate change challenges. Agricultural meteorology and alternative renewable energy are to promote what WOTR calls 'adaptive sustainable agriculture' (M. Mathur, 3 February 2012, Pune). Following the completion of the pilot project, the goal will be to scale up lessons learnt (Lobo, 9 February 2012, Darewadi). This project also seeks to evolve an answer to the market pressure. Further to educating farmers on the importance of indigenous crops for food security and possibly as a source of revenue in the long term (organic agriculture and green branding) as well as the possibilities of diversification – such as the creation of further revenue options via SHGs so as to reduce dependence on market prices for monocrops – the climate change approach also includes the idea of cluster formation for villages so as to increase the market power of villages (M. Mathur, 3 February 2012, Pune) and value addition and exchange within small regions. The goal is to increase the amount of money spent and flowing in the villages – the 'local money multiplier' as WOTR calls it – as a social analogue to improving water retention in the catchment. At this point it is not yet possible to tell whether this WOTR phase will be able to address the climate and market challenges; however, what is clear is that this is a challenge of learning with others. WOTR has recognized this challenge and aims to play the role of *interface* between local needs and knowledge on the one hand, and scientific and technical knowledge on the other hand.

Least in focus for WOTR is the question of people-drain and, in the language of capitals, the missing recognition of cultural capital in the villages. There seems to be a need for further ideas to make life in the village attractive also in a cultural sense, that is, to make visible its advantages, strengths and importance.

Having returned to Europe from India one would surely not expect to see a *holy tree* on the way home from the airport, but would you hope to see one? And if you do – somewhere, even just a little bit – what is the reason for this hope? Coming back to densely regulated social welfare states, you would not expect local, real social contracts including four-day personal contribution for watershed development. Surely, everyone is too busy for that and there is an expert authority that should do the work. And definitely there will be more than one authority that is responsible for some aspects (and there will be surely some aspects where more than one authority is responsible)! But then, who *is* responsible for basic matters in the watershed as a whole? Renewing the social contract tradition, the real one that is, not least with respect to the basic resources of life, should be worthy of further consideration, in India and just as much in flood and drought-prone areas of Europe, or anywhere else for that matter.

NOTES

1. It speaks to the power of this idea that such practical social contracts can also be studied with respect to further Indian initiatives such as Gram Vikas (Ziegler 2012a).
2. Shri Anna Hazare is a civic activist well known in India for his idea of a model village, implemented in his home village Ralegan Siddhi, and more recently for his activism against corruption.
3. WOTR, undated, p. 2 (accessed from www.wotr.org 31 January 2012).
4. According to Crispino Lobo, the first Executive Director of WOTR, we can distinguish three stages in the evolution of the WOTR approach to watershed development (Lobo, 3 February 2012, Pune). The first stage coincides with WOTR's work as facilitator and co-implementation NGO of the IGWDP. The second stage is associated with the Wasundhara approach, developed in the first half of the first decade of the new millennium and adopted for watershed development projects in 2005. The third stage started in 2009 with the Climate Change Adaption Project, which seeks to improve the capacities of rural communities to adapt to climate change effects. It started as a pilot project (2009–2013) in 29 villages in the Ahmednagar District and the goal is to scale once the pilot phase is completed (a first assessment was begun in 2012).
5. For a more detailed account of the different aspects of the approach, the WOTR homepage offers ample information in the form of handbooks, cases and film material that can be downloaded for free.
6. The SHGs serve for intra-community lending among women. Membership requires a monthly savings contribution. The group savings improve the access to capital for individual or group investments. For example, in the village Mhaswandi the president of the women's committees told us that they obtained a communal Masala-spice grinder and they created a liquefied petroleum agency so as to have cooking gas available (Interview President of the Women's Committee, 7 February 2012).
7. The method is familiar from Participatory Rural Appraisal as developed by Chambers and others (Rauch 2009, p. 330). Here, as elsewhere, WOTR shows a willingness to adopt tools from other approaches for its purpose.
8. For an overview see WOTR annual report 2010.
9. Early on in the Indo-German Watershed Fund, Bacher obtained permission from the Forestry Department to treat forestland in watersheds. As the upper-hill part of watersheds is frequently state forestry land, this permission is an important condition for implementing the ridge-to-valley principle (see Section 5.4).
10. http://www.nabard.org/farm_sector/wat_devp.asp (accessed 3 February 2012).
11. Even if we can also point to more specific, incremental innovations such as participatory net planning.
12. WOTR, undated, p. 2 (accessed from wotr.org 31 January 2012).
13. See Annual Report 2011, p. 48 'The WOTR engine for adaptive sustainable development'. The WOTR 5 capital model is inspired by the Forum for the Future, which developed such a model in the 1990s (http://www.forumforthefuture.org/sites/default/files/project/downloads/five-capitals-model.pdf, accessed 1 May 2012). For each capital the focus is on the benefits obtained from the specific type of capital, that is, the benefits obtained from natural resources and processes in the case of natural capital; health, knowledge and skills in the case of human capital; social relationships and partnerships in the case of social capital; material goods and infrastructure in the case of physical or manufactured capital; and tradable currency in the case of financial capital. In the Forum for the Future model, the focus is on the benefits obtained by organizations from these capitals. Here we take a wider view on benefits in terms of human capabilities and environmental sustainability.
14. Working downhill from the steeper slopes slows down and retains rainwater in the watershed and with it reduces the erosion process. To the extent that poorer people live uphill and therefore benefit first, the principle has a social side effect.
15. This focus on politics and work also affects other capabilities such as bodily health

(via food and shelter), education (if there is a reduction of forced migration), affiliation (via participatory measures) and ultimately even practical reasons, emotions and concern for the environment; nevertheless, the main focus is clearly on political and economic participation, and accordingly the evaluative focus rests here.

16. A key reason is that the more affluent will own land in the lower parts of the watershed and in this location also reap the largest benefits from watershed development.
17. We do not discuss the ridge-to-valley principle as it pertains to the implementation phase.
18. Mono-cropping defined as one crop higher than half of total area.
19. The World Water Forum is a tri-annual event organized by major organizations from the private sector in cooperation with the respective host country.
20. http://ecologic.wotr.org/2011/03/wankute-receives-earth-care-award/.

6. Financing water ecosystem services – Marta Echavarria and EcoDecisión

Marianne Henkel and Justus Lodemann

6.1 INTRODUCTION

As we arrived by plane in Quito, the capital of Ecuador, we flew over an ocean of houses covering a narrow mountain valley that stretches for more than 30 kilometres, seldom wider than 5 kilometres, and is part of the Guayllabamba River Basin. Impressive volcanic mountains, some of which are still active, flank the city. With an altitude of 2800 m above sea level, Quito is the highest capital city of the world – an altitude to which we had to adjust in the first few days.

The population of Quito is growing fast with rural in-migration. From 1950 to 1990 the population grew about six-fold and the city's area about 20-fold. Owing to the expansion of the city, the agricultural frontier was pushed outward into areas of partly protected High Andes grasslands (the *páramo*) and native forests (Vredeveld 2008). The loss of forest cover and degradation of the páramo that is driven by agriculture and cattle grazing – and notably in some regions of Ecuador, by oil drilling and mining – are among the core reasons for the deterioration in local hydrological and other ecosystem services, as well as loss of biodiversity (ibid. UN-ECLAC 2010). These changes not only have an impact on local ecosystems, but also on water users downstream (for example in the case of deteriorating water quality and quantity). As elsewhere around the world, ecosystem protection remains a challenge in Ecuador; it requires controlling land use change and reducing the rate of deforestation, which is one of the highest in the region (UNDP EC, GoE 2007). Also parallel to other parts of the world, here there is a fundamental dilemma between conservation and development: protecting vital ecosystems limits their use for income generation and hence poverty eradication, which is most needed in rural areas.

We visited Ecuador to understand the work of someone who aims to contribute to ecosystem protection for the benefit of human society, using economic instruments to ensure sustainable funding for conservation *and* economic development. Marta Echavarria is the co-founder and executive director of a small consultancy located in Quito called EcoDecisión, which offers consultancy to public and private contractors on economic instruments for biodiversity and ecosystem protection. One of the instruments EcoDecisión specializes in are Payments for Ecosystem Services (PES); this term refers to an arrangement between a user of an ecosystem service (such as water purification and regulation) and a land user (the watershed steward) that aims to compensate the latter for using the land in a manner that ensures the continued provision of the ecosystem service (more on this below). For 14 years now Echavarria has been supporting municipalities and other, mostly local actors in the establishment of local and regional water funds that finance protective and restorative measures in watersheds with financial contributions from water users such as municipal water and energy providers and private corporations. When Echavarria embraced the core concept of PES early in her professional life, she was one of the first in Latin America to do so, and she has engaged in promoting this concept beyond her own contracts. In this chapter we focus on Marta Echavarria's engagement in the set-up of Quito's water trust fund *Fondo para la Protección del Agua* (FONAG), a local watershed PES mechanism, as an example of her work on PES and of her role as a disseminator.

The empirical research for this case study comprises an in-depth literature review and desktop study on watershed PES in Latin America, specifically the case of Quito, and a subsequent five-week field trip to Ecuador in January and February 2011. During the latter, with the help of research fellow Grace Viera Andrade, we carried out 19 semi-structured interviews with stakeholders of FONAG and collected further primary data including maps, contracts and other relevant documents.

We will start Section 6.2 by outlining the genesis of EcoDecisión and the concept of PES, then turn to the development of FONAG against the backdrop of ineffective conservation efforts and a fierce water privatization debate. Following a presentation of Echavarria's approach to water funds, we will discuss her achievements in terms of output and impact. Drawing on this framework, in Section 6.3 we will evaluate her work based on the approach outlined in Chapter 1.

A note on the actor focus: Echavarria's family-run consultancy EcoDecisión will be introduced as the organization she heads and represents, yet it will remain in the background since in the case of FONAG and other water funds, Echavarria carried out the consultancy mainly on her own.

6.2 ECODECISIÓN AND THE CONCEPT OF PAYMENTS FOR ECOSYSTEM SERVICES

A central theme in this case study is societal dependence on ecosystems. The major question for ecosystem conservation – or nature conservation more generally – is whether economic instruments such as PES are effective; ultimately the question is whether economic development and conservation are commensurable. These are the issues that water funds like FONAG touch upon, and that Echavarria seeks to respond to in her work. We will need to delve a little into the economic concept of ecosystem valuation and the question of how and to what extent the economic instruments derived from it can contribute to conservation.

We start with some clarification of concepts. Ecosystem services are 'the services people obtain from ecosystems' (MA 2005, xiv, see Chapter 1). As some ecosystem services are not perceivable to the human eye, especially in the case of cultural services, we may not treasure all of them alike. Yet it is not difficult to see how much humans depend on the ecosystems around them for food, water, the air they breathe and many other things that make our life possible. Biodiversity is the 'variability among living organisms from all sources including, inter alia, terrestrial, marine and other aquatic ecosystems and the ecological complexes of which they are part; this includes diversity within species, between species and of ecosystems' (CBD 1992, Art. 2). It is this biodiversity – the entirety of living organisms on earth – that provides such ecosystem services through a dense web of ecological relationships amongst species, and amongst species and their abiotic environments.[1] The rate of biodiversity loss we are currently witnessing is seriously diminishing ecosystem services, a trend that is currently accelerating (MA 2005). In order to survive we need to protect the natural resources we depend on; what follows is that nature conservation is in the best interest of society.

The economic concern is that conservation to ensure future benefits forbids a range of current resource uses, thereby reducing the economic gains to be achieved today, for example from resource exploitation and land conversion. Traditional conservation approaches that denominate protected areas within which land use is restricted or forbidden altogether have had limited effect where enforcement capacities are weak. Too often the level of protection is lowered by granting concessions for resource exploitation projects; valuable and vulnerable ecosystems are not protected in the first place lest that status hinders further economic development. In short, economic development pressures are ubiquitous and often override concerns for nature conservation. This has led to some 60 per cent of ecosystem services being degraded worldwide, and the trend is further increasing (MA 2005).

Echavarria has dedicated her professional life (and some of her leisure-time) to the conservation of vital ecosystems for the benefit of society. In keeping with her view of the private sector and social entrepreneurship, she has chosen to work as a consultant in her own social enterprise.

EcoDecisión and the Rationale of Payments for Ecosystem Services

Marta Echavarria studied at Brown University, USA where she earned a Bachelors in Environment Studies and a Masters in Development Studies. In her first position, she served as an environmental manager for the Colombian sugarcane association, Asocaña, and was in charge of designing and creating a system of water-user associations and voluntary payments for water consumption in the Cauca River Valley, Colombia. The process was initiated out of a growing concern over water availability and led to a public–private collaboration between the users, represented partly by Asocaña, and the Cauca Valley Corporation, the regional environmental authority (Echavarria 2002).

In 1995 Echavarria and her husband Jacob Olander moved to Ecuador and founded the social enterprise EcoDecisión, taking office in Quito. Echavarria's interest in conservation and the experience from Cauca Valley led her to embrace a conservation approach that was still new at the time and largely unexplored – the economic valuation of ecosystems and the related Payments for Ecosystem Services. An important point of reference for her was an influential journal article in 1997 that attempted to estimate the value of the world's ecosystem services (Costanza et al. 1997, Echavarria 2011b); in the same year a book was published that promoted economic incentives for various ecosystem services (Daily 1997).

Since its establishment, the goal of EcoDecisión has been to provide expertise in the creation of financial mechanisms to conserve ecosystems in the tropics, focusing on the ecosystem services of carbon sequestration (focus of Olander), water flow regulation and purification (focus of Echavarria) and biodiversity habitat provision (both). Coming from Colombia, where entrepreneurs are generally seen as people that move things proactively and innovatively, her own view of the private sector is positive (interview Echavarria 2011b). Being an entrepreneur with a social mission does not present a contradiction to her; Echavarria positions her enterprise between the private and public sector as a 'third way' (ibid.). The core features for her are that as an enterprise, EcoDecisión pays taxes and does not avail itself of philanthropic funding (donations), and as a social enterprise EcoDecisión covers its costs but is not oriented towards profit maximization. EcoDecisión is a small, family-run consultancy; Echavarria wants EcoDecisión to be a 'fun place to work' (interview Echavarria

2011c) and aims to create an environment in which people are motivated to work. There are no clearly established hierarchies within the organization and staff may independently carry out communication with contractors and external project partners. At the same time, everyone has their specific responsibilities and tasks, and the directors make all financial decisions regarding the enterprise.

EcoDecisión provides consultancy services to the public sector, companies and NGOs. Their main clients to date are large international NGOs including The Nature Conservancy (TNC), Conservation International (CI), the Wildlife Conservation Society (WCS) and Fundación Cordillera Tropical (FCT), overseas development agencies, and ministries. Although Echavarria considers private companies important stakeholders in her work, awareness on their part is still rather limited (interview Echavarria 2011c).

We now turn to a clarification of ecosystem valuation and PES. The concept of ecosystem valuation is based on the notion that ecosystems are lost or degraded because their value is not being accounted for in decisions on land and natural resources use, and that this value needs to be made visible through translation into monetary terms in order to effectively protect the ecosystems (Costanza 1997, MA 2005, TEEB 2010).[2] It denominates an assessment of the economic value of ecosystems (or parts thereof, such as specific services or elements of biodiversity) expressed in monetary terms. The methodology of such valuations are often based on users' willingness to pay for that element, on its effect on the price of some marketable good, or on the estimated cost of avoiding damage or adequately substituting for loss.

The rationale of PES contends that the users of an ecosystem service should compensate the stewards of the land that provides the ecosystem service for the opportunity cost of protecting the ecosystem service. PES imply a contractual arrangement between at least one ecosystem service supplier (land user) and at least one buyer whereby the latter provides an incentive to the former to use the land in a way that ensures the provision of the ecosystem service (Wunder 2005, p. 3).[3] Such mutual agreements not only establish an incentive-driven conservation but also change the role of the state, which formerly had the responsibility of governing public goods and common pool resources. It is often suggested that economic instruments are more cost-effective (that is, have greater effectiveness at the same cost) than state-led conservation approaches because they are negotiated between the affected parties and the buyer will himself control whether he gets 'value for money'. Moreover it is often held that PES might contribute to economic development in rural areas; indeed, Echavarria considers that they can and should contribute to a shift of resources from urban users to rural providers.

Both ecosystem valuation and PES have been criticized on various grounds, only some of which will be considered here.[4] Most fundamentally, conservation strictly requires an acknowledgement of the limits to growth (Meadows et al. 1972). Conceptually, PES and ecosystem valuation build on the economic logic of our current capitalist subsistence strategy and draw on compensatory payments from activities spurring economic growth. Economists have raised concerns that aiming at development co-benefits will result in trade-offs with the ecological effectiveness and efficiency of PES (McAfee and Shapiro 2010). Notably, there is little hard evidence to date for the superior performance of PES in terms of cost-effectiveness and success factors (Wolff et al. in press). In terms of governance, the ideal of a contract negotiation between equal and equally informed partners as presumed in the concept is itself silent on the possibility of power and information imbalances between ecosystem service buyer and supplier. Consequently little attention has been paid to PES as a governance process. Finally, strong concern has been voiced that economic instruments will pave the way for the commodification of nature. This framing of nature may result in the privatization of public goods and the trade of ecosystem services and biodiversity in markets.[5]

Despite all that criticism, the problems of insufficient funding for conservation and a lack of ecosystem considerations in land-use decisions remain pressing. Economic instruments such as PES may have a place in conservation policy in alleviating these problems – as one tool amongst others, in a contextually appropriate manner. Echavarria herself is aware of the limitations of PES, and sees them as a means to help conservation cope with the current growth imperative as far as possible (interview Echavarria 2011b). In the face of such contradictions, she has opted for a pragmatic approach that aims to raise broad societal awareness and funding for the conservation of ecosystems and rural development.

FONAG and the Issue of Water Privatization

One of Echavarria's first major engagements in the field of PES in Ecuador was to support the establishment of *Fondo para la Protección del Agua* (FONAG), a local water fund for the municipality of Quito. The establishment of FONAG came out of a growing concern for long-term water availability. Over a period of 25 years starting in the early 1970s, upstream water flows diminished and become more erratic owing to land degradation; increasing levels of sand and other particles presented severe problems for Quito's water provider EMAAP and Quito's electric utility EEQ[6] (interview Cubillo 2011).

Quito's water supply situation is paradigmatic of many other cities and regions on the *Pacifico* side of the Andes range in Ecuador, where large-scale environmental change like climate change combines with local changes in land cover and land-use patterns to the detriment of ecosystem services. Water resources in Ecuador are distributed unequally between the Pacifico and the Amazonico regions: water availability is significantly lower in the Pacifico (the western part of the country), where water consumption is greatest owing to irrigated agriculture.[7] Land degradation further impacts flow patterns and diminishes water quality. Moreover climate change has begun to make precipitation patterns more unpredictable and extreme; a trend expected to aggravate in the future (UNDP EC 2007, IPCC 2007). Efforts have been made to designate protected areas to prevent land conversion and ecosystem loss; however, the protection efforts have proven to be limited in their effectiveness.

In Quito's case there were two protected areas at stake situated to the south of Quito that both protect watersheds of major importance to the city – the national park of Cotopaxi and its neighbouring ecological reserve Antisana. Their status as protected areas and the respective restrictions on land use this entailed did not effectively prevent encroachment upon the forests and the illegal conversion of ecosystems into agricultural land driven mainly by rural poverty. As the protected areas are located outside the municipal boundaries, the enforcement capacities of Quito's authorities are restricted.

In April 1998 the executive director and a staff member of Fundación Antisana, a foundation dedicated to the protection of the Antisana Reserve, jointly with an executive of EMAAP came up with the idea of creating a financial mechanism that would generate funds for conservation activities, which eventually became FONAG. Shortly afterwards, Roberto Troya left Fundación Antisana as executive director to become the director of the new Ecuadorian office of The Nature Conservancy (TNC), a North American conservation NGO, and decided to develop the idea further with outside support. Because of Echavarria's experience in the establishment of a financial mechanism for watershed protection in the Colombian Cauca Valley (see above), she was hired as a consultant by TNC to help with the design and implementation of the idea. At this time water funds (and the concept of PES in general) were not known in Ecuador or at least there was no earlier example of a fund.[8] The only well-known example of a watershed PES programme was in the Catskill Mountains, established in the early 1990s to benefit New York City's potable water supply. This scheme served as a point of reference in the development of FONAG.

One of the first successes of the initiators (including Marta) was to convince city counsellor Roque Sevilla to join the initiative. Shortly afterwards when the mayor unexpectedly died, Sevilla became mayor of Quito from 1998 to 2000. Sevilla, who had earlier established a foundation for the protection of nature, became an important ally for the fund's initiators in terms of winning the needed political commitment in the city council (interviews Lloret 2011, Echavarria 2011a). The two main water users, EMAAP and EEQ, are municipal enterprises; bringing them on board required the support of the city council.

The idea of the trust fund and the process to establish it began to take shape mostly among Roberto Troya, Roque Sevilla and Marta Echavarria (interview Troya 2011). It was decided that the trust fund should serve mainly as a financing mechanism for protective measures in the watershed and as a platform for the main water users in Quito, both public and private, and the land users from the watersheds around the city to negotiate and agree upon water and land use as well as the deployment of the fund's financial resources. The fund should be an independent entity under private law so as not to be touched easily by partisan political interests and political whims, and because the initiators generally considered private entities to be more flexible and efficient (interview Echavarria 2011a). The fund should tender out the interventions decided upon by the board and evaluate project success. As an endowment trust it should invest only its interests, while the stock capital should remain untouched to ensure long-term sustainability (interviews Lloret 2011, Echavarria 2011a).

Achieving consensus on member contributions turned out to be difficult. An initial estimate was made on how much was needed for the effective protection of the protected watershed areas, Cotopaxi and Antisana, as these were considered most crucial for Quito's water supply (interview Echavarria 2011a). The results were not considered in the discussion, however. In the international sustainability discourse it was generally held that a large company should dedicate 5 per cent of its sales to environmental management, one-fifth of which (1 per cent of sales) to water issues (interview Echavarria 2011a). After objections from the water users' side, it was finally determined that EMAAP would contribute 1 per cent of its sales to the fund, while the other fund members – EEQ, Tesalia (a private water bottler) and Cervecería Andina (a beverage producer) – would contribute a fixed amount much lower in terms of percentage of their annual turnover. Essentially, the contribution of most members was determined based on willingness to pay rather than required funding, with the public company EMAAP giving the lion's share and rather symbolic contributions from the other public company and the two private corporations. FONAG has not yet succeeded in bringing on board further corporate water users in the Quito area that rely on safe water supply but have their own wells and hence are not contributing through EMAAP (interview Lloret 2011). Additionally, substantial funding for the start-up phase was acquired from US development agency USAID and TNC, both interested in supporting a new instrument that would secure sustainable funding and thus enforce protection for so-called 'paper parks', national parks that are designated but not effectively protected.

As a consequence of the above, the capitalization of the fund took longer than anticipated. Since the trust was to use yields only, for the first few years no activities were undertaken for lack of funding. Eventually, USAID as a major donor urged for results and the first projects were implemented in watershed communities (interviews Zavala, Cedeno 2011, Echavarria 2011a). Regarding the governance structure, the fund's water users make up the board as the strategic decision-making body, which currently encompasses four contributing companies (see above) as well as TNC and Consortio Camarén, a rural development NGO. Decisions in the board are usually taken unanimously, although majority vote is possible. However, EMAAP's role as the fund's largest contributor implies that de facto other members usually do not oppose the company even where they might disagree (interview Lloret 2011). The watershed communities as water suppliers have an advisory function through their representation in the technical committee, but do not have decision-making power; only those who contribute financially can make decisions on the use of the funding.

Although Echavarria has kept in touch with FONAG staff and board members beyond her contract, her direct consultancy to the fund's initiators under a TNC contract ended in 2001, the year following the institutionalization of the fund. In her role as consultant in the early stages of FONAG, Echavarria was involved in the conceptual design of the fund, but not the conception or implementation of conservation programmes. Since her work with FONAG, Echavarria has consulted and accompanied further initiatives for watershed funds to varying degrees in Ecuador, including the Loja region (FORAGUA), Espìndola (Fondo de Agua de Espìndola), the province of Zamora (ProCuencas), Tungurahua (FPTLCP), as well as outside of the country in Bogotà, Colombia and Lima, Peru.

As mentioned above, at the time of FONAG's establishment there was little awareness in Ecuador of Payments for Ecosystem Services. There was, however, a stringent discourse on water privatization at the time, encouraged notably by the World Bank and IMF under their structural adjustment policies, and strongly opposed by a number of NGOs. In 1994 a concessional loan of the Inter-American Development Bank (IDB) pushed the Ecuadorian government to grant a concession for water supply in Ecuador's largest urban area, Guayaquil, leading to mass lay-offs of the previously communal enterprise's staff and rising water prices without the promised substantial investments in coverage and water treatment (Swyngedouw 2005, Acosta w/o year). The negative example of Guayaquil spurred criticism and fear of further water privatization in the country.

In that context both NGOs and government had clear reservations against FONAG as a private entity in the first years after its establishment (interviews Lloret 2011, Echavarria 2011a). The fund was set up as a trust fund under private law in hopes of greater political independence and efficiency; this notion of an efficient, goal-oriented management of public affairs suggests that business is the ideal towards which state bureaucracy should be oriented. This goes hand in hand with the paradigm of multi-stakeholder governance, which has increasingly gained leverage since the realization that globalization processes have effectively reduced the steering capacity of the state. The plausible answer to this challenge is that other sectors – civil society and especially the private sector – should be 'brought on board' to warrant effective and efficient policy-making. Public–private and multi-stakeholder partnerships have gained recognition in the global debate on sustainable development. While the underlying idea of these governance arrangements is to take decisions in consensus and to work for a common interest, there are unresolved concerns over the political legitimacy and effectiveness of such partnerships and over the democratic representation and power (im)balances within them (Dobner 2010).

Although FONAG's manager considers that doubts over the fund being a private entity have been cleared through its transparency towards authorities and the wider public (interview Lloret 2011), some consider it unlikely that today a water fund would be set up as a private trust fund (interview Paladines 2011). Representatives of EMAAP and the Ministry of Environment think that FONAG should be placed under stronger public authority in the future (interviews Romero 2011, Villegas 2011).

What becomes evident in our research on Echavarria is that the ideal she pursued with her colleagues in establishing FONAG – multi-stakeholder governance with a strong role for the private sector – has not fitted easily with the prevailing attitudes in civil society and government. Echavarria is aware of this. Although she is convinced that the uncompromisingly strong role of the state forgoes potential cooperation not only with the private sector, but also civil society (interview Echavarria 2011c), the question of private or public is not of central concern to her concept of water funds, or PES more generally.

Innovation at the Core: Marta Echavarria's Approach to Water Funds

Echavarria's main concern is securing a steady source of financing for conservation rather than focusing on a specific form of governance. While institutions of participatory water management such as watershed councils are commonly known, these often fall short of securing sufficient financial resources to remain operational.

Unlike TNC, who have begun to replicate the FONAG model in several

Latin American countries, Echavarria does not advocate for one specific economic model or institutional structure for a water fund, nor necessarily for water funds in principle. Her approach to the institutional problem is to integrate what she considers core functions into the locally specific institutional environment on the ground.

In Colombia she opted for water-user associations as the core institution of the financial mechanism, whereas in Quito she helped conceive of the idea as a trust fund. While the fund model realized in Quito was inspired by the understanding that private entities are typically more effective and efficient than public administrative bodies (see above), Echavarria has also provided advocacy to fund initiatives that are explicitly designed as public entities or that only involve local government. Her conception of funds also varies in terms of management structures, scope of activities and size or number of watersheds covered. For Echavarria, the essence of the PES concept lies in the (contractual) relationship between upstream watershed stewards and downstream water users, which establishes economic incentives for watershed protection and a multi-stakeholder governance framework warranting key functions. These key components are the technical secretariat in charge of operations and implementation, the board as the decision-making body and a routine of project evaluation and adaptive management of watershed resources (Echavarria 2011c). These functions may be taken up by newly established or existing institutions such as member organizations' offices. This deliberately flexible framework is to be adapted to local circumstances; rather than a fixed model, Echavarria's PES approach relies on constant innovation and co-creation by local stakeholders. These co-initiators, who are mostly her contractors, that is, principals, play a major role in determining the fund's governance arrangement in regards to stakeholders' specific representation, rights and responsibilities in the fund and roles (rights, responsibilities) in the fund. As it is suggested that endogenous or locally adapted institutions fit more easily with established norms, and thus enjoy greater legitimacy and effectiveness (REF; see also legitimacy thesis), it is also plausible to assume that Echavarria's adaptive approach represents a strength in itself.

Regarding the process of establishment of any water fund (or other local water PES scheme), what is important in Echavarria's view is the succession of several phases: 1) political negotiation to win the support of core economic and political decision-makers followed by 2) the evaluation of financial means needed and available as well as of the legal framework (national water and conservation law, relevant municipal statutes, and so on) within which the fund is to be established, and finally 3) the operationalization during which the agreed-upon institutions and activities will be put in place. The greatest relevance of this three-phase model lies in its implications for stakeholders' roles and involvement. While her governance ideal is strongly influenced by the multi-stakeholder paradigm (see above), and participation of the watershed communities is a cornerstone of that ideal in principle, what needs to be gained first when taking a pragmatic stance is the buy-in of political and economic decision-makers: '[I]n the initial stage . . . the participation is not so important, you need more the buying-in – the political buying-in – of the decision makers . . . but as you develop the water fund, as you institutionalise it, the participation is very important' (Echavarria 2011c).

As the institutionalization of FONAG was completed and operationalization began the upstream land users were involved, yet their participation is currently limited to an advisory role. Echavarria suggests that these communities should ideally become full members of the fund by contributing financially, thereby gaining representation on the board and in decision-making (interview Echavarria 2011b).

Echavarria's notion of the role of business in conservation, and environmental management at large, is shaped by her own positive image of entrepreneurship (see above) as well as the works of the World Business Council on Sustainable Development (WBCSD) (interview Echavarria 2011c). In her understanding, pointing out the business case for protecting natural resources vis-à-vis the private sector is often more effective than state-led policies that lack the funding for implementation. The experience of FONAG, however, seems to indicate that even if the business case is clear, private firms prefer to free-ride where collective action is required: only two of the numerous corporate water users in the Quito metropolitan area are currently members of the fund, with rather symbolic financial contributions.

Echavarria's approach to water funds – or more generally, water PES – includes a secure financing mechanism based on water user contributions, a set of core functions that need to be institutionalized, one of them being a multi-stakeholder governance body for decision-making, and a sequence of phases in which stakeholders are pragmatically involved in the order of their importance for the fund. The flexibility in the institutional set-up – public or private entity, creating new institutions or embedding functions in existing ones – is a potential strength, allowing for adaptation to local conditions. The case of FONAG is a good illustration of that approach in many respects.

Goal Achievement (Output and Impact)

What merits our attention next is how far Echavarria is able to realize her approach in her role as a consultant and, beyond her concrete consultancy assignments, in her role as a disseminator of the concepts of water funds and PES.

Her degree of involvement with any water fund initiative varies strongly. In the case of FONAG, she was involved intensively over the course of three to four years; in other instances she provided feasibility studies. As a consultant Echavarria's role is to help develop the idea and the model of each fund, and to counsel on the process of institutionalization; she sees herself as 'catalytic at that initial stage' (Echavarria 2011c). Having taken up her profession out of personal commitment, she frequently supports initiatives through her knowledge of their history even after her contract is fulfilled. In the case of FONAG, she sees herself as having an 'important role in keeping the institutional memory of everything that was being done as actors came in and out' (Echavarria 2011b), a view corroborated by other key stakeholders (interviews Lloret 2011, Arroyo 2011).

There are nevertheless limitations to her role as a consultant. Despite her strong involvement with FONAG, her goal for water funds to raise broad societal awareness of the importance of ecosystems is not yet achieved. In spite of her recommendation, EMAAP chose not to disclose the watershed fee on the water bills, meaning that the majority of households are in fact not aware of it (interviews Echavarria 2011a, Lloret 2011, Ribadeneira 2011). Regarding the functions she considers crucial for a PES mechanism, monitoring and evaluation are not yet institutionalized. In 2011 TNC and the FONAG secretariat commissioned an evaluation of the fund's socio-economic impacts (see below) but a thorough assessment of its ecological effectiveness, let alone cost-effectiveness, had not been carried out by early 2012. Instead of a monitoring routine assessing water flows or water quality of the various sources, proxies like the size of reforested area are used as indicators of FONAG's effectiveness. Surprisingly, board members nevertheless unanimously stated that they considered the fund to be ecologically effective (interviews Cubillo 2011, Uzukovich 2011, A. Arroyo 2011, Romero 2011). Moreover, the number of private sector contributors to the fund is far smaller than the number of actual water users. This is a typical free-rider problem: all water users benefit from the measures financed by only a few. It seriously diminishes FONAG's prospects for financial sustainability in the long term and raises questions of legitimacy. This is a drawback for Echavarria's goal of getting the private sector to recognize and internalize its environmental costs.

Finally, the watershed communities' participation in the fund has not been institutionalized according to her ideal. While the watershed communities have an opportunity to offer their views on foreseen projects through a technical committee, they are not involved in decision-making. Echavarria holds that the communities should be more involved than they are: 'I would say the group that has been most marginalized are the communities in the watersheds that have been . . . out in the field' (interview Echavarria 2011b).[9]

Echavarria views these aspects as shortcomings, yet considers the current state of things as one step of a longer process in which some things have been achieved while others need to be pursued. Looking at the achievements, the fund is operational, it has generated an awareness at least among some economic and political decision-makers in Quito and the communities in the watershed (TNC and FONAG 2011), and it has received a high level of attention among water managers nationally (Kauffman 2011, Lloret 2011).

To what extent Echavarria has contributed to the dissemination of (watershed) PES nationally, regionally and globally should be considered in relation to the context of the development of the concept of PES (see above). Echavarria was one of the early promoters of PES in Latin America. She had an important share in shaping and promoting FONAG in its initial stages, which was one of the first two water funds in Ecuador and has gained significant importance as a role model for replication in the region (see above). It was also the first water fund project undertaken by TNC, who has now adopted the approach almost as a hallmark, replicating it with IDB funds in several Latin American countries (Echavarria 2011a).

Internationally, Echavarria has likewise contributed to the growing awareness of PES in the discourses on conservation, water and development. FONAG is one of the most often-quoted cases of watershed PES in the literature for policy advocacy on ecosystem conservation (for example Landell-Mills and Porras 2002, WWAP 2006, UNEP 2011) and Echavarria's own publications are referenced in a number of publications by major organizations in nature conservation and water management (for example Landell-Mills and Porras 2002, ITTO 2004, IUCN 2006, WWAP 2006, UNEP et al. 2008).

Echavarria certainly has an impact on disseminating the concept of watershed PES nationally and internationally. It is a strength of her role as a consultant that working with many different water funds over the years has yielded a considerable experience. In that respect, her role is uniquely positioned between those of full-time practitioners, who seldom have the time to publish, and those of full-time academics or office staff, who do not have the same first-hand experience and long-term insights into the initiatives.

6.3   EVALUATION – GETTING THINGS DONE SUSTAINABLY?

This chapter sets out to look at the work of a social entrepreneur dedicated to watershed conservation, taking an approach to conservation that also allows for rural development – the classic image of sustainable development. Paradoxically, Echavarria herself does not believe in sustainable development, or more precisely in the possibility of achieving it. This finding is at the heart of the contradictions pervading the analysis, and it may be the hope for this impossible goal that constitutes the core argument for the pragmatic solution.

Strong Sustainability

> [O]ver the years, I became very much . . . a skeptic because of the issue of limits . . . . Unfortunately the concept [of sustainable development] highlights win–win situations, but doesn't talk enough about the losses . . . . Unfortunately there are moments to say you cannot have more economic growth without having social welfare being affected, and without having environmental loss. (Interview Echavarria 2011c)

According to Marta Echavarria, the concept of sustainable development – in the prevailing understanding of three equally important dimensions – fails to acknowledge the unavoidable limits to economic growth. If environmental sustainability is to be taken seriously as a requirement, this understanding is going to have to change.

Ecosystem valuation and PES do not question economic growth conceptually; rather they build on current economic thinking and methods to let nature appear in cost–benefit analyses where otherwise it would not be taken into account at all (see above). PES as a concept does not seek to guarantee constant natural capital; in the extreme, it prioritizes or shifts conservation efforts according to current solvent ecosystem users' preferences. The justice dimensions of sustainability have to be revisited here. An incentive-driven conservation necessarily focuses on current generations (those who are able to remunerate the ecosystem benefits they value) and thus has a blind spot on the principle of inter-generational equity. As future generations cannot yet express their preferences, the conservation choices guided by today's ecosystem service usage patterns may substantively differ from future priorities. Under certain circumstances, the conservation priorities expressed in PES mechanisms may also conflict with concerns over intra-generational justice. In the case of the water funds in Latin America, the ecosystems protected are almost always those upstream of urban centres and important agricultural areas, where households and industries constitute a critical mass of solvent water users.

Arguing the case for her approach, Echavarria points out that the drivers of ecosystem loss – in her context, rural poverty and lack of awareness – need to be addressed in order to solve the problem. PES create incentives for local land users to conserve ecosystems and manage land sustainably, financed by the ecosystem service beneficiaries. Since other conservation efforts have not been sufficient to slow biodiversity and eco-system loss (globally and in Ecuador), addressing the economic incentives to save what can be valuated may not result in constant natural capital, but is arguably better than losing still more. What remains unanswered is whether economic valuation and PES will ultimately lead to a more stringent commodification of nature, appropriation of common goods and the risk of market failure in ecosystem and biodiversity markets (see above). In Echavarria's view, the strength of ecosystem valuation and the PES concept lies in making the economic value of ecosystems visible to society and generating the financial resources required for their protec-tion, which other instruments tend to lack (such as underfunded protected areas). Aware of the conceptual limits and the limited practical experience with PES, Echavarria suggests PES as one among several instruments in a policy mix.

Again, her role as a consultant brings about certain limits regarding her responsibility for the eventual outcome of her work. While she can advocate for a given use of the financial means, to what degree decision-makers in those funds endorse her goal of raising societal awareness and her holistic attitude to conservation is beyond her influence. In the case of FONAG, the main goal of its board members is not primarily environ-mental sustainability in a comprehensive sense, but the ongoing provision of ecosystem services – in this case, water – as a precondition for economic activities. This focus may direct resources to areas less rich in biodiversity but more important for specific sources.

Echavarria's approach to conservation is characterized by an attempt to change incentives and to thereby put ecosystem protection on (eco-nomically) firm ground in a system oriented towards growth and natural resource exploitation. Since she has limited influence over decision-making as a consultant, especially in the operational phase when her contract is over, it is important to distinguish between a conceptual assessment of her approach and the shape of the water funds for which she worked.

Capabilities

Regarding the contribution of her work to human capabilities, we find it useful to distinguish between the goal level and the approach level. The goal of Echavarria and her enterprise EcoDecisión is to establish financ-ing mechanisms for long-term nature conservation, which is in principle very compatible with the notion that intact ecosystems and the provision of ecosystem services are a precondition for human capabilities.[10] In addi-tion, Echavarria and EcoDecisión seek to reward environmental stewards, who in the Ecuadorian context are often poorer rural communities. Her concept of and approach to watershed PES have the potential to benefit social and economic development in rural areas, and hence to expand a number of capabilities, including bodily health, life of normal length and others.

Securing the availability of safe drinking water for the long term is clearly an important goal that is directly connected to these human capabilities of bodily health and leading a life of normal length. In urban centres the municipal water provider should be able to eliminate pathogens and other harmful substances from the water so as to ensure good water quality for households. The lower the quality of the raw water, the more costly the water treatment will be and the higher the risk of health hazards if treatment facilities are insufficient. Moreover, Echavarria points to the gap between access to safe drinking water in urban and rural areas, and makes it a priority in her advocacy work that watershed communities be provided access to safe water in turn for protecting the water sources. Her work certainly has an achievement there.

In her view the measures carried out by the water funds in the watersheds should further contribute to better living conditions in the watersheds by increasing income, health and nutrition. In the case of FONAG, an evaluation among beneficiary communities in 2011 has not yielded significant health effects to date; however, in one of four beneficiary communities, an increase in household incomes owing to FONAG's activities has indeed resulted in better nutrition (TNC and FONAG 2011). Owing perhaps to the specific implementation of her concept in FONAG, which is not within her control, that potential has not fully materialized.

PES at its core is about making the economic value of nature tangible to human society, which may contribute to the capability of being able to live together with concern for nature and in relation to other animals, plants, and the world (Nussbaum 2006). By paying for the conservation of ecosystems, private households and institutional actors might become aware of the role of ecosystem services at large; however, this has yet to be achieved (see above). FONAG board members, the paying contributors to the fund, are indeed aware of the necessity to protect the watersheds, but they do not necessarily seem to endorse a more comprehensive concern for nature or rural development beyond this (Romero 2011, Cubillo 2011). In the watershed communities, the environmental awareness-raising undertaken by FONAG seems to have increased understanding and corresponding changes in behaviour in some respects, such that some groups that have participated in awareness-raising tend to expand their agricultural areas more slowly and to use fewer chemical inputs in agriculture (TNC and FONAG 2011). The findings are not homogenous for the four evaluated communities; here too achievements present a mixed picture (ibid.).

An important aspect that has been discussed above is the representation and participation of upstream land users in the funds, which pertains more to Echavarria's specific approach to setting up a fund than her goals. Such representation and participation has implications for the capability of having control over one's environment. As mentioned above, the PES concept embodied in the water fund model builds on a voluntary agreement between an ecosystem service supplier and a buyer who have symmetric access to information and should be free to accept or not accept the offer; it does not make any statements regarding PES as a process of environmental governance. Echavarria's approach is more explicit here regarding the governance dimension, notably regarding the timing of involvement of stakeholders in different phases and the institutionalization of a multi-stakeholder platform for continued decision-making.

The PES mechanisms can materially benefit both the downstream water users by ensuring that their property rights (for example titles to land used for agricultural production) are not diminished in value through lack of water, and the upstream watershed inhabitants to the extent that the funds' activities actually benefit them economically (for example increased and diversified income via paid work opportunities, alternative livelihood trainings and higher-value marketing channels for organic products). In the case of FONAG, the projects financed by the fund have contributed to an increase in overall household income for beneficiary households in some of the communities (TNC and FONAG 2011). The socio-economic impacts of FONAG's activities vary widely amongst the four communities considered, with some displaying hardly any significant impacts and others influenced more strongly (ibid.). Overall, FONAG seems to reach out especially to poorer households in the selection of beneficiary households (ibid.) so that the material capability of control appears strengthened to some degree.

The political dimension of control is no less important; this includes the capabilities of being able to participate effectively in political choices that govern one's life and having the right to political participation. While the commitment of political and economic decision-makers is arguably a precondition for the establishment of the fund, bringing in the affected communities after the institutional decisions have been taken and only granting them consultative status does not offer a possibility of participating effectively in political choices. If their involvement begins after the set-up phase is completed, their participatory rights and roles will have been constituted by downstream water users. As a mechanism designed to influence land use in watersheds, then, water funds potentially increase the control of downstream water users over areas upstream. In the case of FONAG, the watershed communities were not informed about the creation of the fund itself until the fund was eventually established, in keeping with Echavarria's approach. The fund's activities immediately affect the lives of land users, for example by reducing the size of pastures for cattle grazing if fences are put up around water sources on common lands. If they are not able to effectively participate in the planning process, their control is then limited to cooperating or not cooperating with the project implementers. While the decision-making process and stakeholder participation vary amongst funds, with FONAG the watershed communities have by and large not been able to participate in the decision-making process of the board (interview Consortio Camarén 2011). According to Echavarria, communities should ideally be represented in the board as paying members of the fund. Seeing as those communities have little financial means, that contribution would necessarily be substantially smaller than that of EMAAP, the largest contributor, which de facto determines the fund's strategic planning decisions. It is hard to justify that the communities should have to buy their right to participate in decision-making, notably when their vote can be overruled by one single veto-player, and when it is them who should be compensated through the fund.

The flexibility of Echavarria's approach is a potential strength in that it allows for adaptation to local conditions, co-creation of the institutions by local stakeholders, and increased legitimacy and ownership. However, this co-creation is limited to decision-makers and it is largely up to them how and to what degree to engage upstream land users as Echavarria's ideal of a multi-stakeholder platform is not explicit on the concrete steps and degree of participation. It seems desirable to complement the strength of flexibility with safeguards to ensure that the water funds actually develop into a forum for joint decision-making with balanced decision-making power for all stakeholders affected. Such safeguards should build on a clearer concept of participation. How can communities be enabled to participate in the process, for example through community organization and capacity building? Can they be engaged earlier on in the process so that they can take part in decisions on roles and competences in the fund's governance? How can a balance in decision-making power be warranted so that not only financial contributions to the fund are recognized, but also the affected stakeholders' right to participate in decisions that govern their lives? In Echavarria's consultancy assignments, such safeguards would obviously be non-committal, but should be part of the elements in the phases and functions that form the core of her approach.

To summarize, Echavarria's work has the potential to contribute to a number of capabilities including health, political and economic participation and concern for other beings, although that potential does not always fully materialize. Her pragmatic approach to the process of establishment is a strength in getting the financial mechanisms up and running but falls short of recognizing the political aspect of empowering or disempowering different actors in the long run. This should be reflected better in her concept of a multi-stakeholder decision-making body and the three-phases model.

Echavarria as a Political Actor

The picture that emerges of Echavarria as a political actor is framed to a large degree by her role as a consultant and international expert. Beyond consultancy assignments for water fund initiatives, her contribution to promoting the concept of PES regionally and internationally through publications and advocacy has already been highlighted. Echavarria has certainly been influential in promoting the concept of water funds (and watershed PES) regionally and to some extent internationally.

Output legitimacy

In most of the water funds Echavarria has worked on, she is involved as an expert with profound knowledge, yet has limited and indirect influence on what happens on the ground, especially beyond the start-up phase. In the case of FONAG she effectively contributed to shaping the fund conceptually in its early stages. For reasons outside Echavarria's influence, however, the fund's environmental effectiveness has not yet been properly assessed. It is very likely that the fund's various activities, such as reforestation and awareness-raising, have had positive environmental effects, but a coherent assessment is needed, especially to ensure an adaptive management.

The fund's very existence testifies to an increased awareness among water users of the importance of healthy ecosystems for water supply, although this does not translate into a sizable willingness to pay on the part of the private sector, whom Echavarria views as an important stakeholder. According to an external evaluation (TNC and FONAG 2011), the fund's socio-economic impacts are mixed: while in some communities interventions have had positive effects on beneficiaries regarding household income, nutrition and environmental awareness, the level and kind of impact vary between communities. Echavarria's work has gained output legitimacy in so far as it has contributed to an increased awareness of the value of ecosystems among water users and to the establishment of water funds that (most likely) have positive effects.

Social accountability

Accountability is clearly an important aspect of Echavarria's self-image as an entrepreneur; in her role as a consultant, however, she is accountable first and foremost to her contractor. In the context of her engagement, an important aspect is raising awareness among core stakeholders (political and economic) of the need for watershed protection; Echavarria considers this a precondition for the fund's establishment. Yet this awareness-raising and direct communication will typically only include the watershed communities that have already organized themselves as active members of the process. She is not a local actor in the above sense, although she does try to adapt the specific model of each fund to the local situation (Echavarria 2011b) to increase the embedment of the institutional solution.

Since her involvement with many water fund initiatives is defined mainly through a contract with one of its initiators, she cannot be held accountable for informing or educating further stakeholders, but only for her advice in this regard. She considers participatory governance and environmental awareness-raising important and advocates for these in the conception of the fund activities; however, it has been pointed out that this aspect should be strengthened.

A related and important criterion of democratic governance is transparency, an essential requirement for stakeholder inclusion and accountability. Echavarria strongly recommends transparency in the initiatives, in the case of FONAG, for example through making explicit the extra fee for watershed protection on private households' water bill. Diverging interests may lead to this advice not being heeded or followed inconsistently. While FONAG's annual accounts and further operational information are partly available on its website, the fee apportioned to water users is not disclosed on the water bill. Board members do little else to raise awareness; as a result few households in Quito are aware of the fund's existence.

Empowerment

Marta Echavarria can certainly be understood as a transition agent or facilitator. As a consultant, she typically works with local government agencies or water companies, and while she does advise for engagement of the watershed communities this is not part of her assignment, and usually takes place after her involvement is concluded. As mentioned above, Echavarria has a clear idea of who should be involved at what stage in the set-up of a water fund, the ideal being that the fully operational fund would at the same time serve as a multi-stakeholder governance mechanism balancing powers and interests, or would become an integrative part of an already existing mechanism as such. In practice, as a consultant her influence over the process is limited.

Outside recognition

In Echavarria's opinion, outside recognition has added to her international standing more than her national reputation. She was assigned senior fellow by Ashoka in 2006, has been a member of the Advisory Committee of the Ecosystem Marketplace since 2008 and of the Steering Committee of the Tropical America Katoomba Group since 2006, was selected as Rainer Arnhold Fellow by the Mulago Foundation in 2007 and between 2004 and 2008, she was a member of the board for Fundación Natura in Ecuador.

The stakeholders involved with FONAG who know her involvement in the early years of the fund see her role as that of an expert whose legitimacy derives from her knowledge in the field and from the fact that she fulfilled an assignment as a paid consultant (interviews Arroyo 2011, Troya 2011, Sevilla 2011, Jervis 2011, Lloret 2011). To some, her independence from any institutional or economic interests has further added to her credibility. Echavarria does not see a problem of legitimacy in her work, but one of restricted influence owing to the fact that she does not represent an organization with high leverage, like a public authority. In her view it is her credibility as a competent expert – her knowledge, experience and perseverance – that has gained her recognition at the national and international level.

6.4   CONCLUSIONS AND OUTLOOK

On the plane back to Europe, a last glance over the valley and foothills over which Quito stretches out, flanked by green mountain slopes, once more invoked the picture of our sphere of economic activities encroaching evermore on the natural resources on which we depend. Should we expand this sphere consciously in valuating nature to slow its loss? Can we achieve effective conservation without rejecting the growth imperative? Convinced of the ecological limits to growth, Echavarria has chosen the former approach and it is her strength to build on what she considers achievable. Her contribution to sustainable water management is in raising awareness on human dependence on ecosystems and attracting funding for the protection of ecosystem services. The concept of PES was innovative at the time she started out and her flexible approach results in local variations of the core model adapted to the institutional, legal and stakeholder context. While a thorough monitoring of ecological effectiveness is still lacking for FONAG, the fund has raised awareness for the value of ecosystems among some decision-makers and watershed communities, and it has to some degree improved living conditions in those communities.

In principle PES are based on voluntary agreements, which require that all stakeholders join because they see a value in the ecosystem services at stake. Moulded by her personal background and the corporate social responsibility debate, Echavarria is convinced of the business case for ecosystem conservation. A voluntary solution to a collective action problem may, however, result in a substantial degree of free-riding by private sector stakeholders, as in the case of FONAG. This clearly is a limit to the practical use of voluntary PES.

Echavarria's pragmatic approach to stakeholder engagement and adaptation of the concept is effective in establishing water funds. However, it is rather open regarding the concrete engagement and representation of upstream land users and hence does not fill the lacuna of the PES concept regarding environmental governance as a political process. This deserves reconsideration.

Echavarria's role as a consultant characterizes her achievements. While not all her advice is heeded and materialized in the water funds she supports, her experience of working with different initiatives has enlarged her expertise. This expertise makes her a good disseminator of the water fund concept (and PES at large) in regional and international networks. Looking at her approach to watershed PES and the example of FONAG has helped us better understand the benefits and limits of PES as a tool in environmental governance embracing conservation and rural development.

NOTES

1. The relationship between ecosystem services and biodiversity is more complex than that and subject of an academic debate. It cannot be fully dealt with in the context of this chapter.
2. As a concept, PES has gained increasing recognition internationally since the publication of global assessments such as the Millennium Ecosystem Assessment (MA 2005) and The Economics of Ecosystems and Biodiversity (TEEB 2010).
3. Apart from this so-called 'Coasean' PES concept, there exists a 'Pigouvian' concept as present in governmental, national-level PES schemes. Since the former is of interest in the context of local-level water funds, we do not discuss the latter. For a good overview of these concepts and current literature on both see Matzdorf and Schomers (in press).
4. We do not discuss, for example, the relationship between ecosystem functions and services, questions of methods and their accuracy, issues of price formation (marginal utility vs. absolute value), cultural inappropriateness of a purely economic view of man–nature relationship and that of crowding out non-incentive-driven motivations for conservation.
5. A thorough analysis of these points of criticism is not possible here, but see for example Norgaard (2009), van Hecken and Bastiaensen (2010), Muradian et al. (2012).
6. Empresa Municipal de Agua Potable y Alcantarillado de Quito (EMAAP-Q) is the municipal water provider; Empresa Electrica de Quito (EEQ) is the local energy utility.
7. Some 130 000 hm^3 of water are available in the seven Amazonico water basins, while less than 17 000 hm^3 are received by the 72 Pacifico basins. By contrast, 90 per cent of national water demand accrues to the Pacifico side, where most of irrigated agriculture is located (UNDP EC, GoE 2007).
8. Incidentally, in 2000, at the time FONAG was formally established, another fund was set up in the province of Pimampiro; since Marta Echavarria was not directly involved

with the initiative, this is not being considered in the analysis. For details see Kauffman 2011.

9. In her view, it would be good if the communities joined the board – FONAG's decision-making body – as financial contributors, with consideration of their financial capacities, in order to resolve the potential conflict of interests that might arise when including beneficiaries in the decision-making (Echavarria 2011b).

10. In this context, Holland (2007) speaks of 'sustainable ecological capacity' as a meta-capability.

7. Musketeering for drinking water – Viva con Agua de St. Pauli

Jana Gebauer

7.1 INTRODUCTION

When we arrived in St. Pauli, Hamburg – supposedly the liveliest part of town – there was nothing but peace and quiet. We had just got off the train from Berlin and found ourselves in a sunny, relaxed idyll a stone's throw from Millerntor Stadium, home venue of the 'cult-club' FC St. Pauli (*talkin' football here*). Both district and club are widely known for their special sense of life – pointedly offbeat, open-minded and left-hearted, a shimmering fusion of fighting the bad and partying for good. However, at 10 a.m. on a weekday this sense of life is hard to discover. Why, then, were we there so early? We were meeting with an offspring of that sense of life, an initiative with the image of a flag-waving *fun guerrilla*, dedicated to fighting world thirst.

Viva con Agua de Sankt Pauli is a multi-faceted non-profit organization that aims at improving access to water and sanitation wherever this is severely limited or non-existent. Their motto 'Water for all and all for water' borrows from Dumas's musketeers and captures well the mission and spirit: access to clean water and sanitation shall be granted to everyone and everyone shall engage in this mission. Viva con Agua (VcA) mainly acts as a donation broker and income generator to realize *water for all*. With a targeted engagement in campaigning and fundraising in Germany, as well as a social business selling bottled water on the German market, VcA supports the international water projects of *Welthungerhilfe*, one of Germany's biggest private aid organizations, which has a history of 50 years in development cooperation. *All for water* refers to the way donations are collected and income is generated; VcA pursues an accentuated collaborative approach to mobilize, involve and enable as many supporters and skills as possible – as activists, donors, multipliers, investors and corporate partners. The *fun guerrilla* image stems from the formats VcA chooses to radiate joy and get people going, such as parties, sports events and whatever might work. VcA follows its very own *all-profit thinking* in all of its activities; everyone shall benefit one way or another. Along with water, of course, this means having fun, finding new friends, learning together and gaining a new zest for life.

Viva con Agua is a St. Pauli home-grown player. Initiated by the football club's then midfielder Benjamin Adrion, it grew out of St. Pauli's particular community spirit and managed to spread all over Germany, as well as to Austria, Switzerland and even Spain. This chapter aims to capture what VcA itself calls the *VcA cosmos*. After giving a short profile in Section 7.2, we will introduce VcA's general approach to change in Section 7.3. In Section 7.4 we will give an overview of VcA's international water projects in collaboration with Welthungerhilfe. In Section 7.5 we will describe the different approaches VcA is developing to raise money for water projects and to mobilize and sensitize its target group in Germany. Relating to our theses described in Chapter 1, we will then assess VcA's innovativeness (Section 7.6) and its approach to scaling (Section 7.7); in Sections 7.8 and 7.9 we will evaluate VcA's sustainability contribution and its legitimacy, respectively. In the final section we expand on what we gained from this analysis.

The analysis presented in this chapter draws on semi-structured interviews with VcA staff, partners and supporters in 2010, 2012 and 2013 as well as desktop research. Notably, VcA provided us with access to its intranet. We also analysed the transcripts of interviews and the results of an online survey conducted by our colleagues in the course of the SESAM project.[1] Finally, our desktop research includes open information originating from websites, social media and general media.

7.2   BIG BANG FOR A NETWORK – VIVA CON AGUA'S BEGINNINGS

At a 2005 sports camp in Cuba, Hamburg's then third-division football club (FC) St. Pauli prepared for the season. Midfielder Benjamin Adrion's attention, however, was also caught by the drinking-water problems in the country. Back in Germany Adrion did some research and partnered with Welthungerhilfe; first fundraising and publicity successes led to water dispensers for 153 Cuban kindergartens and four sports schools within one year. These results, and the fact that injuries limited Adrion's future prospects as a professional football player, mingled in a primeval soup that would bear the concept of an open network of supporters.

Fuelled by the strong commitment and support of the St. Pauli community – in particular by the FC's players, fans and friendly artists – the network expanded rapidly with ever more fundraising activities, such as charity runs, book readings, concerts and festivals. In 2006 the

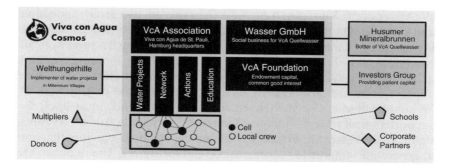

Figure 7.1   The Viva con Agua Cosmos

VcA network was acknowledged as a registered non-profit association; since this time, decentralized cells and local crews[2] have spread all over Germany. After a 'Water March' to Basel, the first non-German cell was founded in Switzerland in April 2009, which eventually grew into a second association – VcA Switzerland. Subsequently, local crews in Austria (Vienna and Innsbruck) were added. In March 2011 the first and so far only non-German-speaking cell was launched in Barcelona, Spain. Instead of expanding further in Spain and throughout Europe, however, VcA's current priority is the stabilization of the network in the German-speaking world.

Over time VcA has developed a varied and interwoven organizational structure. Its centre is the fundraising network, which is made up of more than 3000 volunteers. To complement the fundraising with market-based income, a social business was established in 2010. *Wasser GmbH* is to sell a brand of bottled spring water, *Viva con Agua Quellwasser*, on the German market. The business collaborates with the regional bottler *Husumer Mineralbrunnen* and is backed by long-term supporters-cum-investors. The major part of its profits serves the same purpose as the donations, to finance the water projects of Welthungerhilfe. Along with the business and the investors group, a separate charitable foundation was set up to ensure that VcA's priority is in the common good and to support their long-term survivability.[3] A set of formal rules applies to decision making and money transfer that connects the organizational units of VcA.

7.3   VIVA CON AGUA'S APPROACH TO CHANGE

'Viva con Agua's aim is to bring about positive change through social engagement and through triggering developments in the right direction'

(VcA website[4]). Viva con Agua seeks change on two levels: individual and systemic. On the individual level, people's living conditions are to be improved by changes on the ground in technical infrastructure, hygienic conditions and behaviour; changes that sustainably improve people's access to safe water and sanitation in affected regions (water for all). These improvements are facilitated by directly supporting the project work of Welthungerhilfe in the WASH sector.[5] Also on the individual level, the supporters shall receive 'millions of impulses' (Benjamin Adrion, VcA initiator, CEO Wasser GmbH, 2010) through the manifold activities that aim at generating support for water projects (all for water). The impulses are supposed to trigger changes in people's mindsets as well as in their everyday behaviour, be it in their roles as activists, donors, students, consumers or business partners. These changes relate to people's awareness for water issues and for their own scope of action. VcA's slogan 'You are the drop'[6] suggests without moral pressure that every person can become involved and contribute to social betterment; moreover, the initiative stresses that it can be easy and even fun to engage. VcA's goal is to instil the idea of self-initiative and engagement in young people's minds so that they themselves may become change makers with the claimed prospect of a future sustainable society. Starting from where the people are, VcA wants to spread its mission and spirit on the grassroots level in order to create 'a better mood' among people (Benjamin Adrion, 2010). VcA is aware that not every well built is guaranteed to become a long-term success; the ultimate goal therefore is changing people's mindsets and behaviour (Michael Fritz, VcA co-founder, head of actions, 2013).

The second sphere to change for VcA is on the systemic level. Its fundraising work at first sight seems to fit into the established global system of donor-beneficiary relations; upon closer look, however, VcA aims to inspire change here. In VcA's view, a major shortcoming of the current system of development cooperation is that it generally leaves out options for local activism and engagement in the recipient countries, thereby missing the chance for an advanced conception of 'help to self-help 3.0 or 4.0' (Michael Fritz 2013). VcA would highly welcome, for instance, a VcA network in Uganda.

VcA also wants to induce change in both the business and charity sectors by introducing a different approach to business ownership and profit allocation. Using its Wasser GmbH as an example it wants to prove, first, that a business may successfully be owned and governed by non-profits. In this sense, VcA suggests that rather than just cross-financing isolated social activities, companies could consider establishing a non-profit organization that receives shares of the respective company so that it *actively* benefits from any financial business success (André Lau, sales manager, Wasser GmbH, 2013). The message to non-profit organizations has a slightly different ring: when they establish a social business, they must hold the *majority* of shares in order to ensure true ownership and power of decision (ibid.). Second, VcA wants to stand up to cause-related market-ing[7] and shareholders-only perspectives (Benjamin Adrion 2012) and show that not only some but a significant part of the profits may be transferred to projects that address social problems.

To bring about these changes, VcA pursues a flexible mix of approaches that builds on the four pillars of the association (water projects, network, actions and education), the social business and the foundation. This is where social entrepreneurship comes into play, which is explicitly seen as an attitude of not confining oneself to just one way of doing things (Benjamin Adrion 2010). One should be eager to continuously develop further tools and approaches, for instance exploring new fundraising potentials, tapping new resources for income or enabling and educating people. Collaboration is crucial for all the approaches and their respective activities. VcA sees itself above all as a networker, communicator, facilita-tor and enabler who mediates resources, skills, information and contacts to support those activities that best serve the joint mission. 'We are experts in connecting and activating, that's what we do, [that is] social contagion so to say, building a self-sustaining community. That's our expertise and we very strongly cultivate this' (Benjamin Adrion 2012).

7.4   WATER FOR ALL – VIVA CON AGUA'S ENGAGEMENT IN INTERNATIONAL WATER PROJECTS

Viva con Agua's founding objective is to substantially improve access to clean drinking water and sanitary facilities in so-called developing countries. In many of these countries, an already existent state of natural water stress with scarce and shrinking freshwater resources is exacerbated by demographic pressure, environmental contamination, missing water infrastructure and underdeveloped water governance. In addition, climate change, droughts and lack of financial capital are aggravating these dra-matic situations in many parts of the world. Alongside the lack of access to any (let alone safe) drinking water sources, insufficient sanitary and hygienic conditions present further challenges. Underdeveloped sanitary systems as well as the lack of wastewater treatment and public hygiene result in water-borne diseases (UN 2012, p. 104).

The United Nations (UN) has acknowledged the vital necessity of improving drinking water supply and sanitary conditions and made it a binding responsibility of the world community. On 28 July 2010 the UN adopted a resolution recognizing access to clean water and sanitation as a human right. Moreover, the UN's Millennium Development Goal (MDG) 7-C sets out to '[h]alve, by 2015, the proportion of the population without sustainable access to safe drinking water and basic sanitation'.[8] Achievement of this goal can only partly be affirmed. Global access to safe drinking water has indeed been increased in the last two decades from 76 per cent in 1990 to 89 per cent in 2010 (UNICEF and World Health Organization 2012, p. 55) thus meeting the target 'five years ahead of schedule' (ibid. 2). Closer examination, however, shows notable differences between world regions as well as urban and rural areas. In Sub-Saharan Africa, for instance, coverage raised from a very low rate of 49 per cent in 1990 to no more than 61 per cent in 2010 with a significant difference between urban (83 per cent) and rural areas (49 per cent) (ibid. 55).

The sanitation target of providing 77 per cent of the world population with improved sanitation by 2015 will most likely not be met as only 63 per cent were reached in 2010 (ibid. 54). Only about 56 per cent of the population in so-called developing countries was using some form of improved sanitation in 2010 (ibid.). Again, Sub-Saharan Africa belongs to the region with the least coverage (30 per cent) and there is a significant difference between urban (43 per cent) and rural (23 per cent) populations (ibid.). Consequently, Sub-Saharan Africa is of highest priority to VcA's water projects.

There are various NGOs already active in the respective regions; VcA aims to avoid redundancies by collaborating with Welthungerhilfe in the implementation of water projects (Christian Wiebe, VcA co-founder, head of water projects and PR, 2013). Primarily fighting global hunger and poverty, Welthungerhilfe also provides water and sanitation services with a number of WASH projects. By raising awareness and funds, VcA supports the implementation of WASH projects in Welthungerhilfe's so-called *millennium villages* (a term that refers to the UN Millennium Declaration). Within the first seven years, VcA has raised about 2 million euros and financed 17 water projects in 14 countries.[9] VcA claims to have thus improved the living conditions of 200000 people.[10] With nine locations out of 17, the main geographic focus of the projects was on Sub-Saharan Africa. Other important regions were Middle and South America as well as South East Asia. For the project period 2012–2015, VcA's geographic priorities still lie in Sub-Saharan Africa (especially East Africa) and have also extended to India and Nepal.

Welthungerhilfe provides VcA with project evaluations on a regular basis. Additionally, VcA representatives usually visit the water projects on-site to help form their own ideas of the specific situations, needs and improvements. Such trips are documented with photos and videos, which are broadly communicated via social media to complement project descriptions and status reports on the VcA website. Along with documenting progress and results, the trips also serve education, networking and publicity purposes by conveying the VcA spirit; football, art and music with the villagers are often part of the travel programme. The trips not only help to build closer connections and mutual understanding, they also strengthen the commitment in the villages thereby supporting the projects' long-term sustainability (Anke Mattern, advisor, Welthungerhilfe, 2013). The efforts of VcA as both a fundraiser and a communicator in the villages add to Welthungerhilfe's implementation services and are greatly valued by the NGO that in turn provides start-up funding for VcA (ibid.). We will describe the actual fundraising work of VcA in the next section, as well as its activities in education and the social business.

7.5   ALL FOR WATER – VIVA CON AGUA'S APPROACH TO RAISING MONEY AND AWARENESS

Viva con Agua as a fundraiser aims at the target group of 14 to 30 years old and in doing so tries to overcome narrow views of charity work, which it thinks hinder younger people from becoming donors. VcA explicitly allows or rather calls for micro-donations and offers a broad range of options for customized involvement both of which fits in well with the general resources and interests of this target group. Furthermore, VcA claims that while seriously helping others, one can still have fun and even personally benefit. VcA likes to characterize its special style as a combination of 'having fun, being creative [. . . and] being able to actually realize unusual ideas' (Christian Wiebe 2010). As familiar to social entrepreneurship, VcA also emphasizes the idea 'to not simply be against something, but to actively engage in something together with others' (Benjamin Adrion 2010). The initiative considers itself consequently not a conventional fundraiser but a social platform to tease out the creativity and self-initiative in young people. In the following, we will describe how VcA puts this approach into action and how it generates additional income with its social business.

Network 'n' Action – Fun Ways to Raise Funds

The beating heart of VcA is the activists' network. In 2013 there were ten cells and 19 local crews in Germany and Austria, two cells and three local crews in Switzerland and one cell in Spain.[11] The cells and crews form a vivid network made up mostly of young, urban student activists who feel attracted by VcA's spirit. By living this spirit – that is, organizing creative, cultural and sportive events to have fun while raising money and awareness for the needs of those who are worse off – the activists attract ever more young people as supporters and donors (Marcel Siewert, VcA board member, 2010).

Becoming a VcA donor is as easy as having a drink at a festival and throwing the empty cup into a VcA bin (or at the artists on stage!). By not raking in the deposit, the donor enables VcA to hand over funds to Welthungerhilfe. To become a supporter is also comparably low-threshold; one might start by carrying the VcA bin and collecting the deposit cups. Any further engagement may be arranged according to time and interest – one can jump from level to level, just like in a computer game, to become a keen activist or remain an occasional supporter (Michael Fritz 2013).

VcA approaches its main target group in places where its members spend a lot of time, and it does this with activities and events the members enjoy – for example clubs, street parties, festivals, concerts, football matches and so-called hitchhiking contests. During the past few years VcA has expanded its target group by broadening its spectrum of activities to appeal to a somewhat older audience – for example readings at theatres and water-literature contests (Christian Wiebe 2010). Altogether, the commitment of the cells and crews can be described as very active. According to VcA, cells and local crews engage in about 425 actions per year (Christian Wiebe 2013) and there was more than 670 000 euros worth of micro-donations in 2011.[12,13]

While the attractiveness of the VcA network first lies in the spontaneity and ease with which supporters can get started – 'clear of obstacles, club nonsense, membership fees and endless discussions' (Christian Wiebe 2010) – its main asset is that it allows for personal development by means of continuous engagement. This holds true for the supporters at the events as well as for all the artists, bands, festival organizers and club owners who feature prominently in VcA activities. FC St. Pauli not only supported the very first hour, it is also a constant official partner and investor; alongside the club, various musicians, artists, footballers and other celebrities joined as multipliers over the years. These actors make another part of the network and add a great deal to VcA's brand awareness by means of benefit concerts, football matches, art auctions, dedicated songs and plenty of free publicity (they even seem to enjoy getting empty cups thrown at them). Notably, some of these celebrities jointly established the VcA foundation. In addition, many companies – outfitters, banks, publishers, studios, agencies, and so on – act as sponsors or work pro bono for VcA. They support VcA for example with cars, merchandise, design work, photo and video shoots.

Education – Viva con Agua's Activists Learn and Teach

We have only touched on VcA's educational work briefly so far; we now go into detail about this relevant pillar of the association. Educational work for VcA has an internal and external dimension of knowledge transfer and activation. Internally, fundraisers first need to be informed about the projects for which they want to raise funds. What is the situation in the region, the plan of the project and the financial support needed? Beyond that, basic knowledge on broader water issues such as water privatization, water conflicts and virtual water are imparted to supporters, for example in network meetings.

While this water knowledge is also available on the VcA website for the general public, there is an even farther-reaching approach to external educational work. From almost the outset, VcA offers a variety of programmes and activities to schools first and foremost, as well as to kindergartens, universities and other educational institutions. These offers usually relate to the work of VcA, namely global water problems, experiences gained during visits to VcA's water projects and opportunities for engagement. VcA's activities in schools, for instance, include workshops, lectures, photo exhibitions and film screenings. The educational work at schools principally involves interactive and activating elements, which are said to reach far beyond a teacher's traditional position and access to kids (Hauke Schremmer, staff, education, 2013). Not knowing all the answers now, jointly posing the right questions while experimenting on concrete solutions (for example water filters) is VcA's way to let kids experience easy and fun ways to be part of a larger process of change. Cooperations with schools are medium to long term, thus allowing for lasting partnerships and development processes. Schools are also involved in VcA's fundraising activities, for example via charity runs where the kids, with the support of teachers, friends and families, try to win donations depending on the number of completed rounds. Charity runs are dedicated to specific water projects and are prepared accordingly. To provide proof that their engagement indeed has an impact, participants learn about how the respective water project improves people's lives in the villages. Unlike most established NGOs, VcA activists experience a very direct accessibility to schools and kids; the students are attracted by the young, relaxed, authentic appearance, the hipness factor, as well as by VcA's method, which involves no textbooks but fun, stories, sports and crafts. To manage the many inquiries received from schools all over Germany, VcA has developed its own training concept for activists. This concept consists of a modular training course, which enables VcA supporters (of age) to teach different water programmes at schools in their region.

So far, the educational programmes mainly focus on the international dimension of water and aim to raise awareness for the fact that clean drinking water is a precious and threatened resource (Christian Wiebe 2010). Beyond that, VcA also wants to draw more attention to local water issues such as the water quality of rivers and lakes (Hauke Schremmer 2013). Only 10 per cent of Germany's surface waters have achieved the 'good' or 'very good' ecological status that is required by the European Water Framework Directive (BMU 2010, p. 22). VcA therefore aims to relate its future educational activities – at schools and within the network itself – to the need to act locally (Hauke Schremmer 2013).

Wasser GmbH – Bottling Water for the Good Cause

Viva con Agua established a social business – Wasser GmbH – next to the association we described above. VcA's business aims to broaden revenue streams and also to reach out to older or less event-oriented people (Marcel Siebert 2010). The business idea, however, was not welcomed enthusiastically by a number of activists and was criticized mainly for being an attempt to privatize water (Christian Wiebe 2013). Such criticisms were discussed within the network and as a consequence, restrictive conditions were imposed: the initial emphasis on drinking tap water shall remain first priority and there shall be no destructive competitive conduct (André Lau 2013). Under these terms, the brand *VcA Quellwasser* was introduced as an additional, second-choice option; if you have to drink bottled water, you may now pick a brand that supports water for all (ibid.).

VcA's collaborative approach also becomes apparent here as Wasser GmbH itself is not the bottler but cooperates with a regional mineral water company. This North-German company, Husumer Mineralbrunnen (HM), bottles and sells VcA Quellwasser on its own accounts; it also takes over administrative tasks (Reinhold Seidel, owner-manager, Husumer Mineralbrunnen, 2013). Wasser GmbH is responsible for marketing and sales – and of course branding. By cooperating with HM, Wasser GmbH gains know-how and profound market knowledge and is able to perform well on the market (André Lau 2013). Most importantly, VcA does not bear any financial risks in this partnership because Wasser GmbH makes no investments of its own and has only a few expenses for staff costs, marketing and sales (ibid.). For its income, Wasser GmbH receives a monthly licence-fee based on sales from its production partner.[14]

Benjamin Adrion of VcA and Reinhold Seidel of HM jointly manage Wasser GmbH. Longstanding supporters of VcA committed themselves as social investors and provided the starting capital. HM belongs to this group of investors; furthermore, the company periodically invests, for example in new bottles and crates (Reinhold Seidel 2013). The investors' interests are bundled and represented by an additionally established, limited commercial partnership that holds 40 per cent of the shares and receives 40 per cent of any profits. To ensure that the business continuously serves the common good, the majority of the shares were transferred from the investors to the non-profits. The German VcA association as a legal entity holds 20 per cent of the shares and provides the network and spirit; the VcA foundation holds another 40 per cent and provides the brand. Both organizations receive percentages of the profits according to the size of their shares, which are in turn transferred directly to the water projects.[15] Moreover, ownership and the power of decision stay within non-profit organizations.

This form of ownership where the majority of shares is held by non-profits is highly relevant for VcA's credibility. It also ensures long-term perspective and stability as it prevents significant changes in majority interest (André Lau 2013). Not least, the ownership is a key factor in sales conversations with prospective customers; it helps VcA's sales department challenge traditional business habits (ibid.). This not only relates to profit allocation but also to listing fees, free products or advertising subsidies, all of which are seen to represent destructive competitive conduct and therefore are a no-go for VcA (ibid.). Since this constitutes a material breach of business customs, sales persons need the backing of the common good interest. Indeed, it makes a forceful argument in sales conversations to refer to the requirements of an association with roughly 3000 supporters who all consider this alternative business conduct a premise for preventing reputational damage to VcA (ibid.). Social businesses that are owned by private persons who are at least to some degree acting in their own benefit and interest have a much weaker position vis-à-vis a purchaser in this regard.

Buyers of VcA Quellwasser are conscious consumers who want to support the good cause (Reinhold Seidel 2013): beverage stores, cafés, bars, and so on, that serve the alternative milieus, as well as beverage markets, commercial beverage wholesalers, large gastronomies and hotels that are beginning to respond to changes in consumer behaviour and seek competitive differentiation and exclusivity (André Lau 2013). VcA's approach to these actors, again, does not follow common business practices: when talking to retailers, for instance, it does not insist on selling its own water; rather it encourages discontinuing any bottled water that comes from places where drinking water is scarce; in gastronomy as another example, VcA does not insist on the exclusiveness of its product (ibid.).

Now that Quellwasser has been part of the VcA cosmos for a couple of years, 'it's almost not possible to imagine [VcA] without it' (Tobias Rau, VcA co-founder, head of network, 2013). While being a great possibility for a charity organization to broaden its financial resources, VcA Quellwasser seems especially convincing as an effective communication tool that helps to reach many more people than networking and campaigning alone. Every bottle a flyer – and with that a 'fantastic multiplier' (Christian Wiebe 2013). People who buy VcA Quellwasser can learn about the mission from the label and also learn easy ways to get involved. Once people get to know and like VcA Quellwasser, so the idea goes, this vehicle could deliver more and more messages (André Lau 2013). The first step just taken is to draw people's attention to drinking more tap water by placing a refill logo on the bottle – yet another market-provoking idea even with the small scale of this business.[16]

VcA Quellwasser is also attracting new partners from the business community, to which NGOs typically have only limited access. VcA points to the fact that many times intermediate or ultimate customers also became donors, sponsors or pro bono supporters (ibid.). Quellwasser is regarded as the new ace-striker in the VcA team, 'scoring the goals . . . we wouldn't have scored otherwise' (Tobias Rau 2013). However, just as the goal scorer is nothing without the team, VcA Quellwasser is nothing without the VcA association and its network of supporters. In the end it is just another merchandising tool, though a good one (André Lau 2013). As VcA sees it, the work of Wasser GmbH is enabling the fulfilment of the overall mission, but VcA itself would still work without it (Michael Fritz 2013).

7.6 INNOVATIVENESS – THE VIVA CON AGUA BLEND

'Viva con Agua is no traditional NGO – Viva con Agua is out of the ordinary!' (VcA website).[17] What is claimed here self-confidently at first glance seems to be justified; VcA appears to be a big mixer, blending customs, communities and formats into a *let's-do-it-differently* approach. Nonetheless, as the initiative grows and undergoes processes of professionalization and stabilization, it also draws on long-known conventional instruments such as membership fees, Christmas donations or classic foundation business. Moreover, there are organizations that are on a similar track as VcA.[18] We look now at the genuine ideas and approaches of VcA that speak for its innovativeness.

Action-oriented Fundraising – An Approach to Reach and Mobilize the Young

Germans donate about 4 billion euros to charities each year, with an average of 29 euros per donation. Donations are primarily collected via advertising letters or via regular payments of members. Established non-profit organizations sometimes address young people via separate youth groups in order to foster political and environmental education, but usually not in order to collect donations. Indeed, more than half of those who donate regularly over a longer period of time are above 60. Young people under 30 donate only occasionally, if at all. People in their 20s and 30s also make up the fewest number of volunteers (all numbers from Deutscher Spendenrat and GfK 2012).

VcA's innovativeness therefore first lies in successfully reaching a new target group for charity by involving young folks in its fundraising activities. Second, according to this target group's financial possibilities, VcA extends fundraising to micro-donations. Third, VcA does this without advertising letters or appeals to people's 'bad conscience'; instead, VcA approaches and motivates future supporters directly through positive messages. Not least, VcA calls for personal initiative to collect donations (see Section 7.5). By establishing a fundraising and campaigning network not only *for* but also especially *of* young people, VcA opens up this group for volunteer work. With yearly rising numbers in supporters and donations, the concept so far is proving to meet a demand of the present zeitgeist, one that is yet unfulfilled.

Open Networking – A Social Platform for Joint Engagement

Unlike charities that bulk-mail transfer slips occasionally, VcA's focus is on the individual supporter and his or her deeds and needs. The claim 'You are the drop' points to the importance of individual step-by-step actions that eventually add up to large-scale changes. This call for personal initiative is clearly publicly perceived. The majority of 334 respondents of an online survey among VcA Facebook followers in 2011 said that their engagement with VcA made them more actively involved with social and environmental issues.[19]

The individual VcA supporter is embedded in a network of personal relations and interactions; this is quite a contrast to those charities that merely provide an online platform for DIY-activism. This real-world network should provide not only more guidance and exchange, but also friendship, community spirit and even a 'family'. Our interviews and VcA discussions at network meetings show that these are indeed explicit motivations for people to join VcA. As the network grows, however, it naturally experiences limits in how personal it can become among members of decentralized units. For example, ties between the headquarters in Hamburg and local crews at the outer edges seem to be rather loose; this assessment was voiced by a crew representative as being not only a matter of geography but also of discriminating between cells and local crews.

Action First – The Promise of Boundless Possibility

Another one of VcA's innovative traits is its focus on actions and activation. Subordinate to this is a sensitizing to create a deeper understanding of the societal challenges addressed and the possible solutions required. This approach differs clearly from the more content-driven lobby organizations, where the message comes first. VcA's laid-back attitude is a matter of principle, to not crash the party until just the right time. Meanwhile, VcA confidently relies on the perceived contagiousness of this concept.

Nevertheless, VcA is intrinsically highly pressurized to come up with ever-newer events and formats that can be connected to its mission. There are indeed key innovations like the cup campaign (see Section 7.5) and the Millerntor Gallery,[20] both of which opened new ways into a system to introduce a societal concern. While the cup campaign seemed obvious and 'only' required a large-scale format that was recognizable and fun, the gallery is an example of how two normally separate contexts – art exhibitions and football stadiums – can be linked by a joint social mission.

Linking various contexts and formats while introducing the donation aspect has become a central pattern of Viva con Agua's work. In this manner, VcA calls for the decentralized, context-specific imitation and adaptation of ideas and activities, as well as for their constant renewal and recombination. There is still plenty of room for creativity here. Yet there also seems to be a tendency to merely modify and relabel any format and activity that has not already been used for (water-related) fundraising purposes. While this is a perfectly worthwhile endeavour, the danger is in becoming arbitrary. This can happen especially if more people are consuming the actions rather than actually developing and organizing them (thus separating donation and personal initiative, see Section 7.5), and if actions are merely following the rationale of a social compensation for the donating guests instead of delivering messages (thus primarily activating for fun(d)raising while missing out the awareness part). Guidelines have been developed in 2012 to support the selection and design of activities; however, these things require continuous refinement in regards to the above-mentioned concerns.

A Collaborative Approach – Mission-centred and Out for All-profit

What is also very innovative about VcA is its accentuated collaborative approach that aims at co-generating and sharing benefits with its supporters and partners. In fact, the apparent success of its open network shows VcA as a platform expert who promotes personal relationships and dynamic interactions. Moreover, stemming from an interest in a division of labour based on core competencies, collaboration is the design pattern for each of the activities VcA performs. While other (water-related) initiatives also pursue a division of labour – for instance, fundraising and communication on the one hand with development cooperation on the other – VcA additionally established multiple relations with a variety of partners for different roles. The common basis is the shared mission (water for all), personal relationships and VcA's all-profit thinking. This last point – *everyone shall benefit* – is unique in its explicitness as a general goal and is regarded as highly relevant to VcA's attractiveness. The concept still needs more clarification as to what are the expectations of all parties involved and the tangible and intangible profits generated (see Section 7.7).

A Social Business in the Hands of Two Non-profits and Their 3000 Friends

The social business Wasser GmbH is a recent development by VcA to better serve the charity purpose of the association. The fact that Wasser GmbH now operates in the black illustrates the successful introduction of a social business concept into the realm of conventional consumer goods. However, the German beverage industry has experienced several alternative start-ups in recent years;[21] some of these companies are role models for VcA. Nevertheless, VcA's ownership and governance structure mark a distinct difference with respect to these mostly manager-owned businesses. In addition, while these alternative companies are often built around the idea of a product with an added social or environmental value, VcA Quellwasser was introduced long after the association was established. The bottled water will internally continue to be regarded as a means to the charitable end, not as an end in itself.[22] The outside perceptions of roles and priorities, as well as the actual multiplier effect of the bottled water, have not been assessed so far.

Summarising, Viva con Agua's activating way of fundraising, its variety of activities and approaches, its special combination of non-profit organizations with a social business, as well as its mission-centred all-profit approach to open networking and collaboration are innovative ideas both in the charity sector and in the context of social entrepreneurship – at least as far as water issues are concerned. While it does implement elements and formats that are new as such, VcA's innovativeness is mainly based on its unusual mix of imitated, adapted and new elements and formats to answer the challenge – how can we raise support for water projects and get young folks actively involved? Although there are several organizations and initiatives that work with comparable elements and formats, the difference mainly lies in the overall picture of VcA. So far, the driving intent to impact systemic change is limited to sending impulses and leading by example to challenge and overcome certain charity and business customs. This call for change is not yet specified in the large set-up, as in the daily implementation; thus this intent still needs to be further operationalized and approached more concretely.

7.7   VIVA CON AGUA'S APPROACH TO SCALING – DEEP AMBITIONS

'[T]he vision for 2020 [is] to be an NGO that is operating as well as known throughout Germany' (Christian Wiebe 2010); '[a] real network in permanent growth constantly generating new synergies . . . and finally becoming an international network' (Benjamin Adrion 2010). With these visions for 2020, VcA clearly shows ambitions for the broad societal level according to our scaling thesis. What looks like a straight pro-growth statement of the organization on the surface contains some more nuanced messages. VcA's mix of strategies and approaches to scaling mirrors the mix of strategies and approaches to its work.

Drop by Drop, Steady but Slowly

Growth is of course a relevant category for VcA as the initiative wants to mobilize ever more people and to support as many water projects as possible. Within the last two years, the VcA headquarters underwent processes of growth and formalization, for example regarding employment relationships. Yet it is primarily the self-initiated cells and local crews that will bring about VcA's expansion as a network.

People who feel attracted by the VcA mission and spirit are invited to establish their own decentralized group of supporters. These groups are officially subordinated to the headquarters in Hamburg, from where the larger picture is drawn and to where the money flow is channelled. Hamburg, however, exercises only limited central control. This applies especially to the local crews, which are under little regulation (see Section 7.2). When it comes to the cells, as the official representatives of VcA, there is an agreement on rights and duties between the headquarters and cell representatives that shows features of a social franchising relationship as a long-term, binding cooperation (cf. Hackl 2009, p. 42). In line with this, the headquarters provides documents on standard procedures, 'how-to' guidelines for standard actions, equipment, merchandise, flyers, profiles on water projects, and so on. Both cells and local crews can draw on the knowledge and experience VcA has already acquired so that the speed of successfully establishing a new group can be increased and the risk of failure lowered (Bradach 2003, p. 20).

While this analogy refers to typical benefits of franchising, it should only be weakly stressed. Process standardization, prototyping and obligations hardly match the VcA spirit and the character of VcA's management approach. The headquarters' rationale is rather to offer a platform to make it easy for people to engage in volunteer work where personal relations come first and 'outcome' is about generating new relationships, friendships and synergies that bear *their own* dynamics, innovativeness and creativity. The headquarters is leaving room for trial and error; it merely wants to facilitate the mutual exchange of experiences and lessons learned.

Nevertheless, in 2012 VcA started a systematic process of structural and cultural self-reflexion and development in order to consolidate a sounder basis for the initiative in its entirety (see Section 7.4). As a result, network guidelines and process requirements were explicated, with corresponding tools and templates developed. Notwithstanding the above, the exchange between headquarters and support groups is now approached in a more standardized and systematic way. This outcome actually matches the articulated needs of supporters and it may already better answer the purpose of a guiding and facilitating platform service for a growing network. On the other side, however, as the network expands and gains momentum, both weaker personal ties and stronger headquarters interventions may pose the threat of trading off the idea of decentralized autonomy for the essence of VcA's mission-related brand or vice versa.

VcA's answer to this threat is another outcome of the above-mentioned self-reflexive development process: any further expansion of the network shall be achieved in a controlled and healthy – that is, limited – way. Presently, the stabilization and interconnection of the current VcA groups and regions is more important than pure cell spreading. In strengthening the quality of the network's relationships and interactions, they seek to prevent mission-drift as well as over-formalizing.

Network by Network, yet All as One

It was in 2008 when the seeds for another entire network were planted. VcA Switzerland can be regarded as a step-by-step replication of the basic principles of the German association and its adaptation to the (German-speaking) Swiss context.[23] As regards to structure, only two of the four VcA pillars were established right from the beginning: *actions* to raise funds for *water projects* that are in turn implemented by Helvetas, a Swiss pendant to Welthungerhilfe. The other two pillars, *network* and *education*, were put on the agenda in 2012–2013. Stabilization has become a key goal for VcA Switzerland, which corresponds to the idea of establishing VcA as *one* network in the German-speaking world. The success of creating a recognizable core based on all four pillars is a precondition for any further developments; VcA Switzerland follows VcA Germany in this regard (Gregor Anderhub, VcA Switzerland, 2013).

VcA Switzerland was set up in a social franchise manner where standard procedures, guidelines, lessons learned, and so on, were transferred and adapted. At the same time, a non-contractual but close mentoring relationship prevailed on the basis of strong personal ties with Hamburg, which had an additional effect of joint development work for the entire network. As this closeness was apparently essential for the success in Switzerland, the quality of network relations may prove to become a crucial factor in VcA's scaling process. VcA therefore needs to pay attention to establishing strong personal ties and close cooperation within the network when implementing current plans to establish an Austrian association (Austrian crews so far belong to the German VcA network) and to reach out to South Tyrol.

Broadening Perspectives, Concepts and Revenues

The increase in network coverage and quality is only one way VcA chooses to scale. Another way is VcA's diversification of activities. Here too, quality precedes quantity. This motto applies especially to the fact that VcA remains open to learning and feedback and that it continuously revises and expands its perspectives and concepts. This kind of learning along the way results in a more holistic approach in realizing its mission. The initial focus on drinking water for projects was broadened by consistently including sanitation aspects; the teaching concept was developed to more systematically approach the next generations; the focus on international water problems was complemented by a view on local water-quality problems; and in the short and medium term, the cooperation with Welthungerhilfe is being expanded to strengthen the empowerment of target groups via joint educational work.

There are other diversification processes that aim at generating more financial support for the water projects, such as earned income and long-term donations. Such developments affect both institutional and target-group variability, and eventually contribute to the long-term sustainability of the initiative (Uvin and Miller 1994, p. 16). However, VcA has somewhat limited ambitions regarding quantitative growth. For instance, like any other, the business needs to achieve a certain sales volume to operate in the black. Beyond that, VcA seeks only small-scale growth.[24] Limitless further increase of sales is not considered necessary thanks to both the social investors' patient engagement and bottler's licence model, which takes the financial risk off Wasser GmbH. By introducing the refill option for the bottles, all sides might even take the (probably negligible) risk of declining sales. Apart from the investors welcoming a return of the initial investment, there are no further profit expectations, at least not on the bottler's side. However, the social business has only now started to generate profits and still needs to prove capable of doing so over a longer period of time, as much as the investors have to prove their willingness to patiently forgo significant financial returns in exchange for social impact.

Also, the role of the social business as a vehicle to generate income, to transport the mission and to lead by example still needs some clarification. Developments so far all seem to be accepted and appreciated, but opportunities as well as risks and conflicts of aims cannot be anticipated without a concise scaling strategy and approach. Very clear indeed is the absolute focus on water: since both the mission and name of the initiative is to *live with water* – not with cola or beer – VcA rejects offering a wider range of products. Finally and notably, all parties involved have agreed that the business will be terminated if it causes reputational damage to the association or if Germany faces a severe drinking water problem. Again, these ideas still need operationalization and monitoring.

Organizational Development

Viva con Agua started with a clear-cut mission and some cornerstones of an organizational profile and structure; the rest was left open to further developments. After going through a long phase of trial and error – learning by doing and partnering, so to say – VcA began to channel those developments more systematically. As mentioned above, last year VcA started an in-depth process of structural and cultural self-reflexion and development. This process aims at capturing and stabilizing the status quo whilst working on visions and ways of further development. Its intended practical effects are to establish organizational structures and routines that allow for an increase in systematic mutual learning and feedback to better use internal expertise and to create internal redundancies, as well as for a continuous refinement and improvement of ideas, strategies and approaches. VcA aims to be in a position to meet specific challenges that are being or will be posed, for example by dynamic decentralized growth, increased public attention or even the imminent generation change (more specifically, the fact that the generation of founders and long-term supporters will soon be growing out of the young target group).

To rise up to such challenges, VcA representatives at their 2013 network-meeting called for a more stable and healthier organization. They outlined this aim with the following approaches: to take the long view and go easy on their resources; to prefer quality over quantity and build on what already exists; to maintain and deepen networks and partnerships; to emphasize the mission as opposed to individual persons; to share responsibilities and promote the young generation; to facilitate participation, know-how transfer, best-practice learning and internal education; and not least, to assure commitment, quality, monitoring and transparency. Within the next 30 years, so the formulated vision aims, VcA should grow into a thick tree instead of shooting forth only thin branches.

Concluding, VcA scales its idea at a broad societal level inasmuch as the network of volunteers is spreading throughout Germany and in other European countries, and its social business is set out to follow the same path by planning on cooperating with additional bottlers in further regions. Notwithstanding this pure increase in coverage, VcA in general clearly follows the so-called new paradigm of scaling (Uvin et al. 2000; see Chapter 1). For a start, VcA sets explicit limits to growth in its various fields of action and emphasizes instead processes of qualitative development. In this way VcA has developed over time a recognizable and replicable core by operationalizing and refining the blend of its mission (water for all) and approach (all for water).

Furthermore, collaboration is the key to VcA's ability to scale. It is the close cooperation with Welthungerhilfe that provides professional on-the-ground project work and Husumer Mineralbrunnen enables the production of VcA Quellwasser; both collaborators also support VcA's processes of learning and diversification. Additionally, VcA receives enormous support through (corporate) partners and multipliers. This proves to be extremely important in gaining additional resources and, above all, public awareness. It is these very diverse partnerships that significantly add to the very momentum VcA needs to multiply and scale at this level. Maintaining those partnerships and the corresponding benefits to VcA requires continuously investing in social relations; likewise, developing new partnerships, for example with another bottler or a would-be network, requires a focus on relationship building.

Finally, VcA puts a strong emphasis on changing its informal environment, to change people's mindsets and behaviour through different measures of raising awareness and mobilizing. VcA hereby avowedly attempts to create a self-sustaining society of people and organizations that shows initiative for the social cause. By laying the ground, it may in turn become easier for VcA to attract supporters and donors in the medium to long term. These effects, however, are hard to verify – as are the intended influences on business partners or 'the business world' in regards to responsible business conduct. It is thus all the more necessary to define corresponding aims and to explicate messages to scaling such that fundamental changes may come within reach. Though it is not intended so far, these messages might even lead to political lobbying and positioning.

7.8   SUSTAINABILITY EVALUATION

Viva con Agua is certainly a *getting-things-done* initiative. The important question for us is: is it also getting things done *sustainably*? Following our evaluative approach outlined in Chapter 1, we first discuss how VcA supports and protects certain human capabilities. We then analyse its contribution to environmental sustainability by taking the example of VcA's social business's partner company that bottles the Quellwasser. We will conclude this section by highlighting some of VcA's organizational characteristics.

Supporting Human Capabilities – Viva con Agua's All-profit Thinking

'Well, there are – just as individual as the people are – the most individual profits' (Tobias Rau 2013). Relating to its origin in football, VcA proclaims *fair play* within its network and partnerships; this is translated into fairly sharing any resulting benefits. All stakeholders along the value chain – especially but not exclusively the beneficiaries in the millennium villages – should profit from an increasing value, be it tangible or intangible. This *all-profit thinking* has been a core feature of VcA from the beginning. It has not, however, been operationalized beyond reiterating the nexus of 'help' and 'fun' within an 'open network'. In the following we take a closer look at VcA's all-profit thinking by reflecting on what could count as 'profit' from the point of view of beneficiaries and activists and by making reference to Nussbaum's (2001) set of capabilities.

The millennium villagers are VcA's initial target group, but they are only indirectly addressed by VcA's fundraising and campaigning work. However, VcA's financial support of Welthungerhilfe projects leads to concrete improvements of their living conditions; Welthungerhilfe regards WASH interventions as a central contribution to alleviating hunger and poverty (Welthungerhilfe 2013, p. 6). Welthungerhilfe has endorsed the WASH sustainability charter[25] and has recently developed an orientation framework to guide its WASH interventions (Welthungerhilfe 2013). Against this background, the water projects contribute for example to preventing child death owing to water-borne diseases, ensuring adequate nourishment, reducing illnesses caused by unsafe drinking water and inadequate sanitation, as well as protecting at-risk individuals (mostly girls and women) against (sexual) assault. The projects thus ideally support and protect the capabilities of *life, bodily health* and *bodily integrity*. The project work aims at help by enabling self-help and hence also touches on the capabilities *senses, imagination, thought* and *control over one's environment*, for example inasmuch as girls freed from collecting water can spend more time at school; in addition the project design includes capacity building (for example training of local technical staff), participation in decision making, as well as establishing and supporting communal institutions to secure operation and maintenance of the WASH services.

In addition to supporting the projects financially, VcA representatives also directly visit the affected villages (see Section 7.4). The way VcA representatives act and communicate on their project trips touches on further capabilities on the beneficiaries' side. The villagers experience (young) people from another continent caring about them, respecting, supporting and attaching to them, and – according to a Ugandan beneficiary[26] – exemplifying that self-initiative is possible for the local youth too. These aspects of VcA's work directly show short-term effects; deeper impacts on the support and protection of capabilities such as *emotions, affiliation* and *control over one's environment* can be expected, but so far cannot be pinned down. VcA's support and appearance in the villages, however, are seen to strengthen the people's commitment and ownership and are thus regarded as a crucial factor for the quality of the projects, especially when it comes to their long-term sustainability (Anke Mattern 2013). Indeed, according to VcA, all facilities that VcA has supported are still functioning and in use (Christian Wiebe 2013). Consequently, Welthungerhilfe and VcA agreed that VcA should become increasingly involved in the post-construction phase supporting the long-term operation, maintenance and administration of the implemented WASH services (Anke Mattern 2013).

As our interviews and VcA surveys from the network meeting in 2013 show, VcA staff and supporters indeed regard the *fun-and-help nexus* as a very relevant individual benefit, which in turn fuels their motivation to engage as VcA activists. With VcA they find ways and means to personally trigger social change in the project regions, as well as in their own environments. They feel the double benefit of helping and having fun at the same time. In addition, the social context of their activities creates another important aspect of their engagement. Staff and volunteers value getting to meet and work with like-minded people and making friends along the way. These personal relationships give them the experience of appreciation, respect, openness, tolerance, diversity and equality. People react to this with a strong commitment to and identification with the VcA community. The perceived social cohesion within the network can thus be regarded as another important individual profit that comes with the personal engagement. However, there seem to be structural limits to generating this profit, for instance, as connectedness and equality appear to diminish at the network's outer edges (see Section 7.6).

While these above effects were (however vaguely) expected and even aimed at from the beginning, there is another aspect that did not come to the fore until later. VcA is not only a social platform but also a learning one, where people get the chance to experiment and to develop and discover new skills. While often facilitated by the headquarters, this is to a great deal through learning by doing; people acquire practical know-how, organizational, communicative and management skills, as well as knowledge and real-life ideas related to MDG, water issues and development cooperation. Along with this expertise, activists especially stated they gained a lot of self- as well as social competence, experienced and used creative leeway, crossed both state and mental borders, obtained trust and confidence and learned that it is very possible to induce social change with an idea started by just a few friends.

Again following Nussbaum (2001) these aspects support, protect or represent the capabilities of *senses, imagination and thought, emotions, practical reason, affiliation* and *control over one's environment*. VcA representatives – staff as well as supporters – can freely choose and create their own ways and activities while engaging in various forms of social interaction. Respect, fairness, non-discrimination and friendship are pivotal here for creating meaningful relationships of mutual recognition and attachment, as well as for forming the social basis of self-respect. With respect to VcA's mission, this may support representatives in forming their own conception of the common good and in reflecting on where they want to go from there. Not least, facilitating self-initiative, free speech and association may foster the general exercise of the right to political participation.

While VcA supporters highly value that they are trusted almost instantly to take over responsibility, they also ask for more orientation through general standards, guidelines and templates, as well as for more mutual exchange and feedback. These aspects need to be further developed and consolidated in order to support the above-mentioned capabilities of empowerment. The current organizational development process takes note of this (see Section 7.4); however, it needs to be more explicit here and should integrate organizational learning and knowledge management into VcA's structure and routines. To prevent trading-off this focus on VcA's role as an enabler against the more mission-related profits of fun, help and social cohesion, VcA representatives need to define their profit expectations more clearly in order to address possible conflicts of interests. This process of clarifying and explicating tangible and intangible profit expectations should be extended to all partners and supporters in order for VcA to operationalize and evaluate the all-profit approach. Only in this way can VcA become fully accountable for its impact and value creation.

Environmental Sustainability – How Does Bottling Water Fit In?

'Yes, we care! Viva con Agua feels obliged not only to social but also to environmental values. Therefore, emphasis in the production and distribution of the water [VcA Quellwasser] is placed on treating nature as carefully as possible'.[27] In its self-conception (and also de facto), Viva con Agua is not an environmental organization. Environmental protection, however, is important for VcA as a crucial factor of the projects' functionality and long-term sustainability (Welthungerhilfe 2013). It is also an aspect of the behavioural routines in office administration, travelling and in the day-to-day life of the volunteers. But environmental protection is especially relevant with regard to the social business – in terms of negative impacts resulting from production, packaging and transportation of the bottled water. In the following we thus limit our discussion of VcA's environmental sustainability to VcA's production partner Husumer Mineralbrunnen.

Husumer Mineralbrunnen bottles natural mineral water for its own products as well as for VcA Quellwasser.[28] Bottling of mineral water is strictly regulated in Germany by the directive on natural mineral water, spring water and table water (Min/TafelWV).[29] The directive requires that the subterranean sources and the bottled water be protected from any contamination (Min/TafelWV articles 5 and 12) and that the procedures implemented do not change the water's distinct properties (Min/TafelWV articles 6 and 10). Compliance with the directive's requirements is enforced through official monitoring.

Husumer Mineralbrunnen's source of mineral water originates from a subterranean reservoir that lies in a water protection area in the North Frisian marsh and pasture landscape next to the national park Schleswig Holstein Wadden Sea.[30] Water protection areas are designated by federal state authorities and regulated by the German Water Management Act (*Wasserhaushaltsgesetz*) to assure advanced drinking water protection within the catchment area of a source. Following the precautionary princi-ple, certain activities that risk polluting the source – for example the appli-cation of pesticides in agriculture – are prohibited in such areas. Again, compliance with these requirements is officially monitored.

In 2013 the German Quality Association Eco Mineral Water (*Qualitätsgemeinschaft Biomineralwasser* 2013) developed a private yet legally acknowledged label for organic mineral and spring water in Germany. The association aims to develop an environmental-quality standard for spring and mineral water that contributes to a sustainable economy. This explicit reference to sustainability in the mineral water context makes the association's standard a possible benchmark for judging the environmental sustainability of VcA Quellwasser. In some respects this standard goes beyond existing regulations for mineral and spring water: it aims to further strengthen water protection by, inter alia, requiring bottlers to promote organic farming within the catchment area of the source, to support water protection beyond their own business operations especially by means of education, to use environmentally optimized packaging and to devise a climate protection strategy. Moreover, the standard stipulates a strong commitment to vocational training, the implementation of an environmental management system and sustainability reporting.

But how does HM compare to this proposed new standard? As HM operates in a water protection area, promoting organic farming does not appear to be a central issue. By collaborating with VcA, the company supports water projects and education. The collaboration also complemented the bottler's growing efforts concerning packaging and corporate climate protection. The company's climate protection strategy aims at CO_2 neutrality for the entire production chain including logistics. HM increased its energy efficiency, switched to renewable energies and installed a photovoltaic system; it also offsets the remaining CO_2 emissions that result from using fossil fuels and from delivery logistics.[31] The bottler also further reduces CO_2 emissions by optimizing transportation in regards to fleet and load factor.[32] In addition, it keeps its hauls short by operating mainly regionally.[33] Selling VcA Quellwasser (across the country) thus actually caused an expansion of the company's sales region (Reinhold Seidel 2013).

Husumer Mineralbrunnen uses returnable glass bottles – the company claims to have cut water usage significantly for cleaning the bottles[34] – as well as PET and PETCYCLE[35] bottles. The initiators of the eco-label mentioned above consider PETCYCLE bottles to be environmentally optimized (Qualitätsgemeinschaft Biomineralwasser 2013, p. 9); however, the system actually came under critique by a German NGO for misleading consumers and misrepresenting environmental data.[36] While VcA emphasizes the adverse environmental effects of PET bottles in general and claims to experiment with alternatives,[37] we found no statement of Wasser GmbH on the specific sustainability issues of PETCYCLE.

Despite their efforts to promote environmental sustainability, HM and Wasser GmbH do not consider the new eco-label as an option and refer instead to the already high level of source protection and water quality (Reinhold Seidel 2013, André Lau 2013). The label, however, additionally requires an environmental management system and regular sustainability reporting. As HM does not have either of these two instruments, it is hard to track its development with respect to objectives set, measures taken, timelines agreed and performance achieved. While there is basic information on these issues available on the company's website, it appears to be rather scattered and incomplete; the website of Wasser GmbH does not add to this information.

In sum, Husumer Mineralbrunnen operates in a highly regulated environment that ensures water purity and source protection. The most relevant environmental issues are addressed with logistics, packaging and climate protection. Not least the support of VcA's activities, up to the refill campaign, show the efforts of the company to go beyond the marketable product and to treat and publicly embed water as a common good that is worth protecting. In order to enhance credibility, however, an increase in formal transparency is essential. With a view to both its production partner and its social business, VcA should work towards an integrated strategy for sustainability management that includes non-financial reporting. Linked to this, it remains to be seen whether or not the sustainability contribution that has so far been achieved with this collaboration can be maintained and even increased when adding further production partners.

Internal Organizational Responsibility

'[F]or a social business or for a NGO of course as well, social action [must] start from within, too' (André Lau 2013). In the mutual day-to-day dealings, VcA's all-profit and fair-play thinking translates into terms of respect and empathy, commitment and positive thinking, as well as responsibility, trust and care. Questions of workload and payment, interaction and understanding as well as transparency and reporting have recently become material issues for VcA. VcA started off with the voluntary work of its founding members. Their investment was and still is high – 'we *live* Viva con Agua' is something we heard in several interviews. As the initiative grew into full-time engagements for the founders, it needed to turn into something that would actually pay the rent. In 2011 the first salaries were paid.[38] The employees jointly decided on a compensation plan with a transparent and planned progression starting from junior positions (André Lau 2013).

As a lesson learnt from the volunteering phase, the headquarters is now focusing more on going easy on individual resources. Everyone is asked to pay attention to his or her workload and also to those of others; breaking points are signalled and discussed openly; functional redundancies have been built up to take the pressure off individuals. This call is also addressed to the volunteers in the cells and crews; for instance, they are asked to align their group's annual planning and operative actions with their personal study and work plans. VcA has also formulated values and guidelines for the day-to-day dealings; these dealings are indeed perceived as being respectful, positive, friendly, open and direct – even from the outside. As a representative from Welthungerhilfe sees it: 'VcA lives up to its mission' (Anke Mattern 2013).

Volunteers need to know how to engage, what their engagement is about and where the financial revenues go. According to our interviews and the results of an online survey conducted in the course of a parallel project (see

Section 7.1), transparency and disclosure are considered highly relevant while at the same time supporters almost unconditionally trust VcA in doing the right thing. This is interpreted in the sense that authenticity is of higher relevance to supporters than transparency (Michael Fritz 2013). Nonetheless, the initiative is taking action in the process of its organizational development to become more publicly transparent; VcA recently disclosed more detailed information on the association's financial transactions online and will now do so on an annual basis. The headquarters also increasingly considers it relevant to report on the social and environmental impacts of VcA's work; developments in this regard are still too new to have become effective.

There is also no summary so far on VcA in its entirety; information on the association's website is limited to activities of its four pillars. The foundation of Wasser GmbH, which resulted in an increase of organizational complexity, certainly makes the need for transparency urgent in order to avoid a threat to VcA's credibility (see Section 7.2). This is acknowledged by VcA, who claims that ensuring transparency, responsibility and honesty is a principle of Wasser GmbH.[39] But information on Wasser GmbH's website is limited to the mission statement and guidelines; the actual performance is not yet reported.

In sum, the analysis of internal documents, guidelines and interviews reveals a strong culture of responsibility in VcA. The basic awareness for certain key issues such as workload, day-to-day dealings and transparency, however, is higher than the degree to which these things are formalized and institutionalized. Currently, the financial and non-financial reporting requires the most urgent consideration to level out any discrepancies in these regards.

7.9   LEGITIMACY EVALUATION – VIVA CON AGUA AS A POLITICAL ACTOR

Viva con Agua mobilizes, involves and incites people to collect and donate money by means of fun actions, which on the surface looks more like amusement than serious engagement. These actions not only generate significant amounts of money; they also involve and affect large numbers of people. We now look at the legitimacy of VcA as a political actor.

Output Legitimacy

According to our introductory remarks on legitimacy (see Chapter 1), we begin by identifying the social dimension in what we earlier identified as VcA's innovations. VcA clearly tackles significant societal problems with its engagement in improving people's access to safe drinking water and sanitation. In doing so, it is in line with MDG 7-C and supports and protects basic human needs. As VcA is not the technical implementer of the respective water projects but only a supporter, its contribution is an indirect one at first. But the actual implementer, Welthungerhilfe, acknowledges VcA as a strong actor who is growing into a more active role; this is seen not only in its well-received on-site visits, but also when VcA explicitly takes on financial and communicative responsibilities in the essential post-implementation phase of the water projects (Anke Mattern 2013).

VcA's direct achievements in terms of broadening the target group for voluntary civic commitment match the interests of Germany's National Engagement Strategy (Bundesregierung 2010). In this sense, VcA promotes societal self-organizing capacities, at least within student groups, and the strengthening of social cohesion by motivating joint engagement in a social cause. We regard this, too, as supporting human capabilities and thus ensuring output legitimacy. This argument, however, rests on short-term indications that need to be substantiated by long-term studies.

When talking about output legitimacy, another, now literally tangible, output is relevant – the bottled water. While the foundation of a social business becomes more and more an accepted strategy among charities to generate revenues in a strongly contested donations market (Anke Mattern 2013), selling bottled water can only be regarded as legitimate under the tap-water-first policy and if the business is sensitive to the sustainability challenges of the sector. As we pointed out before, VcA sets out with its production partner HM to clearly improve the environmental impact of such production activities, as well as to change the business conduct of the sector by promoting fair competitive behaviour.

Social Accountability

Is Viva con Agua a socially accountable actor, both for the people in the millennium villages and for its supporters? The responsibility for planning and implementing the water projects rests with Welthungerhilfe. As one of several financial supporters, VcA is not required to come into play as far as the villagers are concerned. Yet in the spirit of social accountability put forward in this book (see Chapter 1), VcA visits the villages on their own initiative. These visits also serve VcA's need to be accountable to its supporters, donors and partners in Germany. VcA's efforts towards information and its collaborative spirit add to this social accountability.

The network, as we have seen, relies heavily on personal interactions and relationships; the VcA headquarters facilitates personal exchange among supporters and also tries to keep in close contact with the network. Accountability in this regard is probably weakened where geographical distance to the headquarters is large, for local crews at the edges of the network. VcA provides extensive public information on the diversity of its activities. Transparency, however, needs improvement with regard to timely, complete and comprehensible information. While some financial aspects of the association's work are disclosed online, so far neither the work of the other organizational units nor the non-financial aspects such as social and environmental impacts are covered (see Section 7.7).

Mediating Role: Transitional Authority and Empowerment

Does VcA take a role in advocating for the affected communities and in fostering empowered participation? With a view to the millennium villages, Welthungerhilfe's approach emphasizes *help to self-help*, thus facilitating education and training as well as participation in decision making for and communal ownership of the implemented WASH services. VcA aims to add momentum to these mechanisms of empowerment by strengthening its support of the projects' long-term sustainability. With a view to its supporters, the VcA headquarters takes the mediating role of a think-tank and also facilitates knowledge exchange, learning and feedback. VcA thus enables and connects people so that they can take self-initiative as decentralized activist groups. This enabling role is increasingly recognized by VcA and will most likely be strengthened and institutionalized. Beyond this, VcA is also providing jobs to supporters. Wasser GmbH, for example, instead of recruiting external sales persons, banks increasingly on hiring people from the network (André Lau 2013).

Outside Recognition

The strong and very visible commitment of all the supporters including many celebrities, the praising testimonies of the associated partners and not least, the many inquiries by schools from all over Germany testify to VcA's outside recognition. As a more objective measure, several prizes have been awarded to Benjamin Adrion as the initiator and 'face' of VcA and to the initiative itself.[40] Adrion received 'The Order of Merit of the Federal Republic of Germany' in 2009 and was recognized for his social engagement by the media ('Panther Prize' of the *Tageszeitung* in 2006) as well as by civil society and business initiatives ('Utopia Award' in 2008; 'BAUM Environmental Prize' in 2011). VcA as an initiative won the *Startsocial* contest in 2007, was awarded for its innovativeness the same year by the policy-business initiative *Germany – Land of Ideas*, and was given a dedicated quality label in 2010 by the German Council for Sustainable Development for its sustainability approach and strong social commitment.

7.10 CONCLUSION

When we finally arrived at the St. Pauli headquarters of Viva con Agua that morning, the quiet of the environment dissolved as everyone was already buzzing around. This buzz was ever-present in our interviews as well. Accordingly, the most frequently used start to a sentence was, 'Well, the exciting thing about Viva con Agua is . . .' or slightly varied, 'It will become even more exciting when . . .'. While it was difficult to ignore such enthusiasm and emotional dedication, we were looking at VcA as an object of research. We conclude this chapter by reflecting on what fascinated us most while engaging with Viva con Agua in this case study analysis and which aspects of its further development appear most promising.

First, VcA's strong commitment to collaboration and networking bears its actual scaling potential. Scaling here is not a matter of franchise, replication or labour division; rather it is strongly dependent on building actual relationships. This in turn needs organizational capacity building and (most likely) a change in VcA's allocation scheme for revenues, which so far naturally prioritizes the water projects. Second, the all-profit approach turns out to capture more than just the initially claimed help–fun nexus and could in fact provide the basis for an integrated strategy of organizational responsibility. However, this would require more systematic thought and an evaluation of expectations, processes and outcomes for VcA's value generation in its entirety. Third, the VcA style of approaching people with low-threshold fun activities and the right multipliers is impressively contagious. While we see the necessity of maintaining accessibility to the target group, we stress here the need to provide more content and positions for the thematic fields where VcA has aspirations to advance social change. With a view to these three points, we expect interesting further developments from the already launched processes of qualitative scaling. As an outcome we expect even more customized engagement to further strengthen the low-threshold fun part as well as options for deep involvement especially for those who will grow out of VcA's young target group.

Fourth, the transfer of ownership from the social investors to the charities not only translates the mission into an appropriate business governance model, it also backs the fair business conduct in day-to-day business. Fifth, VcA is associated with a high authenticity and credibility; this even compensated for a lack of transparency in the build-up phase of the initiative. The foundation of the bottled water business led to a greater demand for social accountability as an organization. It became apparent here how sensitive perceptions of authenticity and credibility are, for instance, to the legal form. Even though the governance model of the business is explicitly in line with the common good mission, at least to some extent there is a public perception that VcA has 'changed sides'.

All of these points coalesce to the question of whether or not VcA will succeed in developing an integrated strategy of organizational responsibility. Such a strategy would have to be in line with the mission, the approach to change and collaboration and the all-profit thinking. It would also have to materialize in reporting that is systematic, consistent, responsive, easily readable and intelligible to all. These are fairly high expectations on Viva con Agua – or on almost any social entrepreneurship initiative – given its organizational capacities. Developments in this regard will probably not only take their time but also require stronger external support. As a recompense for such efforts, however, Viva con Agua can expect to be better positioned in situations like this: 'People are searching for something that is good; they just like to do so. It's only that when they think they have found it they keep searching until they find something that is not okay about it and then [they] say "See, I knew it: it's still dumb"' (André Lau 2013).

NOTES

1. SESAM (Social innovation and its diffusion: Social marketing and social entrepreneurship) was a parallel project carried out by members of our research group GETIDOS, which aimed at identifying success factors of new and target-group-specific marketing strategies for social entrepreneurship. As part of the SESAM project, interviews were conducted with VcA representatives in 2010 and with supporters and guests at a band contest. In addition an online survey among VcA's Facebook followers was performed in 2011.
2. Cells and local crews are decentralized supporter groups. Cells are the official VcA representations and conclude an agreement on rights and duties with the headquarters. Local crews are smaller groups of activists without this articled level of commitment and governance.
3. The circle of founders comprises prominent figures and long-term companions of VcA. In the long run, more and more donors are expected to add to the endowment capital, but so far the work of the foundation is put on hold. We therefore do not further discuss the foundation here.
4. http://www.vivaconagua.co.uk/index.htm?post?1 (accessed 17 September 2013).
5. WASH refers to a sector in the context of international development cooperation where services to improve access to safe **WA**ter, **S**anitary facilities and **H**ygiene education are provided. WASH also emphasizes the understanding that activities in this field have to be integrated in order to be effective. http://www.vivaconagua.org/index. htm?post&id=1594 (accessed 17 September 2013).
6. 'Du bist der Tropfen' (http://www.vivaconagua.org/index.htm?machmit, accessed 17 September 2013).

7.   Cause-related marketing refers to a company's financial support of a non-profit organization that both strengthens the organization's social cause and directly serves marketing and publicity purposes of the company.
8.   http://www.un.org/millenniumgoals/environ.shtml (accessed 17 September 2013).
9.   In total, Welthungerhilfe received 36.8m € in donations in 2012 (Welthungerhilfe 2013, p. 49). The NGO usually applies for co-funding by public donors in order to implement larger projects.
10. http://www.vivaconagua.org/index.htm?spenden (accessed 17 September 2013).
11. The following discussion refers to the activities of VcA Germany unless otherwise indicated.
12. http://www.vivaconagua.org/index.htm?post&id=1995 (accessed 17 September 2013).
13. Actions contribute roughly 70 per cent to the revenue of the association; further sources are partnerships and cooperations with companies (20 per cent) as well as online donations (5 per cent) (Christian Wiebe 2010).
14. With sales figures doubling every year for the last two years, the Wasser GmbH started to operate in the black at the beginning of 2013 (André Lau 2013).
15. Even when still in the red, Wasser GmbH already donated money according to sales figures: 20 000 euros in the years 2010–2012 (http://www.vivaconagua.com/nachhaltig-keit/oekonomisch/, accessed 17 September 2013).
16. The unusual call for refilling the store-bought water bottle is in line with VcA's tap-water focus; all parties involved jointly made this decision, with the condition to break even as a signal of market acceptance. As of late summer 2013, the refill campaign started (http://www.vivaconagua.com/refill-please/, accessed 17 September 2013).
17. http://www.vivaconagua.co.uk/index.htm (accessed 17 September 2013).
18. See for instance European River Network (ERN), WASH United, German Toilet Organization (GTO), Charity: Water, One Drop, Earth Water, LEMONAID & ChariTea, Premium, Quartiermeister, and so on.
19. The online survey was conducted in 2011 within the context of the project SESAM – see note 1 in the introductory part to this chapter.
20. Millerntor Gallery is a big annual art exhibition at the FC St. Pauli arena where artwork that has been donated by international artists is sold to support VcA's cause.
21. See for instance LEMONAID & ChariTea, Premium, fritz-kola and Quartiermeister to name but a few.
22. There is the fear, though, that VcA Quellwasser might dominate the public perception of VcA, thus reducing the initiative mainly to a product (Michael Fritz 2013).
23. By the way: Dumas's 'one for all, all for one' phrase that acts as a model for VcA's mission was also used in Switzerland in the nineteenth century for a country-wide aid campaign for joint action and solidarity to recover from heavy storm-floods and still is an acknowledged Swiss motto (http://en.wikipedia.org/wiki/Unus_pro_omnibus,_omnes_pro_uno, accessed 17 September 2013).
24. 'Until 2018, we want to collect 1 000 000 Euros with the water and provide more than 300 000 people with clean drinking water!' (http://www.vivaconagua.com/die-idee/, accessed 17 September 2013). The sales projection for 2013 is 6.5 to 7.5 million bottles (André Lau 2013).
25. www.sustainable-wash.org (accessed 17 September 2013).
26. Interview in the documentary 'Blue Uganda', available at http://www.vivaconagua.org/index.htm?post?1968 (accessed 17 September 2013).
27. http://www.vivaconagua.com/nachhaltigkeit/oekologisch/ (accessed 17 September 2013).
28. 'Quellwasser' is German for spring water. The decision to label the mineral water as spring water was taken in order to have more leeway in future searches for additional bottlers (namely those that do not have mineral water in their assortment) (Benjamin Adrion 2012).
29. The so-called 'Verordnung über natürliches Mineralwasser, Quellwasser und Tafelwasser' (BMJ 2006).

30. http://www.husumer-mineralbrunnen.de/startseite/ (accessed 17 September 2013).
31. http://www.aquanordic.de/projekte/umgesetzte-projekte/ (accessed 17 September 2013).
32. http://www.aquanordic.de/projekte/geplante-projekte/ (accessed 17 September 2013).
33. http://www.aquanordic.de/start/ueber-uns/ (accessed 17 September 2013).
34. http://www.aquanordic.de/projekte/umgesetzte-projekte/ (accessed 17 September 2013).
35. PETCYCLE GmbH & Co. KG aims at a closed materials cycle using special pool-crates to keep one-way PET bottles within a bottle-to-bottle recycling system. PETCYCLE is an association of beverage, machine and packaging manufactures; Husumer Mineralbrunnen is also a member of PETCYCLE (http://www.petcycle.de, accessed 17 September 2013).
36. *Deutsche Umwelthilfe* states that the deposit and crate system makes consumers believe that those one-way bottles are actually returnable ones; the self-processed recyclate rate is not proven and doubtful; the material-cycle is actually not closed and the pool-crates system even causes higher transport-related emissions (http://www.recyclingportal.eu/artikel/25561.shtml, accessed 17 September 2013).
37. http://www.vivaconagua.com/nachhaltigkeit/oekologisch/ (accessed 17 September 2013).
38. In 2013 nine employees were working for the association in the Hamburg headquarters and five for the Wasser GmbH (http://www.vivaconagua.org/index.htm?team, accessed 17 September 2013).
39. http://www.vivaconagua.com/nachhaltigkeit/leitplanken/ (accessed 17 September 2013).
40. http://www.vivaconagua.org/index.htm?about (accessed 17 September 2013).

8. Getting things done sustainably? Synthesis chapter on social entrepreneurship and water

Rafael Ziegler, Jana Gebauer, Marianne Henkel, Justus Lodemann, Franziska Mohaupt and Lena Partzsch

8.1 INTRODUCTION

This book was an intellectual and physical journey for us into social entrepreneurship initiatives dealing with water challenges in drinking water and sanitation supply, in agriculture and industry, as well as for entire ecosystems. This journey opened us up to the diversity of water challenges and to the variety of ways of addressing these challenges – from toilet monuments for public sanitation to river jumps for water conservation. The social entrepreneurs and their organizations were just as heterogeneous: we met social activists and political lobbyists, consultants and businessmen, architects and hydrologists (with social entrepreneurs frequently wearing more than one hat), and their NGOs, companies and networks. To acknowledge this diversity of persons and organizations, we speak here of *social entrepreneurship initiatives* (SEI) to cover both the social entrepreneur and the organization or network. As we met a diversity of problems, people and organizations, we need to be cautious and acknowledge the difficulty of generalization.

In this synthesis chapter we revisit our initial theses and our working conception of social entrepreneurship (see Chapter 1) with a view to our final conception of social entrepreneurship and its role for sustainable development. We first present our findings from the case studies for the theses proposed in the introduction (Sections 8.2 to 8.4). In the final section, on the basis of these findings, we state our own conception of social entrepreneurship, revisit the Ashoka approach and draw conclusions for the role of social entrepreneurship in sustainable development worldwide in relation to the Millennium Development Goals (MDG) and the post-MDG process. We close with a reflection on our role as scientists in sustainable development research.

In September 2012 we invited the initiatives studied in this book to the River Main in Frankfurt for a preliminary discussion of findings. These discussions with the SEI greatly benefitted the chapters in this book, including this synthesis chapter. Frankfurt is not only a centre of global finance, it is also the birthplace of the poet Goethe, who once said, 'grey is all theory, and green the golden tree of life'. Our working conception of social entrepreneurship for this book is taken from *life*; fittingly, Ashoka chose a green tree for its logo. Is the *golden tree of life* growing in directions of greener and more social purposes, especially in matters of entrepreneurship and investing in it?

8.2 WATER FUNDING – CONTRIBUTING TO STRONG SUSTAINABILITY AND HUMAN CAPABILITIES

Strong Sustainability

The water cycle ideally ensures the regeneration of available freshwater as a non-living fund, thereby providing a constant supply for ecosystems. Human actions and their consequences can (and do) interfere with this regeneration process in such a way that freshwater quantity or quality is threatened. On the global level such threats are owing to economic growth and population growth, which together lead to an increased demand for freshwater, particularly in agriculture. Economic growth has led to an increase in greenhouse gases, which in turn impacts the climate via an increase in severe weather events such as floods and droughts. The exponential increase in human water use along with the uncertainties owing to climate change creates major challenges. Along with agriculture, this affects access to water for drinking and sanitation, not least in rapidly growing cities and poor rural areas. There is no doubt that these trends also threaten water availability for other species, and the very existence of entire ecosystems.

In the previous chapters we saw many examples of this growing need for freshwater, both in good quantity and quality. In Quito, Ecuador, the continued pressure on land for agricultural conversion is in conflict with a rising water demand in urban centres. In Nairobi, Kenya rapid growth makes it very challenging for urban planners to provide equal and good access to drinking water and sanitation. In Maharashtra, India climate change poses an additional threat to poor, rain-fed farmers. Extreme weather events in Europe increase the risk of floods and droughts; this is intensified by heavily modified rivers that 'flush' the water out of the land, an effect of the twentieth-century perspective on water as predominantly an economic resource.

In the introduction to this book we mapped the contribution of SEI in relation to various aspects of freshwater use – for drinking water, sanitation and private consumption, for agriculture and industry, as well as freshwater in the ecosystem as a whole. With a view to this last and most comprehensive issue, we found SEI to provide practical ideas for investing in water as a natural fund, thereby emphasizing the long-term ecological perspective even where short-term economic and social issues call for everybody's attention. Drawing on his new water paradigm, Michal Kravčík and collaborators designed a Green New Deal focused on local water retention in Slovakia. Somewhat complementary, WOTR aims at increased water availability as a precondition for economic and agricultural activities in the arid climate zones of five Indian states. Marta Echavarria also focuses on the sustainability of ecosystem services as a precondition for economic and social activities; to this end she puts the idea of payments for ecosystem services into practice via financial mechanisms in Latin American cities.

In view of these practical ideas for the maintenance and restoration of water as a regenerating fund, we can call SEI such as those just mentioned *water funders*. In social entrepreneurship theory and practice, investment is typically associated with financial investments and the capacity of SEI to attract such investments. The water funders remind us of the ecological dimension of investment; water is a regenerating fund that provides essential services for ecosystems and the living beings therein. They advocate taking the ecological dimension of investment seriously in entrepreneurship and they propose practical ideas demonstrating possibilities even if the long-term impact is unknown and dependent on unpredictable internal and external factors.

Although this long-term investment in the fund is of great social importance, a qualifier is needed. Recall the work of Roberto Epple and other water conservation activists for free-flowing, living rivers. While Epple no doubt endorses the importance of the water cycle as a self-regenerating fund, the language of the *living river* makes it particularly clear that the issue here is not only instrumental value for humans but also the life of the fish in the river and the river itself. In view of this larger concern with living beings and lives, we need to keep in mind that the *use* perspective of natural capital does not have to exclude this recognition of value. We constantly instrumentalize each other to some extent in everyday life, yet this does not preclude us from recognizing that others are always also an end and never just a means. Epple urges us to seriously recognize that the human-use perspective does not exclude attention to other life or indeed even the river as such. Water funding need not be narrowly construed in anthropocentric or even monetary terms.

That being said, human needs, especially the basic needs linked to drinking water and sanitation, are of great moral importance. Ecotact's search for appropriate solutions for ecological sanitation in urban spaces in East Africa has a predominant practical focus on the human need, not the ecosystem as such; yet Ecotact acknowledges the larger ecosystem and seeks to foster meeting a basic human need with a reduced ecological footprint. Likewise, Viva con Agua seeks to comply with environmental standards in both its water projects and its social business; it considers both the direct human needs and those of ecosystems in the respective context.

In conclusion to our theses on environmental sustainability and capabilities from Chapter 1, we find SEI to provide practical ideas for promoting strong sustainability and associated central capabilities of their target groups. These ideas focus on different challenges with a view to the complex task of sustainably living with water, from the restoration and maintenance upstream to the basic needs in mega-cities typically located downstream.

This finding suggests that these practical ideas could complement and reinforce each other for the promotion of sustainable watersheds. We see the watershed as a metaphor for innovation. Water flows from a diversity of sources through brooks, streams and rivers, and finally to the ocean. Like the watershed that draws from many sources, many ideas and approaches are required for sustainable watershed management. There is 'upstream' work for the regeneration of the water cycle, for example flood prevention and water supply, just as there is 'downstream' work, for example creating awareness and promoting sustainable production and consumption processes. We need many fresh sources to promote the sustainable use of water and strong interwoven networks to live together sustainably in watersheds.

Such a need was recognized in our collaborative session with the SEI during the Frankfurt conference. Likewise, Ashoka emphasises *group* entrepreneurship and collaboration.[1] In regards to water issues, there is an awareness of the need for group entrepreneurship and the inclusion of ideas from others to the extent that they fit with one's own mission; however, we found no evidence in practice of SEI working together in watershed management that would come even remotely close to the sustained work on an issue that the SEI are known for in regards to their own ideas.

Capability Innovations

'Sanitation is more important than independence', a slogan Ecotact adopted from Gandhi, captures well a pragmatic, entrepreneurial spirit that prioritizes the meeting of basic needs such as sanitation over formal questions of political independence and formal participation. Take the case of WOTR: if upstream farmers must move with their families several months a year for seasonal work, then stable political participation in the village is not possible. However, we must not misunderstand the pragmatic spirit captured in the slogan as an exclusive focus on sanitation, drinking water or whatever specific issue. To the contrary, the practical ideas of SEI relate a problem, such as inadequate access to sanitation, to other human capabilities, thereby creating new space for experiences and discussions. This point is well illustrated by another Ecotact slogan: 'thinking beyond the toilet'. Ecotact's *toilet monuments* link sanitation access to the creative use of public space; the toilet is reconceived as a landmark and a meeting point. The integrated *toilet mall* concept links sanitation to the provision of services (shoe-shine, mobile phone, beverages) and thereby creates economic options. The health issue of access to sanitation is thereby combined with affiliation in public space and possibilities of economic participation (Ziegler, Dietsche and Karanja 2013). In contrast to the classic Schumpeterian concept of innovation, which focuses on the product and production processes in terms of recombining elements, here the focus is on linking and mutually strengthening human capabilities. To highlight this difference, we speak of *capability innovations* (Ziegler 2010).

Drawing on our case studies, we can further characterize such capability innovations in terms of three aspects closely related to central human capabilities. A first central challenge for these innovations is reconfiguring the perceived problem – to think of the toilet as a monument, of river conservation in terms of Big Jumps or of technical watershed development in terms of a social contract. Developing new ways of seeing a problem and the associated development of ideas is a central aspect. It concerns a change in their mindsets as well as the effective invitation of others to see things differently. 'Il faut changer les cervaux' ('You have to change minds'), says Roberto Epple. This change creates the space to practically experience capabilities; for example in Epple's case the interrelation of play, public participation and a sense for the environment.

Second, this reconfiguration of problems speaks to the capacity to aspire. This is understood as overcoming normative, cultural frames that prevent individuals and groups from expanding their capabilities; for example, expectations of what the poor deserve and can do, or what is appropriate to do in relation to nature.[2] Ecotact aims to change the taboo of public sanitation as a topic; David Kuria hopes the Ikotoilets improve what people can expect in public space (as one visitor wrote in an Ikotoilet guestbook, 'makes me proud to be Kenyan'). Consider also the Big Jump: it provides citizens an entry into the expert-dominated field of river conservation via a simple event of humans together in and at rivers that (until recently) were too dangerous and dirty for swimming. An intriguing aspect of this case is the sense of joy and celebration, something that is also clearly present in Viva con Agua's approach. German water expert (and Big Jump participant) Michal Bender puts it this way: 'It is about putting things into one's hands, achieving something in a concrete situation for water conservation and thereby making a contribution that one can be proud of' (Bender, 8 September 2012, Berlin). This point is not only about local aspiration. As flash jump co-organizer Kathrin Mangelsen says: 'I think it is amazing what we achieved. All the kids that were there; and if they carry the topic further into their classes, then we have really achieved something, and sensitized people for the topic' (Mangelsen, 10 July 2012, Hamburg).[3] Here the experience of what one can do, even in relation to an 'expert issue', contributes to self-esteem as well as to a sense of empowerment.

The capacity to aspire is closely linked to the attempt to empower affected people. This leads to a third aspect, where those involved in an issue are enabled to deal with the issue themselves – in Gandhian terms, *to be the change*. Kravčík's Green New Deal placed central importance on enabling mayors to deal with flood prevention in their villages and on training and paying people from the villages to engage in practical flood prevention work. WOTR has a central community principle and has developed a set of tools to educate people and to create institutions that empower them to carry out watershed development. At an even more fundamental level, Epple seeks to overcome mental oppositions to enjoy rivers as a way to foster the public participation demanded by European law. In these cases, cooperation with local municipalities and village councils is very important, along with the creation of new micro-institutions (for example the Village Development Committee under the umbrella of the established village council in the WOTR approach) or the definition of new roles (for example the *water masters* in Kravčík's Green New Deal). The case studies provide an antidote to the frequently encountered association of social entrepreneurship with Big Business (we will return to this point below). While we did not find evidence for SEI opposing such business collaborations, we did find that the collaboration with local level governance (village, municipality, city administration) played a key role in carrying out the practical ideas.[4] Accordingly we think the local public level deserves much more attention than it currently receives in social entrepreneurship research and in the practice of SEI investors.

This emphasis on collaboration with local government in no way precludes higher-level networking and advocacy. To the contrary, successful advocacy on the national or even international level can create the resources to carry out local cooperations. The Green New Deal was supported from national and European levels: in the WOTR case from the national and global development cooperation level, in the Ecotact case from a private international foundation and in Echavarria's case from an internationally operating NGO; all of these examples helped support the respective local implementations.

The intention to empower does not mean that full and equal participation is actually achieved (see the discussion of legitimacy below). For example, in the Quito case, the approach strengthened already powerful actors downstream but hardly empowered actors upstream. Even in the very participatory approach of WOTR, the organization encounters difficulties overcoming wealth, culture and gender inequalities, which are a barrier to equal participation. It is important to make the associated normative issues explicit so that they can be dealt with as part of the process.

The Target Group: Getting Organized

When we began our research we found it useful to distinguish the impact of SEI on the respective target group and the capability and sustainability issues within the SEI (compare our theses on internal organizational responsibility in Chapter 1). With respect to this initial organizational focus, we found little evidence of integrated policies for staff or environmental guidelines, and we often found – as is familiar in social entrepreneurship research – relatively low incomes and difficulties in providing a stable income for employees. The shining exception notwithstanding, the SEI in our case studies are still a long way from integrated, systematic policies regarding their organizational responsibilities.

This result suffers from the tacit presupposition of *the* social entrepreneurship organization. In practice there are consultants, NGOs, networks of people, social businesses, and so on. We did find something interesting amidst this diversity – the blurring of target groups and actors. In a sense this point already follows from the observation on empowerment above, yet it is worthwhile to make explicit. We found a common aim of SEI approaches is the creation of collaborations that allow the target group to take care of the issue itself: to carry out watershed development and flood prevention in the cases of WOTR and Kravčík, to carry out joyful events for water conservation and human needs in the cases of Epple and Viva con Agua. Empowerment is a classic goal for NGOs, especially in development cooperation. What we found striking beyond this important goal were those cases – most vividly illustrated perhaps by Viva con Agua – where the target group becomes part of a network that can co-create the value in the respective place. It gets organized. This is not to say that everything is a network and organization does not matter. To the contrary, the capacity of the SEI to help the target group organize proved to be very important (see next section).

As seen in this section, we view the contribution of SEI to sustainable development in terms of their practical ideas for strong sustainability and central capabilities that reconfigure perceiving problems and that empower, notably via the improvement of the capacity to aspire, and in terms of the capacity of communities to organize themselves.

8.3 INNOVATION, SCALING AND EARNED INCOME

When introducing our approach to our case study analyses, we emphasized the focus on the *social innovation as such*, that is independently of the presence or absence of earned-income strategies. This manifested itself in the selection of our case studies: all our initiatives are officially and explicitly recognized for their ideas and innovativeness. Did our analyses confirm this preconception that the selected initiatives developed innovative approaches to tackle water problems and that they aimed at and implemented their approaches at the broad societal level (see our theses on innovation in Chapter 1)? Did the analyses also confirm that the forceful engagement of an individual entrepreneur is an essential driver for spreading the innovation (that is our further thesis in relation to the school of innovation from Chapter 1)?

Innovativeness was confirmed to be a vital characteristic of our SEI, which all feature ideas that are relevant to address pressing water-related problems. The SEI take up a variety of perspectives and implement their ideas at very different levels, which mirrors the complexity of problems related to water and sanitation. Kravčík lobbies for decentralized water resource management by re-emphasizing the closing of small water cycles according to former local traditions; WOTR implements and offers training on participatory watershed development; Echavarria introduces financing mechanisms for watershed protection and does consulting work for water trust funds; Epple and Viva con Agua aim at sensitizing and mobilizing people for water issues and a key aspect for both is to promote personal initiative via networking and campaigning; and Kuria tries to break ground for an economic and cultural re-conceptualization of public toilets in favour of high-quality public sanitation in urban centres.

These approaches are all new relative to their temporal or regional contexts. The initiatives show a general attitude to blend ideas and contexts in unusual ways in order to form their own approaches. They also tend to keep doing this, thus continuously adopting and adapting further ideas. Our analyses revealed a strong willingness to improve the approaches. The dedication to improvement in order to take on further challenges and to better deal with problems is a maxim for all the SEI assessed. However, as only a few of the initiatives installed systematic processes of evaluation and learning, there are quite some limitations in actually exercising continuous improvement.

Before we turn to this issue, a few words on the different aspects of scaling are in order. Our case study initiatives usually aimed to scale at the national level or beyond. Indeed, most of them were able to scale out their idea beyond their area of origin. Epple's network of river jumpers grew quickly across Europe, Viva con Agua's network of fundraisers spread rapidly throughout Germany and replicated in Switzerland, Kuria has been able to replicate his toilet monuments in urban public spaces across Kenya, WOTR scaled its participatory approach across fives states of India, and Echavarria initiated water funds in various Latin American cities. Nevertheless, especially in the context of sustainability, we not only focus on scaling impact in terms of spatial spread but also in terms of temporal depth. We found serious obstacles in this latter sense of scaling. For example, local activities within Epple's network of river jumpers are often one-time shots; Kravčík's Green New Deal was rapidly scaled out via the government and then came to a sudden stop with a new government; or consider our largest organization, WOTR, who has been the most systematic at evaluating and learning, yet acknowledges post-project sustainability as an issue. In short, scaling in time and not just in space is a serious challenge.[5]

The SEI aim at fundamental changes to what they identify as root causes of water-related problems. They focus on underlying problems such as a lack of participation, knowledge and empowerment, as well as inappropriate economic mechanisms and adverse regulations, behavioural routines or taboos. Typically this means they are not just focused on scaling out a specific product or service, but also on what we call *the conditions for scaling out*. For example, they lobby to improve political conditions for their mission or campaign to change public perception and cultural attitudes. Assessing the impact of these efforts is much more difficult because the underlying mechanisms of change are rather indirect; it is nonetheless critical to keep them in view. The scaling discussion in social entrepreneurship research is still too focused on the growth in impact of a product or service and how to achieve such impact more efficiently. As a result, the political and cultural efforts of SEI tend to receive insufficient attention, as do the very different problem-specific ways impact can be achieved (lobbying, campaigning, educating, and so on).[6]

The focus on conditions of scaling out also highlights the difficulty of estimating actual impact. Change that goes beyond increasing participant figures or building new infrastructures and institutions (such as wells, toilets and economic incentive systems) can only be observed in the medium to long term. As approaches are complex in themselves and as there are many external factors that can foster change, causalities between the spread of an approach and the perceived changes may be questionable or at least hard to identify.

Organizational Capacity for Achieving Impact with Others

Most of the SEI need to put more emphasis on strategic reflections and concrete scaling mechanisms that would spell out their scaling ambitions. If SEI are to trigger innovation processes, an initial, systematic and integrated consideration of scaling as an explicit part of the overall approach needs to be the rule rather than the exception. It is necessary to build up at least a minimum organizational capacity that would allow for feedback and evaluation processes. To be sure, however, the obstacles to this are numerous. Beyond a lack of resources, a higher level of standardization and institutionalization can be perceived as interfering with the SEI's general spirit of decentralized activism and may be approached rather tentatively. Also, as long as investors are mostly attracted by the *new idea* (presented by an enthusiastic entrepreneur), organizational development with a view to scaling the idea is a bad seller.

In our view, it is owing to limited organizational capacities that almost all SEI studied here had a limited opportunity to engage in continuous trial-and-error processes, let alone for the systematic development of their approaches. Solely WOTR aimed from the beginning to implement structures and routines for knowledge management and integrated evaluation schemes – notably driven by the initial, multi-year support within the context of development cooperation. Viva con Agua is now cautiously taking a path of standardization and institutionalized learning after having reached a critical size as a network; here processes of qualitative development became necessary to counter the threats of mission-drift and randomness. The build-up of organizational capacities can thus be regarded as both a direct and an indirect facilitating condition for scaling. It also reduces the dependency on a charismatic founder. Where there is a more or less dominating individual entrepreneur, there are typically problems in moving from the new idea to an operationalization that generates externally perceivable and replicable approaches that are aligned to the mission but not dependent on the necessarily limited efforts of one individual.

Earned Income

Almost all our SEI (with the exception of WOTR) lack the resources required to build up the organizational capacities to conceptualize and design standards, checklists, handbooks, mentoring or training activities and the like in a sustained manner. The initiatives all encounter financial challenges. The dependence on external financial support such as donations, philanthropic investments or public funding strongly influences the work of SEI. Public funding in the context of development cooperation or governmental funding schemes is typically project-bound; these situations are additionally subject to political dynamics with (sometimes sudden) swings in themes, strategies and preferred actors. The support granted usually covers a short time span of three to five years, with long-term engagements being the exception. Philanthropic investors tend to favour *the new idea* over its continuation and improvement. Our 2012 conference in Frankfurt confirmed the specific difficulty in funding organizational capacity building, be it from private or public sources.[7]

So is market-based income the way out? When it comes to a public good such as water, marketable products and services often can only emerge after an investment has been made, for instance into water funds and approaches to regenerate these funds (Ziegler and Gebauer 2012). The generation of earned income usually comes second and seems to be an option for the target groups rather than the SEI themselves (for example in the case of WOTR). SEI that operate in the context of development cooperation and poverty reduction need to deal with the limits of a market-based approach in the water sector, both in socio-economic terms and in ethical ones. Similar questions arise for our initiatives in the global north: what is the tangible value of networking and political lobbying for achieving medium- to long-term change in regulation, mindsets, education and social engagement? Who is legitimately going to invest?

In summation of the cases studied, earned income options were developed by three out of six initiatives (earned income is not central to the other three). While Kuria proves that earned income is possible for public toilets in urban centres, his model is not working in schools and slums, where the ethical challenges are more pressing. Echavarria earns her living as a consultant; yet her personal consultancy work does not generate income for organizational capacity building, the challenge identified in the last section. Viva con Agua's social business has started to add profits to donation-based revenues, yet it is at this point still an open question how central this social business will be for Viva con Agua, its mission and scaling approach. What can be concluded here is that our SEI cannot, certainly not fully, cover their expenses with market-based income; thus they depend on philanthropy and public funding especially when it comes to those contexts where innovative and scalable solutions matter the most.

New and Old Paradigms of Scaling

As noted in Chapter 1, we can distinguish between two scaling paradigms with a view to generating societal impact: organizational growth (old paradigm) and collaboration (new paradigm).[8] Social entrepreneurship is assigned to the latter and our analyses generally confirm this assignment. With WOTR being the relative exception – it rapidly grew to a staff of some 150, and then preferred to launch new organizations rather than grow as an organization – the SEI analysed only show limited organizational growth. Notably, this 'non-achievement' is most often a matter of attitude and of understanding one's role as a *catalyst* for others to grow or as an *enabler* within a network. Our SEI put a strong focus on collaboration – with their target groups or their implementation and production partners. By cooperating, SEI can gain additional expertise and access to local networks and communities, they can extend and strengthen core skills and they can expand possibilities and compensate for a lack of interest to grow as an organization. This focus on working with others must not be understood as a neglect of internal organization. In order to achieve impact together with others, organizational capacities are still required on the side of the SEI. The dynamics and momentum gained within networks cannot replace this; an (ever so small) organization is necessary to facilitate exchanges and interactions between partners, continuous alignment to the joint mission, relationship building, as well as processes of monitoring and evaluating achievements and impact.

The focus on collaboration with others is important for a critical appreciation of scaling. Working together with others means a relative loss of control compared to scaling via the growth of an organization. At the same time, such a loss of control is necessary if SEI are to empower affected people to find ways of dealing with challenges that suit their contexts (even if the result seems to have little resemblance to the innovator's idea). From this perspective, slow, complex and messy scaling is just as much an indicator of actual collaboration as rapid scaling is an indicator of a non-participatory, one-model-fits-all approach. A key question for the future theory and practice of SEI is how they can develop organizational capacities internally and participatory ways of scaling, thereby initiating innovation processes with others.

8.4   SEI AS POLITICAL ACTORS

We have seen that SEI can be powerful change agents. They perform functions and provide services considered until recently (or still) to be the sole authority of states (for example Ecotact constructs public sanitation infrastructure). SEI also convince many people of their ideas (for example Epple motivates some hundred thousand people to demonstrate for cleaner rivers). They are innovators *for* the public inasmuch as they act on behalf of others. Hence our investigation of what legitimizes their power into authority, that is legitimate power (see our legitimacy theses in Chapter 1).

The first and main source of legitimacy is the SEI's respective innovation inasmuch as it is a social one (*output legitimacy*); there is a tight link here to the prior discussion of capabilities and environmental sustainability. Following our approach to sustainability, SEI need to contribute to strong sustainability and human capabilities. Ecotact builds toilets for others, providing people with access to sanitation in dignity. Echavarria's funds, Kravčík's new water paradigm and WOTR's participatory watershed development seek to improve ecosystem stability and living conditions in poor rural areas. When Epple or Viva con Agua mobilize and enable people, they support human capabilities as well as solutions to problems of water scarcity and insufficient water quality. Nevertheless, in each case there are societal conflicts of interest, value diversity and non-inclusive public spheres, which became visible in our analyses. The SEI have generally faced public opposition; not everybody shares their visions.

On the one hand, all the SEI studied here contribute practical ideas to more sustainable practices in watersheds. On the other hand, their innovations have not (yet) achieved systematic change where it is needed most. While Ecotact has successfully replicated its approach in urban centres, it has run into difficulties in slums, where sanitation problems are most urgent. Or in the case of Epple and SOS Loire Vivante, some interviewees only spoke of an ex-post recognition of the initiatives' achievement to cancel four hydropower-dam projects at the Loire River and to implement an alternative. When SEI take action, the actual output or social impact that could legitimize their agency lies in the future; it is not clear yet if each SEI will be able to convince his or her adversaries and to overcome public opposition. To be sure, we should not underestimate their potential to *initiate* processes of future change; nonetheless, the innovations of SEI frequently can only be considered a potential source of legitimacy.

The second source of legitimacy we proposed is social accountability. While the SEI are not elected by those on whose behalf they take agency, they can be held accountable in a more informal and social manner, for instance by praising or shaming and by supporting or withdrawing participation. There is a civic quality to persons and organizations working within a community doing what is urgent and important. In our case studies, SEI mostly exercised power from within local communities, thus within reach of the affected people (at least more than international experts who come to install their product and leave the community afterwards). Kuria is a Kenyan working in Kenya and Echavarria an Ecuadorian working in Ecuador; though Bacher was born in Switzerland, he made Maharashtra his home early in life; Kravčík is very much involved with the mayors of his native region in Slovakia; Epple still lives in Le Puy and organizes annual cycling trips in the Loire watershed with stops and discussions in villages and towns; finally, personal ties are essential to Viva con Agua's open-network approach and its locally embedded supporters. All social entrepreneurs analysed here travel a lot and involve themselves with people (both advocates and opponents). However, we have found little transparency and no systematic documentation of what the SEI actually do on behalf of others. Only in the WOTR case study did we find systematic evaluation of projects on a regular basis (notably, though, Viva con Agua is very communicative and well documented). Support organizations such as Ashoka concentrate on success, while the opportunity to support the change agents to learn from defeat is not on their public agenda. The SEI lack the time and means for a systematic evaluation; hardly any money is available to systematically evaluate projects once they are implemented. SEI can thus only be considered socially accountable to affected people in a limited sense.

Participation offers a third potential source of legitimacy. Participation refers to the involvement of affected people in a project's decision-making and implementation process. In each case study the SEI has a mediating role by advocating for the affected communities. They are significant inasmuch as they promote a scaling of basic principles and are transition agents who do not simply exercise power for the sake of domination and self-interest. Kuria plans to hand his toilet monuments over to the public municipality after five years. Echavarria is involved in the set-up of new water funds and not in their long-term control and maintenance. WOTR creates local institutions such as the Village Watershed Development Committees, which make major decisions themselves. Viva con Agua calls for decentralized activities that develop their own dynamics. Kravčík and Epple are transition agents who transfer ideas and knowledge on more ecological and decentralized water management through their networks. In some cases at least, the SEI focus on ideas enables the uptake of these ideas elsewhere and independent further development. The Big Jump is a particularly good example of this: an increasing number of events outside Europe demonstrate how Epple's innovation has developed a life of its own. However, while SEI enable participation and ownership, they cannot necessarily guarantee equal participation.

We analysed the outside recognition of SEI as a fourth criterion of legitimacy. If outsiders take an interest and consider innovations valuable, this may increase the local acceptance of an agent vis-à-vis other agents; it also makes it harder to ridicule new ideas. This criterion relates to the second criterion of local embedment and social accountability. Such recognition can be seen in the selection of Echavarria, Epple, Kuria and Kravčík for Ashoka or Schwab fellowships, Marcella D'Souza's Kyoto Water Prize and Benjamin Adrion's 'The Order of Merit of the Federal Republic of Germany'. All of the SEI analysed received various awards, also sometimes in the name of their NGOs and social businesses. Only in one case did we find evidence for negative responses with respect to one award. However, there is a tendency when reporting on such awards in the media to reduce the SEI to a particular project, especially if that fits the pre-established expectations (for example Kuria is mostly recognized as a social entrepreneur in slums even though he is mostly active in urban centres). Thus the attention gained does not necessarily reflect the major activities of the SEI, such as Epple's political advocacy work or Kuria's more beneficial projects in Nairobi's business district. Outside recognition is a further source of legitimacy for each SEI analysed, however at the cost of possibly narrowing down their perception to a specific project.

We arrive at an ambivalent conclusion on the legitimacy of SEI. First, while their innovations potentially contribute to solve public water problems, their ideas usually face opposition and systemic change has not yet happened. We should not underestimate the fact that SEI initiate processes of change. Second, while the local embedment allows affected communities to hold SEI socially accountable, we have found little transparency and no systematic documentation of what the SEI actually do on behalf of others. Third, the SEI are mediators and sometimes their innovations develop a life of their own, enabling others to address water problems. While they enable participation, however, SEI cannot guarantee equal participation. Fourth, outside recognition tends to promote local acceptance but risks oversimplifying perspectives.

8.5 CONCLUSIONS

Reviewing our above results, we come to an understanding of SEI as pioneers who develop and aim to spread novel ideas in collaboration with others for the public good, and also partly succeed in doing so. *Ideas* for the public good in the sustainability context refers to relatively new, practical solutions to challenges regarding strong sustainability and central capabilities. These ideas usually come with an attempt to reconfigure problem perception with a view to central capabilities and environmental sustainability. They typically bank on cooperations at the local level and they aim at empowerment, in particular with a view to improve the capacity of communities to organize themselves and to promote individual and group capacities to aspire. *Pioneer* here refers to the development and testing of new ideas and processes, in the sense of providing an initial proof of functionality as well as making efforts to create or change political, economic and cultural conditions with a view to the respective social mission. *Pioneer* here also refers to achieving the impact with others, where the pioneer – be it a person or organization – needs organizational capacities to trigger and facilitate such collaborative processes. As pioneers for meeting social-ecological challenges, their innovations provide them with a potential source of output legitimacy. Empowerment, social accountability and outside recognition are further potential sources of legitimacy. The actual legitimacy of SEI remains ambivalent partly because the aims are still in the future (output legitimacy is not yet fully clear), partly because there is a lack of transparency and systematic documentation (reduced social accountability) and partly because empowerment may yield only unequal participation possibilities.

Investing in Social Entrepreneurship – The Ashoka Approach Revisited

From a global perspective, no organization has done as much to promote investment in social entrepreneurship as Ashoka, and hence no organization has been as important for defining what 'it' is that ought to be promoted. In view of our conception of social entrepreneurship arrived at above, it is worth revisiting the Ashoka approach, which has remained remarkably stable over the years that we conducted our research project.[9]

Ashoka's focus on the individual and the new idea has proven fruitful in that it allows us to explore social entrepreneurship irrespective of a specific organizational form. With the variety of organizational forms in diverse institutional contexts worldwide, this focus enables a prima facie inclusive approach and avoids *one-size-fits-all* thinking. Yet this also introduces a constant irritation. How are SEI different from organizational forms such as NGOs, businesses or political parties? We have analysed SEI in terms of their initiation of an innovation process rather than an organizational form; this process can be triggered via an NGO, a private consultant, a businessperson, an activist network or anyone with the initiative. Yet if this process initiation is reduced to an individual – the social entrepreneur – then the chances are high that the ability to achieve change is radically limited owing to a lack of organizational capacity. So if change is to be achieved, is there then not an organizational form required? When Ashoka writes they are looking for 'the Andrew Carnegies, Henry Fords, and

Steve Jobses of the citizen sector' (ibid.), we ask: Carnegies, Fords, Jobses *without a company*? The analogy of the business entrepreneur is misleading inasmuch as it understands impact achievement in terms of the old paradigm, that is, organizational growth. This covers up a key question emerging from our case studies: what are the organizational capacities required to achieve change with others? More subtly, what does *in the company of citizens* mean? As far as we can tell, neither practice nor theory has provided answers to these questions. What does seem fruitful is the promotion of strong organizations and networks rather than individuals only.

In regards to the second part of Ashoka's approach, our case studies showed the focus on the new idea (the 'knock-out criterion') to be a possible way to study processes of change in society. The question remains how exactly this new idea is linked to social entrepreneurship. 'Rather than leaving societal needs to the government or business sectors, social entrepreneurs find what is not working and solve the problem by changing the system, spreading the solution, and persuading entire societies to take new leaps'.[10]

According to our conception of social entrepreneurship, the danger with such statements is the creation of misleading expectations. Societal problems are not solved by one actor, let alone one individual. What social entrepreneurs can do, together with their organizations and networks, is initiate processes of change. For this to be successful SEI need to collaborate with institutions, organizations, communities and the people 'in' them. In relation to water issues, we found the collaboration with local and regional government to be a particularly important and no doubt difficult field. A juxtaposition of social entrepreneurship and government, even if not intended, is empirically misleading. It is also normatively problematic: if social entrepreneurship is all about the 'citizens sector', we should remember that citizens ideally govern themselves, that we are the government. As one citizen put it in relation to water conservation problems in Europe: 'The [water] authorities in the widest sense is no one else but us' (quote from Lodemann 2013).

In light of these last two points, it is quite important to note that in more recent work, Ashoka members have argued for a new paradigm of scaling focused on social entrepreneurs achieving impact *in collaboration with others* (McPhedran Waitzer and Paul 2011). Our case studies suggest that this momentum does not likely originate from group entrepreneurship understood as the collaboration between social entrepreneurs;[11] at least in relation to water challenges, we could not find much evidence for this.[12] In practice SEI create networks with groups from civil society, business and government that are directly relevant to the problem they seek to tackle.

While the SEI studied here all demonstrate creativity and ethical fibre, our case studies suggest that it is important to also translate such characteristics from the personal level to the organizational one. If 'ethical fibre' is understood as a matter of trusting the entrepreneur, then on the organizational level such trust calls for transparency and accountability. This point is particularly important when societal change is aimed for in contested societal issues such as access to and distribution of freshwater. In our case studies we found only limited evidence for such transparency and accountability; we see here an opportunity for those who seek to promote SEI. Many have recognized this opportunity already; our point here is to emphasize how important this is. Transparency and accountability cannot be taken for granted however sympathetic or likeable the idea or entrepreneur.

In this book we have followed the school of social innovation (see Chapter 1) and saw that earned income from the market plays only a limited role for SEI in initiating change processes. In the cases analysed we encountered a recurrent difficulty for the initiatives to secure financing. In view of the importance of government for our initiatives and for achieving large-scale change in matters of the public good, we see here an important field for further practical and theoretical work. How can governments from various levels provide space for experimenting with and scaling ideas that improve livelihoods for communities and help restore or maintain ecosystems? This question takes us to the MDG and post-MDG process.

The Millennium Development Goals and the Potential Role of SEI in the MDG and Post-MDG Process

Since the Rio Earth Summit in 1992, *sustainable development* is being widely adopted as a goal by government, business and civil society. Yet it remains controversial and contested. Sustainable development seems to replace the primary focus on economic growth in favour of an integrated social-ecological perspective. While nature conservationists worry this is de facto not enough priority for nature conservation with development (as economic growth) remaining the priority, development groups criticize prioritizing nature conservation at the cost of not paying attention to development demands, especially of the poor worldwide.

Against this background, the *Millennium Development Goals* notably achieved a formulation of development goals that take into account (even if in a limited way) environmental sustainability and human development needs, especially of the poor. The means to achieve these goals, however, were left open. In view of the diversity of historical, natural and situation-specific contexts, the openness towards a diversity of means can be easily appreciated. Yet in practice, this is not what happened. A focus on economic growth as the major strategy for achieving the ends quickly re-emerged (Vandemoortele 2009, p. 364), along with a donor-centric view that focuses on the monetary costs of achieving the goals in 'less developed' countries. 'Estimating a fixed price tag or setting a specific rate of economic growth is symptomatic of the misconception that the MDG can be achieved through a scientific, apolitical and rational process which can be manipulated from the outside and accelerated by external actors' (ibid. 366).

Moreover, this focus on growth left little attention on inequalities. Constructive contributors to the post-MDG debate hence call for a better inclusion of this topic in the formulation of collective responsibilities (Nayyar 2013).

In this predicament with a view to post-MDG goals, what can we say about the role of SEI? First, their advocacy of new ideas for thinking about and dealing with societal challenges provides an antidote to a primarily monetary focus on growth. The lack of organizational specification or growth model allows the identification of SEI in very different contexts worldwide as they emerge in relation to different challenges, thereby preventing the *one-model-fits-all* preconception. Global goals such as the MDG are not of immediate relevance for SEI; their realization in specific contexts is. As we have seen in our analysis of legitimacy, SEI are typically not perceived as powerful outside experts but rather as actors endogenous to a problem context. They encounter problems with the medium-term durability and impact of their approach, yet they are typically still there in that context and can worry about possibilities of backstopping and further adaption of their approaches. This role of the local and endogenous implies that scaling *by the SEI* beyond the region or even globally is a questionable desideratum as it necessarily diminishes this local embedment. The challenge of scaling and diffusion *with others* appears as the true challenge. In short, SEI fit well with the MDG process. 'MDG call for fundamental changes and transformations that must be endogenous. They will seldom be rapid, rational or linear because they will have to address complex political, cultural and ecological constraints' (Vandemoortele 2009, p. 366). In view of the discourse on sustainable development and the contested views on economic growth, justice and environmental protection, social entrepreneurship is a discourse contribution that adopts the economic language of entrepreneurship and innovation, yet necessarily provokes normative questions regarding 'the social' or 'public' beyond technical efficiency and effectiveness. Introducing normativity into economic discourse contributes to a discussion of sustainability beyond 'business as usual' and in favour of collaborative innovation processes oriented towards the common good. The innovations emerge from societal challenges, regarding water in our cases; SEI collaborate because they typically have neither the economic resources of corporations nor the legal power of governments. Empowerment of the target group is also of instrumental importance. Moreover, as societal challenges in the respective contexts are complex and messy, SEI focus both on scaling out and on the conditions of scaling. Rather than limit themselves to a specific sector, SEI use their ideas to invite a reconfiguration of a problem by linking various aspects.

This normativity as a matter of discourse, however, is ambivalent. Powerful donors from the business community along with SEI investors[13] promote a conception of social entrepreneurship that in analogy to business is focused on innovativeness and rapid 'solution' potential. This stands in stark contrast to the messy, contextual approaches we encountered in our case studies. It is noteworthy from a sustainability perspective that while such promotion tends to associate Big Business with the 'good' SEI, to our knowledge it is not yet linked to a simultaneous and sustained debate of the sustainability contribution of business actors themselves and what they might learn from much praised social entrepreneurship. In view of these observations, the increased attention paid by government and regional entities (such as the EU) to SEI and to social innovation promises an interesting enrichment of this debate; it will also hopefully add to an understanding of the role of a proactive state to provide a fair space for experimentation and scaling of ideas.

This takes us to our observation from the introduction of this book that SEI are currently only partly promoted in correspondence to where public needs are most pressing (as understood by the MDG). In particular, Sub-Saharan Africa stands out as an area of many 'white spots' in terms of promoting water-related SEI (see the water maps in Chapter 1). This indicates a potential for further promotion of SEI and once again invites the question why civil society and private donors appear to have focused less in these areas despite the well-known needs.

In sum, we find SEI to promote the global goals of the MDG via context-specific realizations that introduce normativity into the (still frequently) growth-focused and donor-focused MDG and post-MDG debates. They do this along with many other actors from civil society. The actual impact (and hence partly the legitimacy) of this contribution is difficult to evaluate. We can observe that SEI encounter difficulties in overcoming inequalities and achieving empowerment, that they face challenges with medium- and long-term financial security and that this in turn further constrains their organizational capacity to learn, monitor and promote innovation processes. In short, we see a distinct yet modest role for SEI. The approach of SEI-supporting initiatives to cluster themes – be it water, nutrition or the environment more generally – is an interesting proposal that the general public will have to critically discuss for the post-MDG processes. Our research in the water sector suggests that such clusters, if they are to be collaborative efforts for social-ecological change, are better conceived not only as potential for group entrepreneurship amongst SEI but also as collaborations of diverse actors from civil society, business and government with SEI as idea proponents.

Sustainability Science and Research Outlook

The research in this book has been carried out under the umbrella of a research programme for sustainable development. Such research acknowledges the normative dimension of sustainable development as a goal as well as the temporal aspect of urgency this may include. It typically seeks to proceed in a way that includes different disciplines as well as partners from outside academia (see Section 1.6). Accordingly this synthesis chapter closes with a brief reflection of our research as an attempt in sustainability science.

While our evaluative conception and its relation to the MDGs in the discussion above have already clarified how we deal with the challenge of normativity in an urgent context, the cooperation with non-academic partners in the research invites some further reflection.

Our focus on a small number of in-depth case studies is a typical feature of transdisciplinary research (Krohn 2008). The focus on the case in its context and singularity facilitates a shared perspective with actors from practice that puts primary emphasis on dealing with their respective practical problems. At the same time, the focus on the case is in tension with the demand of generality from many disciplines that search for *the* general model or even *the* law or rule. We pursued our research with a theory-thread throughout all cases based on our conception of strong sustainability, human capabilities and legitimacy in relation to a social innovation account of social entrepreneurship.

Still the tension remained, and at times a powerful one, between the sympathetic personal encounter in a case and the distance required by an interdisciplinary approach that seeks to explore theory-based hypotheses and a conception that not all partners will have time or interest to learn more about. From the perspective of each case, or each social entrepreneur, we no doubt could have invested much more into the specific case and its practical development (something we were only able to do with respect to the Big Jump, see next chapter). Especially as the SEI were generally welcoming and helped us to 'study them', there always remained the worry of legitimizing a mission in a way that is beyond the role of scientists. In addition, the dynamics of innovation and the many obstacles encountered by SEI make it very difficult to plan research; some cases unexpectedly evolved and the SEI moved further before we could get a hold on our 'research object' or could ensure that our results were heard.

In this light, it is worthwhile to briefly re-examine the reasons for cooperating with non-academic partners (as stated in Section 1.6, subsection on justified inclusion of non-academics). The first reason – direct cooperation with partners of practice adds a dimension of local and tacit knowledge about the way things get done that enriches the understanding of the researchers – is clearly something we experienced throughout the case studies and in the extra feedback round in Frankfurt. Second, the discussions with social entrepreneurs, their teams and the people they work for with no doubt also helped adjust our understanding of social entrepreneurship. It showed us the complexity of the phenomenon to the point that there were moments of asking whether it is meaningful to speak of something unifying all these cases. Third, the exchange with SEI and their supporters – groups that care especially about the practical implications of research – taught us the importance of some distinctions that we may have been theoretically aware of but were not practically paying sufficient attention to. An important example is the discussion launched by Marcella D'Souza in Frankfurt regarding the question of earned income: for whom? For the SEI or for the community? Who ought to benefit and under what conditions can we legitimately expect SEI to benefit if they work in contexts of poverty? Fourth, working with SEI is a source of creative, wild conjectures for scientists; 'new water paradigm', 'reconciliation with the river' and 'toilet monuments' are all examples of bold yet rich ideas to be examined in applied research in hopes of enriching our understanding of sustainability issues. Finally, it was important for us to discuss our evaluative claims with the SEI prior to the publication of this book. Evaluation is inevitably normative and as there are no final authorities in ethics, this discussion was particularly important with respect to evaluative claims.

It is difficult to evaluate the impact of our approach on the respective SEI, especially with a conceptual approach focused on strong sustainability, human capabilities and legitimacy. At least some of our SEI found this approach helpful, particularly the questions of heterogeneous value that the capabilities approach made available for discussion. The strength here is not a common metrics for operationalization in the sense of measurement, but rather a wide perspective on the various and interrelated aspects of the common good and their realization in problem contexts.

At the workshop in Frankfurt in September 2012, we first made a boat trip with the SEI along the River Main. It was a hot day and our boat was packed; many people were walking along the river. Michal Kravčík took pictures. 'Isn't it great', he said, 'for people to be directly at the water?' He wished people everywhere would have more walking and boating options at their rivers. From the river the land takes on a new perspective. With this we turn in the final chapter to our own, collaborative effort to enter the river, the Big Jump Challenge.

NOTES

1. https://www.ashoka.org/promote (accessed 27 August 2013).
2. Here we expand Appadurai's (2004) concept, introduced in Chapter 5, to the more general ethical framework of the capabilities approach.
3. A flash jump on a bridge rather than a river jump was chosen because the security measures that the jump organizers would have had to meet were too demanding, not least with a view to the uncertain number of participants.
4. As always, there are exceptions. Cooperation with local villages and towns need not be the central means for empowerment. A case in point is the Viva con Agua open-network approach that attracts people at very low threshold levels of involvement, such as micro-donations at rock festivals, then offers increasingly deeper ways of getting involved in civic engagement.
5. Justice demands that we are impartial with respect to the consideration of different generations. As scaling affects (or does not affect) future generations just as much as current generations, we highlight this point with the expression *scaling in time*.
6. In a general discussion of the scaling literature, this point is well argued by Anna Davies and Julie Simon (2013).
7. As part of the conference we organized a workshop on capacity building together with Ashoka and the Siemens Foundation.
8. However, a similar paradigm discussion can already be found in the earlier development cooperation literature (Uvin, Jain and Brown 2000).
9. https://www.ashoka.org/support/criteria (accessed 12 September 2013).
10. https://www.ashoka.org/social_entrepreneur.
11. https://www.ashoka.org/promote.
12. At the beginning of this research project, we explored the Ashoka Mosaic approach in cooperation with David Strelneck. However, we found it difficult as a research group to explore and justify patterns of water-related social entrepreneurs independently of a specific theoretical approach, and also found the approach to meet with little interest from the side of the SEI. Therefore, we did not pursue this approach further.
13. See Drayton 2006, and for discussion Boddice 2009.

9. Getting things done together? From collaborative competition to collaborative campaigns

Rafael Ziegler

9.1 INTRODUCTION

The Big Jump Challenge emerged from a confluence of developments. In May 2010 Big Jump inventor Roberto Epple (see Chapter 3) visited us in Greifswald to talk about river conservation and how to achieve sustainable change. We could not leave this as only a talk and miss the opportunity for the first ever Greifswald Big Jump. It was a grey day, cold with fog and rain; nevertheless, students, university staff and journalists came out (with their umbrellas) for a walk along the Ryck. Landscape ecologist Wendelin Wichtmann shared information about various aspects of the ecology in and along the Ryck. At noon colleagues and students jumped into the Ryck, which offered a refreshing swimming opportunity at about 16°C. Since then, collective Ryck jumps have followed in 2010, 2011, 2012 and 2013; all subsequent ones, however, have been held in the summer.

Before Epple's visit we had already discussed the goals, achievements and limitations of a collaborative competition with Ashoka staff and the betterplace lab, a think (and do) tank associated with the German social entrepreneurship initiative betterplace. We presented the results of our analysis of collaborative competition and discussed the possibility of conducting such a collaborative competition in the German language (the Ashoka competitions are not available in German). Finally, we put the analysis results of collaborative competitions together with the inspiration for the Big Jump and decided to launch the Big Jump Challenge as a socio-ecological experiment for sustainability in the water sector.

Collaboration and cooperation are frequently demanded to improve results and outputs within civil society, and between civil society, business and government for the benefit of society as a whole. A recent contribution to this demand from the sphere of social entrepreneurship is experiments with collaborative competitions, which mix cooperation with the individual participant's ambition to succeed.

At first sight the idea of collaborative competition seems counterintuitive, a seemingly paradoxical mix of cooperative and antagonistic elements. To be sure, in capitalism *competition* is constantly called for, not just in the economy but also as a means for more innovation, efficiency and accountability in other social spheres.[1] Just as frequent, however, are objections to the extension of competitive mechanisms to civil society and politics. *Collaboration*, though used less frequently, is spoken of when competitors work together, for example in the purchase of inputs of their respective production. There is also collaboration in science when people from different disciplines (and even from outside academia) work together for an improved understanding and way of dealing with problems, such as social and environmental ones. Sustainability science as an applied science explicitly devoted to sustainable development as a normative goal is an example of such collaboration between disciplines and specialities, especially between natural and social sciences (De la Vega-Leinert et al. 2009, Bettencourt and Kaur 2011) as well as between scientists and other societal groups (Funtowicz and Ravetz 1993, Ziegler and Ott 2011).

In this chapter we first introduce the idea of an online collaborative competition as pioneered by the Ashoka Changemaker Initiative (ACI). We present the results of an analysis of a collaborative competition held by the ACI in the domain of drinking water and sanitation, particularly our findings of limited evidence for collaboration (Ziegler and Hamker 2011). In 2012 we conducted the Big Jump Challenge as *collaborative campaign* inspired by the idea of collaborative competition while seeking to improve on its collaborative aspect. We report on this experiment we carried out in an effort to make our findings productive and to learn from them. The analysis of the experiment takes on the theme of a new paradigm of scaling (Chapter 8) and explores its possibilities and limitations within a practical experiment for human capabilities and environmental sustainability.

9.2   IN SEARCH OF A COLLABORATIVE SPIRIT

In the context of social entrepreneurship, the theme of collaborative competition was pioneered by the ACI, which presents itself as the 'world's first global online "open source" community that competes to identify the best solutions to social problems'.[2] The initiative has run more than 45 collaborative competitions on social and environmental issues – including maternal health, women and sport, new media, tourism, and drinking water and sanitation. This last issue is particularly interesting for our research interests; for this chapter we thus focus on the drinking water and sanitation competition.

While contributors to the competitions include social entrepreneurs who were already generally selected by Ashoka as fellows, the competitions are not limited to Ashoka fellows, but open to anyone (with access to the Internet). The design structure of the competitions follows a four-month schedule: 1) identification of the topic and its key questions; 2) online launch of the competition; 3) competition period – online entries, comments, revisions, and so on; 4) selection of up to 15 finalists by a jury (appointed by ACI); 5) vote on the top proposals by the Changemakers Community, that is, all ACI participants, not just the jury. Companies and foundations sponsor the costs of running the competitions; sponsors may also convene follow-up meetings and give further support after the competition.

Recent work in sustainability science has highlighted the importance of an inclusive approach for sustainability projects, including the discovery of new ideas. Silvio Funtowicz and Jeremy Ravetz have coined the term *extended peer-communities* to highlight the importance of moving beyond disciplinary expert perspectives and towards an approach that appropriately includes affected stakeholders as well as local and implicit knowledge (Funtowicz and Ravetz 1993). Drawing on this perspective, we analyse the collaborative competition approach as a public, open, dynamic and reciprocal peer-review process (Ziegler and Hamker 2011). 1) *Public*: All entries and comments are publicly posted. 2) *Open*: Anyone with Internet access can become a contributor (of an idea or of comments on the ideas of others). 3) *Dynamic*: Contributors can respond to comments, which is potentially developmental in that contributors can improve their entries in response to comments. 4) *Reciprocal*: Contributors are simultaneously reviewers.

These categories enable us to track the collaborative quality of the online competition and its potential contribution to discovering and improving ideas. To this end, we analyse in depth the ACI online collaborative competition on the drinking water and sanitation crisis.[3] There were 263 ideas for dealing with the water and sanitation crises made by proponents from 52 different countries. Out of the 263 entries, 143 were commented upon; however, the distribution of comments was skewed and 12 of the entries received almost a third of all comments. In total, 694 comments were made. We also found that in the final vote the jury and the online community did not consider refining and enriching, as part of a developmental process, a necessary condition for winning proposals: none of the finalists had responded to criticisms or suggestions before being selected for the final vote. This result was confirmed by an examination of four other randomly chosen ACI collaborative competitions.

Nevertheless, we did find evidence for reciprocity. About 60 per cent of participants, 150 persons of the 254 persons posting an entry, also commented on other entries. Less than a third of all persons posting an entry replied to comments on their entries (72 persons). Generally the distribution of comments was skewed, with about three-quarters of all entries receiving zero to three comments, and a few entries the majority of comments (Ziegler and Hamker 2011, Section 9.4). Some online collaboration was thus in evidence, but not amongst the winners and very uneven in distribution.[4]

Our analysis suggests that online competition gives global visibility to ideas. It 'surfaces' them, as the organizers put it. The key innovative aspect of collaborative competition is its way of making ideas visible to a worldwide community of people interested in change, rather than the collaborative effort to discover ideas and improve proposals.

From a practical perspective, this raises the question: can the collaborative aspect be improved upon? Our analysis above of the ACI competition suggests that strengthening the collaborative spirit might be achieved via the following improvements. 1) *Offer of different awards*: Contributors to the competition vary from speculative proposals to ideas already manifested in projects of several years' time, hence the competition is like one in which the local football lover competes with the professional football star. Different awards could deal with this; alternatively, the target group could be narrowed down so as to promote a level playing field. 2) *Change of competition design*: Collaboration could be promoted via rules, if eligibility as a finalist depends on collaborative behaviour such as commenting on other entries and responding to comments, or refining one's proposal; alternatively the competition theme could be chosen in such a way that collaboration is required or makes intuitive sense. 3) *Improvement of online platform*: Make the linkage between proposals and comments easily visible so that dialogue can be traced without difficulties.

Yet, such improvements are more easily suggested than implemented. Based on our analysis of the ACI competition, we decided to experiment further with the idea of collaborative competition. Following discussions with Ashoka, the advisory board of our research group, other scientists and civil society organizations, we decided to explore the idea further in terms of a collaborative campaign to be designed and carried out together with French social entrepreneur Roberto Epple and his European Rivers Network (ERN), the betterplace lab, Viva con Agua, the Grüne Liga Berlin, the Deutsche Umwelthilfe and the Global Nature Fund (with its living lakes programme). The experiment was in German only (language is an important practical barrier for communication online and offline).

9.3 THE BIG JUMP CHALLENGE – A COLLABORATIVE CAMPAIGN

In view of our analysis of the ACI collaborative competition, we decided to try out a design that focused on a more narrowly defined target group and a more narrowly defined topic with active encouragements and possibilities for collaboration (compare suggestion 1 above). This resulted in the Big Jump Challenge as a collaborative youth campaign for water conservation, accompanying the already established European Bathing Day (see Chapter 3). We focused on youth between the ages of 14 and 21 thereby eliminating participation of experienced water conservation experts in favour of a focus on students. Only this age group was allowed to enter the competition. The topic we focused on is public participation in water conservation for Europe in the context of the European Water Framework Directive (EWFD; see also European Commission 2003 and Chapter 3 in this book). The EWFD mandates the good condition of European rivers and lakes by 2015 and is widely acclaimed as a piece of progressive environmental legislation, not least because it requires the active involvement of the public for achieving water conservation. However, it is far from clear that implementation will be achieved on time. For example, the German government stated in 2011 that as of 2009 only about 10 per cent of rivers and lakes had reached a good ecological condition and that by 2015 only an additional 8.5 per cent would reach the target.[5] Thus further public participation and even public pressure is called for in the implementation of the EWFD.

Roberto Epple, a French environmental activist and social entrepreneur (see Chapter 3), developed the idea of a *Big Jump* as a practical way to make water conservation public. His idea is that the experience of swimming together in lakes and rivers across Europe at the same time (the Big Jump) has the potential to reconcile people with their rivers and lakes and to foster the desire for participation and involvement in water conservation. How a Big Jump happens at a particular lake or river, however, is a matter of good ideas for carrying out fun and educational events. With a view to scaling, the collaborative campaign offers a way of further scaling out the idea in a way that encourages the original adaption of the idea in regards to the respective river or lake. Moreover, these variations of ideas ideally reinforce each other and result in a collaborative Big Jump across many rivers and lakes (compare suggestion 2 above). The term collaborative campaign here is meant to indicate this priority of joint action over individual success. In a nutshell, we recombined the lessons from our ACI analysis with Epple's Big Jump idea and our analysis of it (Chapter 3).

For the ACI water initiative, collaboration was encouraged in the first place via an online platform for entries and comments. Our analysis of this collaborative competition as well as discussions with our partners when preparing our collaborative campaign suggest that online collaboration alone may not be the most effective, and possibly not the most important, way of collaborating. In the case of water conservation, the achievement of water conservation strongly depends on effective water authorities that are able to implement the EWFD. Encouraging collaboration with those authorities – who are mandated by the EWFD to involve the public in their efforts to fulfil the EWFD requirements – therefore seemed a natural addition. Local jump organizers were invited to contact their local authorities in advance so as to become informed about the status of their rivers and lakes, as well as the implementation stage of the EWFD, and to post the results on the online platform along with a rating of the reply (if they received one). In this way they would challenge, in a friendly way, the authorities regarding the EWFD implementation, and they would also be better informed for the preparation of local jumps creatively adapted to their context. This addition finally gave rise to the name of our experiment: *Big Jump Challenge*.

The best Big Jump teams were then invited to a final *river parliament* in Berlin, where they presented their results, requests and recommendations to members of Parliament.[6] They were selected by an independent jury according to the following criteria: originality of the jump, contact with local authorities, number of participants in the jump, publicity created in terms of media attention and local integration of the jump (for example with the municipality, local associations, and so on).

The Big Jump Challenge was launched in March 2012 with an online platform that allows participants to register, post their ideas and comment on those of others. The platform also includes background information, teaching materials, assistance for contacting local water authorities as well as the possibility to upload and comment on the answers provided by the authorities. The online design and provision of materials was made via a view to the target group. The Big Jump of students took place on 17 June 2012 (the last weekend before the summer vacation in German schools) and the river parliament in Berlin on 17 October 2012 (see Figure 9.1 for the structure of the challenge).

This collaborative campaign was coordinated by a network. Scaling out of the platform thus followed the new paradigm of scaling (see Chapter 8). Roberto Epple and the ERN provided the initial idea and from an early stage (January 2012) onwards we discussed the goals of the campaign with all of the organizers. The actual organization employed a network of established organizations seeking to complement their experiences: the social-ecological research group GETIDOS took on the role of coordinator in

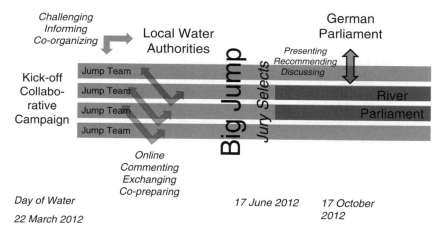

Figure 9.1   Collaborative campaign structure

Germany, the betterplace lab designed the online platform, the Deutsche Umwelthilfe, Global Nature Fund and Grüne Liga Berlin provided expertise and experience with water conservation, the ERN helped disseminate and organize the campaign, and Viva con Agua contacted schools and youths in general drawing on their already established network of young volunteers.

The next section turns to the analysis of results.

9.4   THE BIG JUMP CHALLENGE 2012 – FINDINGS

As a deliberate experiment in collaborative competition, we accompanied the Big Jump Challenge 2012 with an evaluation that focused on the individual level of the participants, on the societal level of the affected community and on the organizational level of the Big Jump Challenge coordination network. The intermediary results of this evaluation were presented to participants for an internal feedback session during a meeting prior to the river parliament in Berlin. The evaluation results along with the participants' feedback inform our critical discussion at the end of this chapter. Information for the evaluation was gathered via an online participant survey conducted after the Big Jump,[7] an analysis of media coverage on the Big Jump Challenge between March and July 2012, as well as interviews with our network partners.

Individual Level Results

On the level of participants, our goal was to better understand the impact of the Big Jump on personal capabilities of participants. These capabilities are political participation (engaging), play (having fun), education (being informed) and concern for the environment (being concerned).

Engaging: Of the 55 registered groups, 30 contacted their local authorities (for the remaining groups we lack information), thus engaging prior to the Jump by using their right to get informed about the state of the water conservation implementation at their given river or lake. In the survey, about 40 per cent of participants according to their own assessment had not been involved in nature conservation prior to the jump; of these, more than a third (37 per cent) stated that they would further engage in water conservation after the Jump.

Having fun: Survey participants were asked to rate their enjoyment of the Big Jump on a scale of 1 to 10, with 1 being an activity that one really does not enjoy and 10 being one's most preferred personal activity. Respondents rated the Big Jump with an 8.5 on average. Thus, the Jump contributes a fun activity. About 85 per cent of all participants said that they would jump again.

Being informed: Teachers were offered an educational package as a free download so as to prepare and motivate students for the Jump. However, only five groups (out of 55) downloaded or requested the package. About 65 per cent of students participating in the Jump rated their increase in knowledge as average (12 per cent as low, 23 per cent as high).

Being concerned for the environment: In the survey, participants were asked whether, following the Jump, rivers and lakes had become a more frequent topic of conversation with friends and whether they followed reports on water conservation in the media with an increased interest. About three-quarters of all participants (74 per cent) agreed with at least one of the two statements.

The Big Jump as a playful and fun activity is thus a central aspect of the Big Jump Challenge. The capability of engaging (political participation) calls for further promotion, as indicated by almost half the participants likely not contacting their authorities. To be sure, this political participation is not a usual action students would engage in, and in this sense the participation rate can be interpreted as a relative success, yet one to be further promoted with a view to the EWFD goals for public involvement.[8] The Jump appears to have particularly promoted a sense of concern for rivers and lakes. The results were least impressive for education. This may be owing to the difficult and technical nature of the EWFD, and water conservation more generally; at any rate, the apparent promotion for a concern for the environment suggests that there is much space to improve the educational options offered as part of the Big Jump Challenge, in particular if the concern for the environment in its local context can be addressed.

Societal Level of Collaboration

The Big Jump Challenge focused on collaboration in two main ways. First and foremost, collaboration happened via the contacting of water authorities for information and possible cooperation. There were 30 jumps that contacted their authorities (for the remaining groups we lack information); of those, 23 received a response from their respective authorities. In the survey the groups that received responses could rate their satisfaction as to how well they felt informed by the response (satisfied, neutral or dissatisfied): 43 per cent felt satisfied, 36 per cent neutral and 21 per cent dissatisfied. In a few cases – the Jumps at the Nagold, the Mühlenriede and the Spree – there was active exchange between jump organizers and authorities in the form of face-to-face meetings, the provision of additional information and help with the organization of the jump. The result was above average jumps (with Nagold and Mühlenriede as finalists).

Second, the collaboration between jump organizers via the online platform followed a pattern familiar to the ACI. Almost half of all jumps received no comments at all, whereas most of the others received some (on average three) and the few remaining received most of the comments (up to 14). Comments were mostly focused on getting informed (73 comments) and congratulating others (12 comments). Thus, while participants may have learnt from others – for example, the Mühlenriede Jump uploaded extended information about their jump and the opening of a nature conservation path to be opened with the jump – there is no online traceable evidence of extended discussion and mutual learning. This result confirms the analysis of the ACI competition. In the feedback round of the Big Jump Challenge, a majority of participants declared themselves dissatisfied with the homepage design for collaboration. They saw a lack of or insufficient exchange of ideas, and also an inadequate homepage design for this purpose.[9] In short, in our experiment we were not able to live up to our own suggestion for improvement 3 in Section 9.2 above.

Media attention on the local jumps was generally quite impressive. More than 70 media reports about local jumps appeared in newspapers (and their online platforms) as well as on local TV and radio. The majority of these reports clustered on the day of the Big Jump. Creative jumps received special attention – for instance, the 'dry jump' in the form of a flashmob that happened next to the Alster in Hamburg after the authorities had prohibited an actual jump. About 80 per cent of jumps were announced or reported in the media.[10] The topic of water conservation was well covered in all reports; the EWFD was explicitly referred to in about 60 per cent of all reports. About 45 per cent of articles published prior to a jump also referred to the collaboration with authorities.[11]

Organizational Level of Scaling the Big Jump Challenge

On the organizational level, the network succeeded in scaling out the Big Jump according to the following criteria:

a. *Spreading the Big Jump* – only 9 per cent of the jumps took place in towns that had participated in Big Jump activities prior to the jump (in comparison to the general ERN Big Jump taking place in 2011). Thus, many new participants were found.
b. *Deepening the Big Jump* – collaboration with the authorities, along with the possibilities of online collaboration, are novel features that likely contribute to the impact of the jump on both the personal level and the societal level (see results above; see also for comparison the media analysis in Chapter 3).

Excursus: Jumping – A Good Investment?

The Big Jump Challenge 2012 was also accompanied by a *Social Return on Investment* (SROI) study.[12] The investment for the challenge from March to October 2012 included the costs of staffing the organizing institutions, travel and the dissemination of materials such as flyers: the investment totalled 30 277 €. We additionally calculated an average cost for local jumps based on the mean of known costs at five jumps; this came to 224.80 € per local jump for hiring security staff (typically from the German Life Saving Association DLRG) and totalled 10 116 € for all jumps. Thus a rough estimate of the total investment comes to 40 393 €.

Outputs and outcomes also were tracked following the SROI methodology; however, main outputs and outcomes – such as the ones introduced above on the personal level – are difficult to monetize. The SROI therefore cannot be seen as a comprehensive tool of social impact, but rather as a communication tool with respect to the economic aspect of the campaign. Nevertheless, two outcomes of the campaign can be monetized in our view:

1. If participants prefer to swim in a river and lake rather than a swimming pool, we can assume that they would be willing to pay at least the equivalent cost of a swimming pool entry for river or lake swimming.

As a medium entry cost for swimming pool entries we calculated 2.87 €, then multiplied this cost by the number of participants we assumed (based on the survey) to have such a preference. This yielded a value of 1767 €.

2. Media attention for the Big Jump (and thereby for water conservation) would have alternatively been possible via advertisement in the respective media. We can calculate the equivalent cost of media coverage that reported on the Big Jump, based on their respective charges for advertisements. We subtracted 20 per cent of this cost because unplanned media attention does not carry the message in the exact way one would like it (however, it is more authentic than an advertisement). We thus arrived at an equivalent advertisement cost of 78 947 €. As we were not able to track all the coverage, this is an underestimate rather than an overestimate.

From these calculations we subtracted the so-called deadweight – in our case, the activities that might have taken place anyway. A comparison with the Big Jump in 2011 suggests that 9 per cent of jumps might have taken place anyway owing to prior acquaintance with the Big Jump. It is highly unlikely that any of the remaining jumps would have taken place without the organization of the Big Jump Challenge (error of attribution). Taking these considerations into account, we arrive at an impact of 71 841 €, and hence an estimate for the social return on investment of 1.77 € for each invested euro.

9.5 GETTING THINGS DONE TOGETHER AND SUSTAINABLY?

What have we learnt from this experiment for getting things done together in a sustainable way? On the individual level of participants, the results on the capabilities of political participation, play, education and concern for the environment were generally encouraging. The combination of engaging in a fun way and becoming informed and concerned for the environment is mutually reinforcing. However, there is much space for improvement with respect to direct and indirect conversion factors. Helping students to convert the available knowledge about aquatic ecosystems into personal environmental knowledge for their respective rivers and lakes is a task where the evaluation results show much space for improvement in terms of appropriate and attractive teaching offers.

Just as important are indirect conversion factors (Ziegler, Dietsche and Karanja 2013), which are those factors required for a stable use of goods and services (such as teaching materials). The campaign showed especially impressive results when schools and teachers got fully engaged and included the water education as part of school teaching. The inclusion of water conservation – and specifically the Big Jump as an action learning possibility – in regular school curricula is an indirect conversion factor for long-term deep impact; in our experiment this was only very partly achieved and shows that a better understanding of teachers' and students' needs would have been required. Just as important are parallel opportunities with associations and clubs that have a direct interest in water conservation, from nature conservation associations to sports clubs for diving and canoeing.

On the organizational level, the open-network approach chosen for the campaign follows the idea of the *new scaling paradigm* with diverse partners that seek to advance the campaign via their competences and networks. Our evaluation shows this approach to be a success in the sense that participants were gained from new regions, and there were more participants over all (in comparison to the same regions the year before). Also, the network approach deepened the Big Jump idea via the creation of an online platform; this makes the individual jumps visible, including the links to their respective water authorities, as parts of a whole water conservation project. At the same time, the experience clearly demonstrates a central challenge for the open-network approach. Each participating organization will usually already have its own mission, agenda and tasks; keeping organizations working together on the practical focus of educational, joyful and participatory local jumps – and not just passing on messages via Facebook and newsletters – is therefore a real challenge, which relies on a coordinator to put in much additional energy exclusively devoted to the coordinating task. It is also very clear that parallel to the personal level of participation – where the real experience of a Big Jump is very important and not just the online exchange – it is hard to substitute for real face-to-face exchange on the organizational level. Regular personal encounters, 'deep networking' as Roberto Epple calls it, is only imperfectly replaced with emails and Skype.

On the societal level, the Big Jump is an example of a constructive, nonviolent way of communicating the implementation difficulties of existing laws and policies, and bringing these issues to public attention. This is a central point in regards to the implementation challenges of practically all major sustainability regimes and policies. Examples include the difficulties of implementing climate policies and biodiversity policies. In view of these challenges, where it is often the case that laws and policies are stuck in the process or not fully implemented, creative ways of informing and empowering the public are one domain for innovators. As our experiment indicates, the media is ready to report. In addition, digital technology such as homepages and social media allows organizers to make actions visible in a relatively cheap and shared way: it is not just a local jump (X) in a particular place (Y), but a visible surfacing of all actions at the same time. However, our experiment again highlighted the difficulty of triggering online collaboration. As in the ACI, evidence for online collaboration remained limited. Finally, this result in no way yields a recommendation to prioritize the competition, or to even drop entirely the 'collaborative' element in collaborative competition. To the contrary, in our experience it highlights as the key challenge to design and communicate effectively the reasons for collaboration for a larger cause. This, and not competition, is a central challenge.

Henry Thoreau made a life experiment: he spent a year alone at *Walden Pond*. He observed the dynamics of the water and the forest, and recorded his own needs. As a thinker he inspired many to reflect on *the good life* in a way that is mindful of our natural environment and to put such action into practice even if it requires civil disobedience. Thoreau suggests that once the needs for food, shelter and so on are met, 'there is an alternative than to obtain superfluities; and that is, to *adventure on life* now, [our] vacation from humbler toils having commenced' (Thoreau 1993, p. 10, italics added). Social-ecological innovations such as the Big Jump provide experimental space for *adventures on life*. While Thoreau himself may have preferred the solitary jump into his Walden Pond, here the adventures are experienced together. Getting things done sustainably is a collaborative challenge.[13]

NOTES

1. No doubt, this point also pertains in particular to social entrepreneurship. In a survey of 200 social entrepreneurship initiatives, Johanna Mair, Julie Battilana and Julian Cardenas find various entrepreneurial models but one common logic of justification for social entrepreneurship: efficiency, productivity and operational effectiveness (Mair, Battilana and Cardenas 2012, p. 363).
2. http://www.changemakers.com/en-us/competitions (accessed 30 April 2010).
3. http://www.changemakers.com/en-us/waterandsanitation (accessed 26 February 2013).
4. These findings on online commenting are limited: the method of analysis did not include collaboration beyond the online platform (emails, phone calls, meetings, effects on social innovators in other domains, and so on).
5. http://dipbt.bundestag.de/dip21/btd/17/080/1708036.pdf (accessed 15 March 2013).
6. There is a parliamentary group with members from each political party specifically devoted to 'free flowing rivers' (name of the parliamentary group).
7. Invitation to participate in the online survey was sent to participants via the jump coordinators after the Big Jump – 48 people participated; 21 of the participants were jump coordinators.
8. Further promotion of political participation, however, need not be narrowly construed in terms of collaboration with water authorities. Some groups may also favour

alternative, different ways of getting engaged publicly, and for this reason not contact their authorities.

9. For example, jump organizers were not automatically notified if somebody posted a comment with respect to their jump outline.
10. For the remaining jumps there was either no coverage or we were not able to track it.
11. The media analysis along with all survey results is published in the report 'Big Jump Challenge 2012 – Dokumentation für Jump-Teams und Partner' (in German) and available for download from www.getidos.net.
12. We followed the approach proposed by the SROI Network (http://www.thesroinetwork.org/publications/doc_details/241-a-guide-to-social-return-on-investment-2012 (accessed 20 August 2013). To this end, two members of the organizing team attended an SROI workshop prior to the Big Jump Challenge. The SROI was chiefly carried out by Lukas Richter and Martin Schreck, and its documentation is also available from www.getidos.net.).
13. At the time of writing the Big Jump Challenge 2013 is running, and Roberto Epple has announced first plans for a European-wide 2015 Big Jump.

References

Alvord, S. H., P. D. Brown and C. W. Letts (2004), 'Social entrepreneurship and societal transformation. An exploratory study', *Journal of Applied Behavioral Science*, 40, 260–82.

Anderson, B. and J. G. Dees (2006), 'Rhetoric, reality and research: building a solid foundation for the practice of social entrepreneurship', in A. Nicholls (ed.), *Social Entrepreneurship: New Models of Sustainable Social Change*, Oxford: Oxford University Press, pp. 144–68.

Appadurai, A. (2004), 'The capacity to aspire: culture and the terms of recognition', in V. Rao and M. Walton (eds), *Culture and Public Action*, Stanford: Stanford University Press, pp. 59–84.

Aquastat, FAO, available at: http://www.fao.org/nr/water/aquastat/main/index.stm (accessed 30 August 2012).

Barlow, M. (2008), *Blue Covenant: The Global Water Crisis and the Coming Battle for the Right to Water*, New York: The New Press.

Bettencourt, L. and J. Kaur (2011), 'Evolution and structure of sustainability science', *PNAS*, 108 (49), December 6.

Boddice, R. (2009), 'Forgotten antecedents: entrepreneurship and the social in history', in R. Ziegler (ed.), *An Introduction to Social Entrepreneurship: Voices, Preconditions, Contexts*, Cheltenham, UK and Northampton, MA, USA: Edward Elgar Publishing.

Bradach, J. (2003), 'Going to scale: the challenge of replicating social programs', *Stanford Social Innovation Review*, 19–25.

Bradach, J. (2010), 'Scaling impact: How to get 100X the results with 2X the organization', *Stanford Social Innovation Review*, 26–8.

Bundesministerium der Justiz (BMJ) (2006), 'Verordnung ueber natuerliches Mineralwasser, Quellwasser und Tafelwasser (Mineral- und Tafelwasserverordnung)', available at http://www.gesetze-im-internet.de/bundesrecht/min_tafelwv/gesamt.pdf (accessed 17 September 2013).

Bundesministerium für Umwelt, Naturschutz und Reaktorsicherheit (BMU) (2010), 'Die Wasserrahmenrichtlinie: Auf dem Weg zu guten Gewaessern', available at http://www.bmu.de/fileadmin/bmuimport/files/pdfs/allgemein/application/pdf/broschuere_wasserrahmenrichtlinie_bf.pdf (accessed 17 September 2013).

Bundesregierung (2010), 'Nationale Engagementstrategie der

Bundesregierung', available at http://www.forum-engagement-partizipat ion.de/?loadCustomFile=Publikationen/Nationale_Engagementstrateg ie_10–10–06.pdf (accessed 17 September 2013).

CCSDPL Common Czecho-Slovak Digital Parliamentary Library (2010), Original text, 33rd Session, 9 July 1959, available at http://fenrir.psp.cz/ (accessed 29 April 2010).

Cho, A. H. (2006), 'Politics, values and social entrepreneurship: a critical appraisal', in J. Mair, J. Robinson and K. Hockerts (eds), *Social Entrepreneurship*, London: Palgrave, pp. 35–56.

Costanza, R., R. d'Arge, R. de Groot, S. Farber, M. Grasso, B. Hannon, K. Limburg et al. (1997), 'The value of the world's ecosystem services and natural capital', *Nature*, 387, 253–60.

Daily, G. (ed.) (1997), *Nature's Services: Societal Dependence on Natural Ecosystems*, Washington DC: Island Press.

Davies, A. and J. Simon (2013), 'Growing and diffusing social innovation: mapping the current knowledge base'. Paper presented at the 2013 International Social Innovation Research Conference, Oxford University.

Dees, G. (2001), 'The Meaning of Social Entrepreneurship', available at http://www.caseatduke.org/documents/dees_sedef.pdf (accessed 11 May 2009).

Defourny, J.and M. Nyssens (2010), 'Conceptions of social enterprise and social entrepreneurship in Europe and the United States: convergences and divergences', *Journal of Social Entrepreneurship*, 1 (1), 32–53.

Department of Land Resources, Ministry o. R. D. G. o. I. (2006), 'From Hariyali to Neeranchal'.

Deutsche Umwelthilfe (2007), 'Zehn Jahre Lebendige Elbe. Ein Jahrzehnt voller Ereignisse bietet Grund zum Feiern', *DUH Welt* (2), 8–17, available at www.duh.de/fileadmin/user_upload/download/DUH_Pu blikationen/DUH_Welt_08/DUHwelt_05_06–07/welt2_07_Internet.pdf (accessed 20 June 2012).

Deutscher Spendenrat and GfK (Gesellschaft fuer Konsumforschung) (2012), 'Bilanz des Helfens 2012', available at http://www.spendenrat. de/filearchive/51f5cc7df589a49c7a7e07dcc149b13d.pdf (accessed 17 September 2013).

Directive (2000/60/EC), Guidance Document No. 8, Public Participation in Relation to the Water Framework Directive Working Group 2–9 Public Participation.

Dobner, P. (2010), *Wasserpolitik. Zur politischen Theorie, Praxis und Kritik globaler Governance*, Berlin: Suhrkamp.

Drayton, Bill (2006), 'Everyone a changemaker: social entrepreneurship's ultimate goal', *Innovations*, 1 (1), 80–96, Winter issue.

D'Souza, M. and C. Lobo (2004), 'Watershed development, water management and the millennium'. Conference Paper.

D'Souza, M. and C. Lobo (2008), 'Restoring ecosystems and renewing lives: the story of Mhaswandi, a once poor village in India', in P. Galizzi and A. Herklotz (eds), *The Role of the Environment in Poverty Alleviation*, New York: Fordham University Press, pp. 121–44.

Dušička, P., T. Hodák and P. Šulek (2010), 'Historical development of small hydropower plants', *Engineering Structures*, professional journal, available at http://www.asb.sk/ (accessed 29 April 2010).

Easterly, W. (2006), *The White Man's Burden: Why the West's Efforts to Aid the Rest Have Done so Much Ill and So Little Good*, Oxford: Oxford University Press.

Ebrahim, A. and V. K. Rangan (2010), 'Acumen fund: measurement in impact investing', Harvard Business School (*Harvard Business School Cases*).

Echavarria, M. (2002), 'Water user associations in the Cauca Valley, Colombia: a voluntary mechanism to promote upstream–downstream cooperation in the protection of rural watersheds', *Land–Water Linkages in Rural Watersheds Case Study Series*, Rome: FAO.

Ecotact, Ecotact Homepage, available at http://www.ecotact.org (accessed 12 January 2012).

Ecotact (2010a), 'Ecotact – Investing in innovations' (company brochure).

Ecotact (2010b), 'Ikotoilet manual: a framework for sustainable management of public Ikotoilet – urban Nairobi', unpublished manuscript.

EcoDecisión (2011), 'What we do', available at http://www.ecodecision. com.ec/html/achievements.html (accessed 18 October 2011).

European Commission (2003), Common Implementation Strategy for the Water Framework Directive.

European Commission (2012), 'The EU Water Framework Directive – integrated river basin management for Europe', available at http://ec.europa.eu/environment/water/water-framework/index_en.html (accessed 20 June 2012).

Federal Ministry for the Environment, Nature Conservation and Nuclear Safety, Umweltbundesamt (2010), 'Die Wasserrahmenrichtlinie – Auf dem Weg zu guten Gewässern', available at www.umweltdaten.de/publikationen/fpdf-l/4012.pdf (accessed 11 July 2013).

Fondo para la Protección del Agua (FONAG) (2013), 'El Fondo', available at http://www.fonag.org.ec/inicio/quienes-somos/el-fondo.html (accessed 5 August 2013).

Funtowicz, S. and J. Ravetz (1993), 'Science for the post-normal age', *Futures*, 25 (7), 735–55.

Gallie, W. (1956), 'Essentially contested concepts', *Proceedings of the Aristotelian Society*, 56, 167–98.

Gebauer, J. and R. Ziegler (2013), 'Corporate social responsibility und social entrepreneurship – Entwicklungen, Debatten und Perspektiven für Forschung und Praxis', in J. Gebauer and H. Schirmer (eds), *Unternehmerisch und verantwortlich wirken? Forschung an der Schnittstelle von Corporate Social Responsibility und Social Entrepreneurship*, Schriftenreihe des IÖW 204/13, pp. 15–67.

Government of India (2005), 'Millennium Development Goals – India Country Report 2005'.

Government of India (2008), 'Common Guidelines for Watershed Development Projects'.

Government of Kenya (2007), 'Kenya Vision 2030, the popular version', Nairobi.

Government of Slovakia, Provision of the Government of the Slovak Republic, No. 183 of 9 March 2011 for the proposal of the first implementation project of the Programme of Landscape Revitalization and Integrated River Basin Management in the Slovak Republic (2011), Material number: 5697/2011.

Grenier, P. (2009), 'Social entrepreneurship in the UK: from rhetoric to reality?', in R. Ziegler (ed.), *An Introduction to Social Entepreneurship: Voices, Preconditions, Contexts*, Cheltenham, UK and Northampton, MA, USA: Edward Elgar Publishing, pp. 174–206.

Grüne Liga (2004), 'Die EG-Wasserrahmenrichtlinie', Berlin.

Hackl, V. (2009), 'Social Franchising: Social Entrepreneurship Aktivitaeten multiplizieren', Bamberg: Difo-Druck GmbH.

Hazare, A. (2003), *My Village: My Sacred Land*, Pune: Ralegan Siddhi Pariwar.

Henkel, M. and R. Ziegler (2010), 'Rain does not fall on one roof alone: a case study in participatory environmental governance', Berlin Conference, FU Berlin, October 2010.

International Panel on Climate Change (IPCC) (2007), 'Assessment Report 4. Working Group II: Impacts, Adaptation and Vulnerability', Cambridge.

International Tropical Timber Organisation (ITTO) (2004), 'For Services Rendered: The Current Status and Future Potential of Markets for the Ecosystem Services provided by Tropical Forests', *ITTO Technical Series* No. 21.

International Union for the Conservation of Nature (IUCN) (2006), 'Pay. Establishing Payments for Watershed Service', Gland.

Jacobs, Michael (1999), 'Sustainable development as a contested concept', in Andrew Dobson (ed.), *Fairness and Futurity*, Oxford: Oxford University Press, pp. 21–45.

Jewler, S. (2011), 'The Wasundhara Approach', available at http://wotr.org/ (accessed 31 January 2012).

Joshi, Lalita and Ratna Huirem (2009), *Participatory Net Planning: Reflections and Learnings from the Field*, Pune: WOTR.

Kale, Eshwer (2011), 'Social exclusion in watershed development: evidence from the Indo-German watershed development project in Maharashtra', *Law Environment and Development Journal*, 7 (2), 97–116.

Karugu, W. (2011), 'Ecotact: affordable sanitation services in pleasant surroundings in Kenya', *GIM Case Study*, No. B060, United Nations Development Programme, New York.

Kauffman, C. (2011), 'Global governors and local governance: the transnational campaign for integrated watershed management in Ecuadorian municipalities'. Paper presented at the 52nd Convention of the International Studies Association, Montreal/ Canada, March 16–19, 2011.

Klíma, I. (1963), 'Hodina ticha', Republished by Academia Praha 2009.

Kolb, F. (2002), 'Soziale Bewegungen und politischer Wandel', Lüneburg: Deutscher Naturschutzring e.V. – Kurs Zukunftspiloten, available at www.stiftungbridge.de/fileadmin/user_upload/bridge/dokumente/mass_studienbrief.pdf (accessed 20 June 2012).

Kravčík, M. (2009), 'Return the lost water back to the continents', in R. Ziegler (ed.) *An Introduction to Social Entepreneurship: Voices, Preconditions, Contexts*, Cheltenham, UK and Northampton, MA, USA: Edward Elgar Publishing, pp. 21–32.

Kravčík, M. (2009), 'Water for people: Global New Deal (GND)'. Paper presented at the Skoll World Forum on Social Entrepreneurship, University of Oxford, March 2009.

Kravčík, M., J. Kohutiar, M. Gažovič, M. Kovac, M. Hrib, P. Suty and D. Kravčíková (2012), 'Po nás púšt' a potopa? – After us, the desert and the deluge?', D. Press Group, s.r.o., Banska Bystrica.

Kravčík, M., J. Pokorny, M. Kohutiar, M. Kovac and E. Toth (2007), *Water for the Recovery of the Climate: A New Water Paradigm*, Zilina: Krupa Print.

Kriš, J. and I. Škultétyová (2009), 'Drinking water supply in Slovakia'. Paper presented on the International Symposium on Water Management and Hydraulic Engineering in Ohrid/Macedonia, 1–5 September 2009.

Krohn, W. (2008), 'Epistemische Qualitäten transdisziplinärer Forschung', in M. Bergmann and E. Schramm (eds), *Transdisziplinäre Forschung:*

Integrative Forschungsprozesse verstehen und bewerte, Frankfurt: Campus, pp. 21–38.

Landell-Mills, N. and I. T. Porras (2002), 'Silver bullet or fool's gold? A global review of markets for forest environmental services and their impact on the poor', London: International Institute for Environment and Development (IIED).

Lodemann, J. (2013), *Flussversöhnung*, DVD, 45 min (accessed at www.getidos.net, 10 September 2013).

Lodemann, J., R. Ziegler and P. Varga. (2010), 'The New Water Paradigm, human capabilities and strong sustainability', *IJW*, 5 (4), 429–41.

Mair, J., J. Battilana and J. Cardenas (2012), 'Organizing for society: a typology of social entrepreneuring models', *Journal of Business Ethics*, 111, 353–73.

MASR Ministry of Agriculture Slovak Republic (2000), 'Green Report 1999', available at http://test.uvtip.sk/ (accessed 29 April 2010).

Mauser, W. (2007), *Wie lange reicht die Ressource Wasser? Vom Umgang mit dem blauen Gold*, Frankfurt am Main: Fischer Taschenbuch.

Maweu, J. M. (2012), 'The morality of profit in business: transforming waste into wealth through the *Iko Toilet* business venture in Nairobi, Kenya', *Thought and Practice: A Journal of the Philosophical Association of Kenya (PAK)*, New Series, 4 (1), 75–89.

McAfee, K. and E. N. Shapiro (2010), 'Payments for ecosystem services in Mexico: nature, neoliberalism, social movements, and the state', *Annals of the Association of American Geographers*.

McPhedran Waitzer, J. and R. Paul (2011), 'Scaling social impact: when everybody contributes, everybody wins', *Innovations: Technology, Governance, Globalization*, 6 (2), 143–7.

Meadows, D., J. Randers and W. W. III Behrens (1972), *The Limits to Growth. A Report for the Club of Rome*.

Millennium Ecosystem Assessment (MA) (2005), 'Ecosystems and Human Well-being: Synthesis', Washington DC.

Ministry of Education (2008), 'Safety Standards Manual for Schools in Kenya'.

Ministry of Environment and Forestry (2001), 'National Action Programme to Combat Desertification'.

Ministry of Environment and Minerals (2011), 'Press Statement on the Prevailing Drought Conditions over Kenya', Kenya Meteorological Department OCHA (2011).

Muradian, R., M. Arsel, L. Pellegrini, F. Adaman, B. Aguilar, B. Agarwal, E. Corbera, D. Ezzine de Blas, J. Farley, G. Froger, C. Garcia-Frapolli, E. Gómez-Baggethun, J. Gowdy, N. Kosoy, J. F. Le Coq, P. Leroy, P. May, P. Méral, P. Mibielli, R. Norgaard, B. Ozkaynak, U. Pascual,

W. Pengue, M. Perez, D. Pesche, D. Pirard, J. Ramos-Martin, L. Rival, F. Saenz, G. Van Hecken, A. Vatn, B. Vira and K. Urama (2013), 'Payments for ecosystem services and the fatal attraction of win–win solutions', in *Conservation Letters*, 6 (4), 274–9.

National Bureau of Statistics (2010), 'Kenya Census 2009, 2009 Population and Housing Census Highlights', available at http://www.knbs.or.ke (accessed 6 February 2012).

Nayyar, D. (2013), 'The Millennium Development Goals beyond 2015: old frameworks and new constructs', *Journal of Human Development and Capabilities*, 14 (3), 371–92.

Nicholls, A. (2010), 'The legitimacy of social entrepreneurship: reflexive isomorphism in a pre-paradigmatic field', *Entrepreneurship Theory and Practice*, 34 (4), 611–33.

Norgaard, R. (2009), 'Ecosystem services: from eye-opening metaphor to complexity blinder', *Ecological Economics*, 69 (2010), 1219–27.

Nussbaum, M. (2000), *Women and Human Development: The Capabilities Approach*, Cambridge, New York: Cambridge University Press.

Nussbaum, M. (2006), *Frontiers of Justice: Disability, Nationality, Species Membership*, Cambridge, MA: Harvard University Press.

Nussbaum, M. (2011), *Creating Capabilities: The Human Development Approach*, Cambridge MA: Belknap Press, Harvard University Press.

OCHA (United Nations Office for the Coordination of Humanitarian Affairs) (2011), 'Horn of Africa Drought Crisis', *Situation Report*, 7, 29 July 2011.

Ott, K. and R. Döring (2004/2008), *Theorie und Praxis starker Nachhaltigkeit*, Marburg: Metropolis-Verlag.

Partzsch, L. and R. Ziegler (2011), 'Social entrepreneurs as change agents: a case study on power and authority in the water sector', *International Environmental Agreements*, 11 (1), 63–83.

Pecho, J., P. Faško, M. Lapin and M. Melo (2009), 'Changes in Precipitation Regime in Slovakia – Past, Present and Future'. Poster available on the website of the Slovak Hydrometeorological Institute, at www.shmu.sk/File/ExtraFiles/KMIS/pub_cinnost/Pecho_et_al_2009_poster.pdf (accessed 30 August 2012).

Pogge, T. (2002), *World Poverty and Human Rights: Cosmopolitan Responsibility and Reforms*, Cambridge: Polity Press.

Qualitätsgemeinschaft Biomineralwasser (2013), 'Richtlinien der Qualitätsgemeinschaft Biomineralwasser e.V. für Biomineralwasser, Bioquellwasser und als Zutat für daraus hergestellte Biogetränke', available at http://www.bio-mineralwasser.de/fileadmin/user_upload/

downloads/BioMW-Richtlinien_v__28_03_13.pdf   (accessed   17 September 2013).

Rauch, Th. (2009), *Entwicklungspolitik. Theorien, Strategien, Instrumente*, Braunschweig: Westermann.

Rawls, J. (1999), *A Theory of Justice*, revised edition, Oxford: Oxford University Press.

Ripl, W. (2003), 'Water: the bloodstream of the biosphere', *Philosophical Transaction of The Royal Society London*, B 358, 1921–34.

Ripl, W. and C. Hildmann (2000), 'Dissolved load transport by rivers as an indicator of landscape sustainability', *Ecological Engineering*, 14 (4), 373–87.

Rivernet (2012), Homepage of the European Rivers Network, available at www.rivernet.org, (accessed 20 June 2012).

Robeyns, I. (2005), 'The capability approach: a theoretical survey', *Journal of Human Development*, 6 (1), 93–114.

Rucht, D. (1999), 'The impact of environmental movements on Western societies', in Marco Giugni, Doug McAdam and Charles Tilly (eds), *How Social Movements Matter*, Minneapolis: University of Minnesota Press, pp. 204–24.

Sachs, W. (1999), *Planet Dialects: Explorations in Environment and Development*, London: Zed Books.

Sainath, P. (1996), *Everybody Loves a Good Drought*, London, New Delhi: Penguin.

Schomers, S. and B. Matzdorf (in press), 'Payments for ecosystem services: a review and comparison of developing and industrialized countries', *Ecosystem Services*.

Schumpeter, J. A. (1942[1975]), *Capitalism, Socialism and Democracy*, New York: Harper Collins Publishers.

SEI (Stockholm Environment Institute) (2004), 'Ecological sanitation', revised and enlarged edition. Editors and co-authors: U. Winblad and M. Simpson-Hébert. Co-authors 2004 revised edition: P. Calvert, P. Morgan, A. Rosemarin, R. Sawyer and J. Xiao, Stockholm Environment Institute 2004, 141.

Sen, A. (2009), *The Idea of Justice*, London: Penguin.

Sen, P. (2007), 'Ashoka's big idea: transforming the world through social entrepreneurship', *Futures*, 39, 534–53.

SNCLD Slovak National Committee on Large Dams (2010), Alphabetical list of registered dams in ICOLD, available at http://www.skcold.sk/ (accessed 29 April 2010).

StAUN (Staatliches Amt für Landwirtschaft und Umweltschutz) (2006), Homepage with reports on the Ryck, available at www.wasserblick.net/ servlet/is/?fields=descriptors%2Cname%2Ctitle%2CcommentC%2Cab

stract&categories=&orderBy=score+desc&class=Entry&command=
search&doIt=yes&terms=ryck&hitsPerPage=10&OK=OK.

Swedberg, R. (ed.) (2000), *Entrepreneurship: The Social Science View*, Oxford: Oxford University Press.

Szolgay, J., S. Kohnová and K. Hlavčová (2009), 'Water management: establishment, purpose, definitions and short history of water management'. Lecture Notes, *Department of Land and Water Resources Management in Slovak University of Technology in Bratislava*, Slovakia.

The Economics of Ecosystems and Biodiversity (TEEB) (2010), 'Mainstreaming the Economics of Nature: A Syntesis of the Approach, Conclusions and Recommendations of TEEB'.

Thoreau, H. (1854[1993]), *Walden and Resistance to Civil Government*, New York: W. W. Norton.

UN Economic Commission for Latin America and the Caribbean (UN-ECLAC) (2010), Millennium Development Goals. 'Advances in Environmentally Sustainable development in Latin America and the Caribbean', Santiago de Chile.

UNICEF and World Health Organization (2012), 'Progress on Drinking Water and Sanitation: 2012 Update', available at http://whqlibdoc.who. int/publications/2012/9789280646320_eng.pdf (accessed 17 September 2013).

United Nations Development Programme (UNDP), Government of Kenya, Government of Finland (2005), *MDGs Status Report for Kenya 2005*, Nairobi.

United Nations Development Programme (UNDP) (2006), *Making Progress on Environmental Sustainability: Lessons and Recommendations from a Review of over 150 MDG Country Experiences*, New York.

United Nations Development Programme (UNDP) Ecuador, and Gobierno Nacional del Ecuador (GoE) (2007), *Segundo Informe Nacional de los Objetivos de Desarrollo del Milenio – Ecuador 2007. Alianzas para el Desaroll*, Quito.

United Nations Development Programme Ecuador (UNDP) (EC) (2012), 'Objetivos de Desarrollo del Milenio en Ecuador', Quito: UNDP, available at www.undp.org.ec/odm/index.htm (accessed 10 October 2013).

UN Environment Programme (UNEP), The Katoomba Group and Forest Trends (2008), *Payments for Ecosystem Services: Getting started: A Primer*.

UN Environment Programme (UNEP) (2011), 'Towards a Green Economy: Pathways to Sustainable Development and Poverty Eradication', Nairobi, Kenya: UNEP, available at http://www.unep.org/greeneconomy (accessed 10 October 2013).

UN (2011), 'The official United Nations site for the MDG Indicators', available at http://unstats.un.org/unsd/mdg/ (accessed 6 May 2011).

Uvin, P. and D. Miller (1994), 'Scaling up: thinking through the issues', available at http://www.globalpolicy.org/component/content/article/177/31630.html (accessed 17 September 2013).

Uvin, P. and D. Miller (1996), 'Paths to scaling-up: alternative strategies for local nongovernmental organizations', *Human Organization*, 55 (3), 344–54.

Uvin, P., Pankaj S. Jain and L. David Brown (2000), 'Think large and act small: toward a new paradigm for NGO scaling', *World Development*, 28 (8), 1409–19.

Vandemoortele, J. (2009), 'The MDG conundrum: meeting the targets without missing the point', *Development Policy Review*, 27 (4), 355–71.

Van Hecken, G. and J. Bastiaensen (2010), 'Payments for ecosystem services: justified or not? A political view', *Environmental Science and Policy*, 13, 785–92.

de la Vega-Leinert, A. C., S. Stoll-Kleemann and T. O'Riordan (2009), 'Sustainability science in concept and in practice. a guide to a new curriculum', *Geographical Research*, 47 (4), 351–61.

Vörösmarty, C. J., P. B. McIntyre, M. O. Gessner, D. Dudgeon, A. Prusevich, P. Green, S. Glidden et al. (2010), 'Global threats to human water security and river biodiversity', *Nature*, 467 (7315), 555–61, doi: 10.1038/nature09440.

Vredeveld, B. (2008), 'Urban growth in peri-urban Quito, Ecuador: challenges and opportunities for comprehensive land use management', *Tropical Resources*, 27, 79–86.

Watershed Organisation Trust (WOTR), 'Watershed Organisation Trust'. Online brochure, available at http://wotr.org/ (accessed 31 January 2012).

Watershed Organisation Trust (WOTR) (2005), 'Drop by drop: the story of WOTR', Pune: WOTR.

Watershed Organisation Trust (WOTR) (2010a), 'What are we in for? Rural dynamics in the context of climate change: a look at Ahmednagar district', Pune: WOTR.

Watershed Organisation Trust (WOTR) (2010b), 'Annual Report 2009–2010', Pune: WOTR.

Welthungerhilfe (2013), 'Orientation framework water, sanitation and hygiene', available at http://www.welthungerhilfe.de/en/about-us/service/media-centre/artikel/mediathek/orientation-framework-wash.html (accessed 17 September 2013).

Westley, F., B. Zimmerman and M. Patton (2006), *Getting to Maybe: How the World Is Changed*, Toronto: Random House Canada.

WGBU (German Advisory Council on Global Change) (2011), 'World in

Transition – A Social Contract for Sustainability', *Flagship Report 2011*, available at http://www.wbgu.de/en/flagship-reports/fr-2011-a-social-contract/ (accessed 31 January 2012).

WHO/UNICEF (2011), 'WHO/UNICEF Joint Monitoring Programme (JMP) for Water Supply and Sanitation', available at http://www.wssinfo.org/ (accessed 7 February 2012).

Wolff, F., C. Schleyer and B. Arts (in press), 'Discourses and politics of market-based instruments for ecosystem services: introduction'.

World Commission on Environment and Development. (1987), *Our Common Future*, Oxford: Oxford University Press.

World Water Assessment Programme (WWAP) (2006), '2nd World Water Development Report: Water – A Shared Responsibility', New York.

WSP (Water and Sanitation Programme) (2004), 'From hazard to convenience: towards better management of public toilets in the city of Nairobi', *Water and Sanitation Programme*, Nairobi.

Ziegler, R. (2010), 'Innovations in doing and being: capability innovations at the intersection of Schumpeterian political economy and human development', *Journal of Social Entrepreneurship*, 1 (2), 255–72.

Ziegler, R. (2012a), 'Capability innovation and the (re)making of social order', in B. Hawa, Y. Martina Hölzchen and N. Weidtmann (eds), *The Capability Approach on Social Order*, Münster: LIT Verlag, pp. 232–51.

Ziegler, R. (2012b), 'Reconciliation with the river: analysis of a concept emerging from practice'. *Greifswald Environmental Ethics Papers*, 2/2012 (final version forthcoming in *Environmental Values*, August 2014).

Ziegler, R. and J. Gebauer (2012), 'Ideas changing minds or money changing hands?', *Stanford Social Innovation Review Blog*, available at http://www.ssireview.org/blog/entry/ideas_changing_minds_or_money_changing_hands (accessed 10 October 2013).

Ziegler, R. and N. Hamker (2011), 'The idea of a collaborative competition: a case study', *Futures*, 43, 441–9.

Ziegler, R. and K. Ott (2011), 'The quality of sustainability science: a philosophical perspective', *Sustainability: Science, Practice & Policy*, 7 (1), 31–44.

Ziegler, R., B. Karanja and C. Dietsche (2013), 'Toilet monuments: an investigation of innovation for human development', *Journal of Human Development and Capabilities*, 14 (3), 420–40.

ZMOS Slovak Association of Towns and Villages (2008), 'Principles of Integrated Water Resources Management in Municipalities and their River Basins', available at http://www.zmos.sk/ (accessed 29 April 2010).

Index